FCE
Use
of English 1

CONTENTS

D1640783

Introduction

The "FCE Use of English 1" is a practice book intended mainly for intermediate and post-intermediate students, but it is also useful for more advanced students for revision and consolidation.

The aim of the book is to help students to understand and use English grammar through structurally graded material and full-colour pictures. In addition the book offers preparation for the new Cambridge FCE Examination or any other similar examinations.

◆ Oral Development sections.

These appear throughout the book and help students practise the grammar structures presented.

◆ Consolidation sections.

Each unit is followed by exercises which provide general practice for the new FCE Examination or any other similar examinations. **Phrasal Verbs** are listed in alphabetical order and the use of **Prepositions** is explained in Appendix 1 at the back of the book. There are also open cloze texts, multiple choice cloze texts, word formation, error correction and "key" word transformation exercises, collocations and tense revision exercises.

◆ Practice test sections.

After every second unit there is a section which trains students to cope with the Revised Cambridge FCE Examination Paper 3 - Use of English or any other similar examinations.

◆ Pre-test sections.

After every four units there is a section which familiarises the students with the format and level of difficulty of the actual tests. These appear in the Teacher's Book and revise all structures taught up to this point.

A Teacher's Book accompanies the Student's Book. This contains the answers to the exercises in the Student's Book and presents useful grammar tips as well as three tests in two separate versions.

Published by Express Publishing

3 Roman Bridge Close, Blackpill, Swansea SA3 5BE
Tel: +44-1792-404855 – Fax: +44-1792-404886
e-mail: inquiries@expresspublishing.co.uk.
INTERNET http: //www.expresspublishing.co.uk.

© Virginia Evans

Design and Illustration © Express Publishing

Second impression 1998

ISBN (set) 960-361-018-6
ISBN 960-361-019-4

1 *Modals*

1 *Identify the use of the verbs in bold, then write a synonymous expression.*

1 She **can't** have left yet. Her coat's still here.   ...logical assumption...   ....I don't think.......
2 I **have got to** meet my boss for lunch.   ....
3 **May** I have a glass of water?   ....
4 **Shall** we go and see Andrea tonight?   ....
5 We **should** be home before midnight.   ....
6 She **can** speak four languages fluently.   ....
7 **Can** I leave early today?   ....
8 You **should** stop spending so much money.   ....
9 They **must** have got married recently.   ....
10 You **needn't** buy a present.   ....
11 Peter **might** be able to come tonight.   ....
12 He **could** have at least phoned me last night.   ....
13 **Would** you like me to make the arrangements?   ....
14 You **can't** leave your bags here, sir.   ....
15 All employees **had to** work overtime.   ....
16 You **don't need to** book in advance.   ....
17 **Can** you give Cathy a message?   ....
18 She **should** phone to confirm her appointment.   ....
19 **Shall** we go shopping at the weekend?   ....

2 *Fill in the blanks as in the example:*

MODAL	USE	SYNONYMOUS EXPRESSION
1 She could swim before she could walk.	...ability...	...She was able to swim before she was able to walk....
2 He .... an actor.	....	I'm sure he's an actor.
3 Shall we have a barbecue tonight?	suggestion	....
4 He .... busy.	....	Perhaps he's busy.
5 .... finishing the report before you leave?	polite request	....
6 .... I show you the way?	....	Would you like me to show you the way?
7 You .... exercise regularly.	....	It's a good idea to exercise regularly.
8 Children mustn't play on the grass.	....	
9 You .... told him the truth.	....	It would have been better if you had told him the truth.
10 You .... wear school uniform.	obligation	You are expected to wear school uniform.
11 He .... tonight.	logical assumption	I don't think he's coming tonight.
12 You may board the plane now.	permission (formal)	....
13 .... borrow your book, please?	polite request	....
14 I .... send the letter today.	....	It's urgent that I send the letter today.
15 She .... lost it.	....	I'm sure she hasn't lost it.

1 Modals

Summary of Functions of Modal Verbs

USE	PRESENT/FUTURE	PAST
ability	He **can** speak Japanese. She**'s able to** make people laugh.	He **could/was able to** speak Japanese. (repeated action - ability in the past) We **were able to** go on a three-month tour of Australia. (single action)
possibility	He **can** still be at work. (90% certain) She **could** be angry. (50% certain; it's possible she is angry) Sally **may** be teaching. (50% certain; it's possible that she is teaching) You **might** need to come tomorrow. (40% certain; perhaps you need to come tomorrow) **It is likely that** Sue will give up working. **Sue is likely to** give up working.	--- We **could have** had an accident. (luckily we didn't) John **may have** broken that vase. (perhaps he did it) Jane **might have** lost our telephone number. (perhaps she has lost it) **It was likely that** she had taken the last train. **She was likely to** have taken the last train.
probability	They **will** be in Spain tomorrow. (100% certain; prediction) We **should** see him there. (90% certain; future only; it's probable) She **ought to** be in Canada by now. (90% certain; she will probably be in Canada)	--- He **should have** finished by now. (He has probably finished.) They **ought to have** started the course by now. (They have probably started the course.)
logical assumptions	He **must** be exhausted. (90% certain - positive; I'm sure he's exhausted) She **can't** be serious. (negative; I'm sure she's not serious) They **couldn't** be on holiday. (negative; I don't think they are on holiday)	He **must have** won the pools. (positive; I'm sure he has won the pools) She **can't have** married Ted. (negative; I'm sure she didn't marry Ted) They **couldn't have** been friends. (negative; I don't think they were friends)
permission	You **can/can't** have a party. (giving or refusing permission; informal) **Could** I be excused? (more polite; asking for permission) You **may** be excused. (formal; giving permission) **Might** I bring a friend to the wedding? (more formal; asking for permission) I'm afraid you **can't/mustn't** have visitors. (informal; refusing permission) Guests **may not** smoke in their rooms. (formal; refusing permission - written notice)	He **wasn't allowed to/couldn't** board the plane. He **was allowed to** see the patient. (not: ~~could~~) --- --- --- --- ---
necessity	I **must** return these books soon. (I say so) She **has to** find a new job. (necessity coming from outside the speaker) They**'ve got to** sell their caravan. (informal) The plants **need** watering. or The plants **need to be** watered. (it's necessary) She **doesn't have to/doesn't need to/ needn't** leave when they do. (it isn't necessary - absence of necessity) We **ought to** reply to the invitation. (it's necessary)	I **had to** return the books to the library. (I was obliged to) She **had to** find a new job after she was dismissed. They **had to** sell their caravan. The plants **needed** watering. or The plants **needed to be** watered. (it was necessary) She **didn't have to/didn't need to** work as hard as me. (it wasn't necessary for her to work as hard as me and she didn't - absence of necessity) She **needn't have** got a taxi. (it wasn't necessary for her to get a taxi but she did)

Summary of Functions of Modal Verbs

USE	PRESENT/FUTURE	PAST
advice	You **should** try to make more of an effort. (general advice; I advise you) You **ought to** keep to the speed limit. (I advise you; most people believe this) You **had better** not keep her waiting. (It's not a good idea; advice on a specific situation) **Shall** I apply for the job? (asking for advice)	You **should have** paid more attention. (but you didn't) She **ought to have** reserved a table. (but she didn't) It **would have been better** if you hadn't kept her waiting. (but you did) ---
criticism	She **could** at least wait until 5 o'clock. They **should** warn us. You **ought to** be more polite to her. ---	She **could** at least **have** waited until 5 o'clock. They **should have** warned us. (but they didn't) You **ought to have** been more polite to her. (It was the right thing to do, but you didn't do it.)
obligation	I **must** get more exercise. (I need to; I say so) I **have to** get more exercise. (I'm obliged to; the doctor says so) We **ought to** give more money to charity. (It's the right thing to do, but we don't always do it.)	I **had to** get more exercise because I was unfit. I **had to** get more exercise because I was unfit. We **ought to have** given more money to charity. (It was the right thing to do but we didn't do it.)
requests	**Can I** use your phone? (informal) **Could I** use your phone? (polite) **May I** make a phone call, please? (formal) **Might I** borrow your pen? (very formal) **Will you** give me a hand? (very friendly) **Would you mind** helping me? (polite)	--- --- --- --- --- ---
offers	**Can I/we** do anything to help? (informal) **Shall I/we** help you tidy up? (informal) **Would you like me** to do it for you?	--- --- ---
suggestions	**Shall we** stop for a drink? **I/we can** always leave early. We **could** eat out tonight if you want.	--- --- He **could have** asked for advice.
prohibition	You **can't** wear jeans at work. (you aren't allowed to) You **mustn't** walk on the grass. (it's forbidden) You **may not** talk during the test. (formal)	They **couldn't** wear jeans at work. (they weren't allowed to) --- ---
duty	All members **must** follow the rules. People **ought to** live in peace. (It's the right thing to do, but people don't always do it.)	All members **had to** follow the rules. She **ought to have** treated us more fairly. (It was the right thing to do but she didn't do it.)

3 *Rephrase the following in as many ways as possible.*

1 She might have misunderstood you. **2** I'm sure they are tired. **3** They ought to pay more attention. **4** I don't think she's sold her house. **5** It's likely that he'll object. **6** We may have to wait for them. **7** I'm sure she isn't Australian. **8** I'm sure he is terrified. **9** We ought to offer to help. **10** They'll probably want something to eat. **11** You can't park here. **12** He should have warned us about the dog.

1 Modals

Mustn't - Needn't

- **mustn't (it's forbidden)** You **mustn't** cross the street when the light is red.
- **needn't / don't have to (it isn't necessary)** You **needn't** worry about it. I'll do it in a minute.

 4 *Complete the sentences using the words in bold. Use two to five words.*

1 Soldiers are forbidden to leave the camp unless they get special permission.
   not Soldiers ...*must not leave the camp*... unless they get special permission.
2 Unauthorised personnel are not allowed to go beyond this point.
   must Unauthorised personnel .... this point.
3 It isn't necessary for Jim to get up early tomorrow as it is a holiday.
   have Jim .... up early tomorrow as it is a holiday.
4 Readers are not allowed to take books out of the library without first filling in a form.
   not Readers .... out of the library without first filling in a form.
5 It isn't necessary for Julie to work today; she can have the day off.
   have Julie .... today; she can have the day off.

5 *Fill the gaps with must, mustn't or needn't.*

"Welcome to "Finest Foods" factory. We are happy that you have come to work for us. Before you start work, I want to familiarise you with some rules and regulations. First of all, you **1)** ...*must*... wear the uniforms which are supplied, and you **2)** .... keep your hair covered at all times. You **3)** .... wear gloves unless you choose to, except in a few special areas. You **4)** .... smoke anywhere in the factory apart from the canteen, and you **5)** .... forget to wash your hands after breaks. You **6)** .... stay in the factory during your breaks, but you **7)** .... clock in and out if you do leave the premises. You **8)** .... work overtime, but we do encourage our workers to do so if they wish to. Last but not least, if you have any problems, you **9)** .... go to your supervisor who will help you to sort them out."

Needn't - Didn't need to - Needn't have

- **don't have to/don't need to/needn't + present infinitive (it is not necessary in the present or future)** You **don't have to/don't need to/needn't** wear evening dress. It's an informal party. *(It is not necessary to wear ...)*
- **didn't need to/didn't have to (It was not necessary in the past and we may not know if the action happened or not.)** She **didn't need to/didn't have to** wear evening dress as it was an informal party. *(It wasn't necessary for her to wear evening dress, and we don't know if she did or not.)*
- **needn't + bare perfect infinitive (We know that something happened in the past although it was not necessary.)** You **needn't have** cooked as much food as you did last night. *(You did, although it was not necessary.)*

6 *Complete the sentences using the words in bold. Use two to five words.*

1 It wasn't necessary for him to write to his mum because she rang him.
   need He ...*didn't need to write*... to his mum because she rang him.
2 We took more luggage than was necessary on our holiday.
   taken We .... much luggage on our holiday.
3 There's no need for you to water the plants this morning.
   have You .... the plants this morning.
4 It wasn't necessary for Arthur to get the train because his brother offered to give him a lift.
   need Arthur .... the train because his brother offered to give him a lift.
5 She came early last night, which wasn't necessary because the party didn't start till ten.
   come She .... early last night because the party didn't start till ten.

Must (affirmative logical assumption) - May/Might (possibility) - Can't/Couldn't (negative logical assumption)

Present Infinitive	I'm sure he **studies** a lot. Perhaps he **will study** a lot.	He must **study** a lot. He may **study** a lot.
Present Cont. Infinitive	I'm sure he **is studying**. Perhaps he **will be studying**.	He must **be studying**. He may/might **be studying**.
Perfect Infinitive	I'm sure he **didn't study**. I'm sure he **hasn't studied**. I'm sure he **hadn't studied**.	He can't **have studied**. He can't **have studied**. He can't **have studied**.
Perfect Cont. Infinitive	Perhaps he **was studying**. Perhaps he **has been studying**.	He may **have been studying**. He may **have been studying**.

7 *Complete the sentences using the words in bold. Use two to five words.*

1 I'm sure she has given up smoking.
have She ...*must have given up*... smoking.
2 I'm sure she isn't feeling sick now.
be She .... now.
3 Perhaps they were working for the enemy.
have They .... for the enemy.
4 Perhaps he will be on time.
be He .... time.
5 Perhaps he was too ill to take part in the race.
been He .... to take part in the race.
6 I'm sure they informed the police about the robbery.
have They .... about the robbery.
7 Perhaps Harry will be sunbathing this time tomorrow.
be Harry .... tomorrow.
8 I'm sure he had warned the soldiers about the coming danger.
have He .... about the coming danger.
9 I'm sure Jenny hasn't been working there that long.
have Jenny .... there that long.
10 Perhaps she was telling you the truth.
been She .... the truth.
11 Perhaps she's been working hard.
been She .... hard.
12 Perhaps she'll come with us.
may She .... us.
13 I'm sure she hadn't prepared her speech.
have She .... her speech.
14 Perhaps he was asleep when we rang.
been He .... when we rang.
15 Perhaps he'll be waiting when we get there.
may He .... when we get there.
16 I'm sure she didn't know about it.
known She .... about it.
17 I'm certain it has stopped raining now.
have It .... raining now.
18 It's possible that Jane has left already.
have Jane .... already.
19 I have no doubt that he was lying to you.
been He .... to you.

1 Modals

Expressions similar to Modal Verbs

- **Be supposed to + infinitive** means "should" but it expresses the idea that someone else expects something to be done. *You're supposed to wear a suit to work. (Your employer expects you to.) You should wear a suit. (It is a good idea because it makes a better impression.)*
- **Be to + infinitive** means "must" but it expresses the idea that someone else demands something. *I am to report for military training. (It's the law so I must obey.) I must report for military training. (If I don't, the army will look for me.)* **Be supposed to** and **be to** are used to express what someone expects about a previously arranged event. *Recruits are supposed to/are to have a haircut when they arrive. (It is scheduled.)*
- **Be likely to** means "may" (possibility). To express possibility in questions we don't use "may", we use: Is he likely to ...?, Is it likely that he ...?, Can he ...?, Could he ...?, Might he ...?. *Is he likely to understand my feelings? Is it likely that he will understand my feelings? Could he understand my feelings?*
- **Would you mind** is used to express polite, formal requests. *Would you mind holding this for a moment?*
- **Let's.../How about...?/Why don't we...?/What about...?** are used to make suggestions. *Let's stay in tonight. How about staying in tonight? Why don't we stay in tonight? What about staying in tonight?*
- **Would you like to/Would you like me to...?** (= Shall I...?) are used when we offer to do something. *Would you like me to read you a story? (Shall I read you a story?)*
- **Be allowed to** is used to express permission, to say what the rule is. *He was allowed to visit the prisoner. (not: He could visit) Was he allowed to visit the prisoner?*

8 How else can we say the following?

1 It is likely that she has got lost. ...*She is likely to have got lost.*...
2 Shall I book a ticket for you as well? ....
3 How about inviting Paul and Helen? ....
4 I am to welcome the guests and show them to their rooms. ....
5 Might he have forgotten all about it? ....
6 You have to wait until dark before you leave. ....

9 Fill in a modal or a synonymous expression and the appropriate form of the verb in brackets.

1 There's no reply when I ring him. He ...*must have left*... (leave) the office already.
2 Don't give up so easily. You .... (do) it if you tried a little harder.
3 That's no excuse! You know you .... (finish) this report by today.
4 He .... (mention) his plans on the phone last night but I really can't remember.
5 Since she crashed the car, she .... (walk) to work every day.
6 If you find something valuable, you .... (take) it to the nearest police station.
7 Passengers .... (not/walk) across the lines. They should use the footbridge.
8 You .... (know) better than to tell her all your secrets.
9 You .... (destroy) the letter as soon as you receive it.
10 You .... (enter) the building if you have a special pass.
11 Can you help me? I .... (find out) what time the London train arrives.
12 He looks very annoyed. He .... (wait) for ages.
13 I .... (take) the library books back yesterday but I forgot and now I'll have to pay a fine.
14 Increased sales mean that all employees .... (be given) an extra Christmas bonus.
15 .... (you/take) grandma to the cinema tonight as I have to go out?
16 When I was at school we .... (not/wear) jewellery.
17 You .... (bring) the map with you so we wouldn't have to ask people the way.
18 Those bags look heavy. .... (I/carry) some of them for you?
19 Don't pretend you don't know that you .... (have) a valid ticket on the bus.
20 You .... (ring) me to let me know you'd be late. I was worried.

In Other Words

- Perhaps he is working now.
  He may be working now.
- I'm sure he hasn't got the letter yet.
  He can't have got the letter yet.
- I'm sure she understood.
  She must have understood.
- Shall I help you do your homework?
  Would you like me to help you do your homework?
- Was it necessary for you to help her?
  Did you need to help her?
- It's forbidden to smoke in here.
  You mustn't smoke in here.
  You aren't allowed to smoke in here.

- He is likely to buy a sports car.
  It is likely that he will buy a sports car.
  He'll probably buy a sports car.
- It isn't necessary for him to work today.
  He doesn't have to/doesn't need to/needn't work today.
- It wasn't necessary for them to buy so much food.
  They needn't have bought so much food.
- It would be a good idea to avoid eating sweets.
  You should avoid eating sweets.
- Let's try doing this exercise.
  Shall we try doing this exercise?
- Would you mind if I used your pen?
  May/Might I use your pen?

10 *Complete the sentences using the words in bold. Use two to five words.*

1 Perhaps the bridge collapsed because of the storm.
   have   The bridge ...*may/might have collapsed*... because of the storm.

2 He'll probably come to the party.
   likely   He .... the party.

3 You mustn't photograph any of the paintings.
   allowed   You .... any of the paintings.

4 It's forbidden to touch the statues in the museum.
   touch   You .... in the museum.

5 I'm sure he didn't cheat in the exam.
   cheated   He .... in the exam.

6 Was it necessary for you to call a doctor?
   need   Did .... a doctor?

7 Shall I carry your shopping for you?
   me   Would .... your shopping for you?

8 I'm sure Ann didn't do it on purpose.
   have   Ann .... on purpose.

9 Might I take some photos?
   if   Would .... some photos?

10 Let's go and see "The Blob" tonight.
   we   Shall .... "The Blob" tonight?

11 It isn't necessary for you to do that exercise.
   need   You .... that exercise.

12 It would be a good idea to eat less high-cholesterol food.
   should   You .... high-cholesterol food.

13 It wasn't necessary for him to take a coat but he did.
   taken   He .... a coat.

14 I'm sure Ann spends all her money on clothes.
   spend   Ann .... on clothes.

15 Was it necessary for you to say that?
   have   Did .... that?

16 I'm sure he knew what he was doing.
   known   He .... he was doing.

17 Perhaps she's busy at the moment.
   be   She .... at the moment.

1 Modals

11 Find the word which should not be in the sentence.

1 You shouldn't to have told him that.
2 Would you have mind helping me with this?
3 We were been able to book a hotel room through a travel agency.
4 Can you please to pass the salt?
5 He might have had left his wallet at home.
6 You are not allowed it to enter that part of the building.
7 Sonia should be know about his refusal to co-operate.
8 They needn't to have spent so much money on redecorating their house.
9 He may be is waiting for the bus.
10 Mr Beaumont is to will arrive at 9.00 am tomorrow.
11 Ellen is likely that to return sooner than expected.
12 How about we calling him to find out if he has been invited too?
13 That can't to have been Richard Gere!
14 You should to go now.
15 Might does he still be waiting for us?
16 She will has to make an appointment to see the doctor.
17 He has had got to borrow money twice already this month.
18 You mustn't to let anyone know about our agreement.
19 She may have had given you the wrong address.
20 Would you mind if my asking you a personal question?

1	*to*
2	
3	
4	
5	
6	
7	
8	
9	
10	
11	
12	
13	
14	
15	
16	
17	
18	
19	
20	

Oral Development 1

Make speculations for the following pictures as in the example:

He is a disabled man. He can't walk.
The lady behind the wheelchair may be his wife.
He may have had a car accident.   etc

Consolidation 1

Phrasal Verbs

be about to: be on the point of
be after: go after; chase
be against: be opposed to
be away: be absent
be back: return; come back
be in: be at home/in one's office etc
be in for: be about to experience (usu bad)
be on: be shown in cinemas, theatres etc
be over: be finished
be up to: 1) be equal to, 2) depend on
• • • • • • • • • • • •
break down: 1) (of machinery) stop working, 2) (of a person) lose control of feelings
break in: 1) (intr) enter by force, 2) **(on)** interrupt, 3) (horses etc) train
break into: 1) (tr) enter by force, 2) burst into (song, laughter etc)
break off: 1) stop temporarily, 2) (tr) end a relationship
break out: 1) begin suddenly (war, disease, fire etc), 2) **(of)** escape from a place
break up: 1) (intr) separate; split up, 2) stop for holidays (schools etc)

12 *Fill in the correct particle(s).*

1 After months of preparation, the director is ...*about to*... start shooting his new film.
2 It's .... you to decide what to do.
3 I thought the match would be .... by now.
4 I'm afraid we're .... a bumpy flight.
5 Your work isn't .... your normal standard.
6 My washing machine is being repaired as it broke .... yesterday.
7 The waiter broke .... our conversation to take our order.
8 She broke .... their engagement because she realised she didn't love him.
9 School breaks .... for the Christmas holidays on 23rd December.
10 He broke .... after hearing the news of his wife's death.
11 Robbers broke .... the bank yesterday.
12 Two dangerous criminals have broken .... jail.
13 Their marriage broke .... after five years.
14 Mr Jones broke .... the interview to answer the phone.
15 The horse must be broken .... before anyone can ride it.

13 *Look at Appendix 1, then fill in the correct preposition.*

1 Catherine was absent ...*from*... school yesterday.
2 Mr King received fifty letters in answer .... his advertisement.
3 She was amazed .... the fantastic view.
4 He is very attached .... his parents.
5 She isn't accustomed .... drinking champagne.
6 She decided to apply .... Jones Ltd ...... the job advertised in the local paper.
7 She accused her son .... taking some money from her purse.
8 My doctor doesn't approve .... smoking.
9 He argues .... his wife .... everything.
10 Do you believe .... ghosts?
11 He was angry .... Ann .... her behaviour.
12 The antique dealer took advantage .... the customer's ignorance and sold him a fake.
13 She was very anxious .... him to arrive.
14 She was so anxious .... her exams that she couldn't sleep.
15 He agreed .... his boss that the office needed reorganising and agreed .... do it himself.
16 Her latest novel is based .... the life of Joan Collins.
17 I can see no basis .... changing our plans now.
18 He enjoys betting .... the horses.

14 *Complete the sentences using the words in bold. Use two to five words.*

1 I advise you to check the details before you sign the contract.
   had   You ...*had better check the details*... before you sign the contract.
2 It isn't necessary for you to drive me to the station.
   have   You .... me to the station.
3 There's no milk left.
   run   We .... milk.

4 Don't blame me if there's no food in the house.
   fault   It .... there's no food in the house.
5 Diana moved to London after finishing her degree.
   since   Diana .... she finished her degree.
6 Our house is an hour's walk from the village.
   takes   It .... to our house from the village.
7 She should be told the truth.
   better   It .... her the truth.
8 I should wash the curtains.
   need   The curtains .... washed.
9 I'm sure he read about it in the newspaper.
   have   He .... in the newspaper.

How to treat Open Cloze Texts

- **Read the whole passage at least once to become acquainted with the general meaning.**
- **Try to find out what kind of word is missing (noun, adjective, adverb, modal, article, preposition etc). Look at the words which are close to each blank or in the same sentence but consider other words as well.**
   a) *They were tired .... they decided to have a rest for a couple of hours. (The second clause is a result of the first clause, therefore we need "so".)*
   b) *He has got .... fastest car I've ever seen. (The adjective is a superlative - it needs "the".)*
   c) *......... awful weather! (The exclamation mark shows that this sentence is an exclamatory one, so we need either "what" or "how" - in this case "what" because there is an uncountable noun after the gap.)*
   d) *He was .... absorbed in the book that he didn't notice that someone had entered the room. (There is a "that" in the sentence, therefore we need to use either "so" or "such" - in this case "so" because there is an adjective but no noun after the blank.)*
   e) *He didn't have .... money to go on holiday. (The infinitive construction shows that we need either "too" or "enough" to fill the gap. The word "money" determines that the appropriate word is "enough" because "too" can only be used with adjectives or adverbs.)*
- **One area that needs particular care is constructions with modal verbs.**
   You needn't .... left so early. (the missing word is "have" - needn't + have + past participle)
- **Another area which needs particular care is constructions with relative pronouns/adverbs.**
   Claire, ... has been in the USA for three years, has come back. (correct answer: who - that cannot be used after a comma.)
   The man .... house belongs to is in Paris. (correct answer: the/this/that)
- **When you have completed the cloze text, read the passage carefully to see if it makes sense and is grammatically correct.**

15 *Choose the correct item.*

1 She has got ...C... loudest voice I've ever heard.
   A this   **B** a   **C** the

2 There were not .... chairs for everyone.
   A enough   **B** quite   **C** so

3 I was .... interested in what the teacher was saying that I didn't notice the time.
   A too   **B** as   **C** so

4 These cars are not as big .... some I've seen in America.
   A than   **B** as   **C** to

5 If cars weren't so expensive, we ..... buy a new one.
   A shall   **B** did   **C** would

6 Jane, ... has just passed her driving test, is having a party to celebrate.
   A which   **B** who   **C** that

7 I had .... little time to go to the shops.
   A too   **B** such   **C** enough

8 The woman .... cat belongs to has gone away for a week.
   A this   **B** which   **C** of

9 This is the beach .... we go every weekend.
   A which   **B** where   **C** that

10 .... tasty food!
   A What   **B** So   **C** How

11 It was .... cold to go for a swim in the sea.
    A as   **B** enough   **C** too

12 You shouldn't .... drunk all the milk.
    A have   **B** had   **C** has

13 After you had given me the money, I put ....
in the bank.
    A they   **B** them   **C** it

14 He is .... a good athlete that he is certain to
make the team.
    A so   **B** such   **C** too

15 .... lovely you look in that dress!
    A Such   **B** How   **C** What

16 They were late .... they decided to take a taxi.
    A so   **B** as   **C** that

17 She was much ...... after she had changed her job.
    A happiest **B** happy   **C** happier

18 I was .... tired to watch television, so I went
straight to bed.
    A quite   **B** so   **C** too

19 If only we .... left earlier, we would have been
there by now.
    A did   **B** had   **C** were

20 The weather in Greece is hotter ...... in England.
    A as   **B** than   **C** like

16   *Think of the word which best fits each space. Write only one word in each space.*

The English Language

Today English is, without doubt, the world's **(0)** ...*most*... important language. One **(1)** .... ten people speak it as their mother **(2)** .... and it has a larger vocabulary **(3)** .... any other language. English belongs to the Indo-European family of languages, **(4)** .... developed from a parent language first spoken about five thousand years ago in central-northern Europe. From there, it spread to the **(5)** .... of Europe and the Middle East, and over time it developed into a series of new tongues. One of **(6)** .... was Primitive Germanic, which later split into old English, Dutch, German and the Scandinavian languages. Old English was later heavily influenced **(7)** .... French following the Norman invasion in the eleventh century. Then, in the sixteenth century, due **(8)** .... the invention of printing, the increase **(9)** .... opportunities for education and the growth of international trade and communication, this form of English, which is known **(10)** .... Middle English, changed into the language we now speak, Modern English. Language change continues to the present day, although **(11)** .... 1800 the major area of change has been in vocabulary **(12)** .... than grammar. Events **(13)** .... as the Industrial Revolution and the two world wars are among the reasons **(14)** .... the expansion of vocabulary. **(15)** .... factor is the growing influence of the media.

17   *Fill in the following collocation grids.*

	an invitation	saying sth	an accusation	help	an offer	knowledge	to work	responsibility
refuse	✓							
deny								

	passport	hand	teeth	lights	flowers	promise	alarm	statement
false	✓							
artificial								

	sky	hands	voice	house	view	clothes	record	conscience
clean								
clear	✓							

18 *Use the words in capitals to form a word that fits in the space in the same line.*

Tropical Islands

Many people dream of a **(0)** .... holiday on a tropical island. They imagine **(1)** .... golden beaches, the **(2)** .... of the sea, and clear blue skies. The **(3)** .... is that a tropical holiday is even more **(4)** .... . Most Caribbean islands are very **(5)** .... . They are clean and **(6)** ...., and the islanders are always **(7)** .... . Although the hotels are often large and **(8)** ...., the welcome you receive is far from **(9)** .... . Most visitors don't want the **(10)** .... of these islands to increase. They want to keep their secret to themselves.

RELAX	
END	
WARM	
TRUE	
ENJOY	
PEACE	
POLLUTED	
HOSPITALITY	
LUXURY	
PERSONAL	
POPULAR	

0	relaxing
1	
2	
3	
4	
5	
6	
7	
8	
9	
10	

19 *Read the text carefully. Some of the lines are correct and some have a word which should not be there. If a line is correct, put a tick (✔) in the space provided. If a line has a word which should not be there, write it in the space provided.*

Spell it as you hear it!

0	Have you ever wondered where the expression	✔
00	O.K., which it means all right, comes from originally?	it
1	In one amusing story the expression said is attributed to the	
2	American President Andrew Jackson who, like to many before	
3	and after him, was a soldier by occupation. Unlike the most	
4	presidents these days, who have spent many years	
5	at college, Jackson's education was not as	
6	complete as that his military training and it	
7	is said his spelling was not as much good as	
8	it should have been. Of course, a great many	
9	papers were been given to the president to	
10	sign but he did not never want to write	
11	much at the bottom of these papers so, when	
12	he agreed with what thing was written, he	
13	would simply write O.K. on to the paper because	
14	President Jackson believed in the spelling of "All Correct"	
15	to be "Orl Kerekt", or O.K. as for short!	

 # The Infinitive/-ing form/Participles

Forms of the Infinitive		Forms of the -ing form		
	Active Voice	**Passive Voice**	**Active Voice**	**Passive Voice**
Present	(to) play	(to) be played	playing	being played
Pres. Cont.	(to) be playing		---	---
Perfect	(to) have played	(to) have been played	having played	having been played
Perf. Cont.	(to) have been playing		---	---

* Passive Present Continuous and Perfect Continuous Infinitives are rarely used.

Forms of the infinitive corresponding to verb tenses

Verb tenses	Forms of the Infinitive
Present Simple/Future Simple she cleans/she will clean	**Present** (to) clean
Present Continuous/Future Continuous she is cleaning/she will be cleaning	**Present Continuous** (to) be cleaning
Past Simple/Present Perfect/Past Perfect/Future Perfect she cleaned/she has cleaned/she had cleaned/she will have cleaned	**Perfect** (to) have cleaned
Past Continuous/Present Perfect Continuous/Past Perfect Continuous/Future Perfect Continuous she was cleaning/she has been cleaning/she had been cleaning/she will have been cleaning	**Perfect Continuous** (to) have been cleaning

20 Write the appropriate form of the infinitive.

1 she finished ...*(to) have finished*...
2 he was driving *To have been driving*
3 it has been taught *to have been taught*
4 they had come *have come*
5 she tries *to try*

6 it is brought *to be brought*
7 they are studying *to be studying*
8 it will be accepted *to be accepted*
9 it was written *have been written*
10 she has left *have left*

21 Fill in the correct form of the infinitive.

1 I've looked everywhere, but the file appears ...*to have been misplaced*... (misplace).
2 He is not old enough .... (allow) to stay out late.
3 Since her illness she seems .... (find) work difficult.
4 Although Jane hopes .... (invite) to the embassy dinner, it is unlikely that she will be.
5 The little dog seems .... (lose) its master.
6 I don't think I'll be able to make it tomorrow. I'm supposed .... (meet) Jane for lunch.
7 She was only pretending .... (read); she was really daydreaming.
8 No one is .... (admit) to the concert without a ticket.
9 The team is said .... (win) the match through sheer luck.
10 I need you .... (help) me prepare the food for the party.
11 The accident is believed .... (cause) by reckless driving.
12 The newspaper received many calls from people claiming .... (see) UFOs.
13 He was the first British writer .... (award) the Nobel prize for literature.
14 Aren't you supposed .... (look after) your sister at the moment?

The to-infinitive is used

- **to express purpose.** *You should take a few days off* **to recover***.*

- **after certain verbs (agree, appear, decide, expect, hope, plan, promise, refuse etc).** *He* **agreed to meet** *us tonight.*

- **after certain adjectives (happy, glad, sorry etc).** *I was* **sorry to hear** *about your accident.*

- **after I would like/would love/would prefer to express specific preference.** *I'd love to visit India.*

- **after certain nouns.** *It's such a* **pleasure to be** *with you.*

- **after too/enough constructions.** *It's* **too early to leave** *the party.* *He's* **rich enough to afford** *a Porsche.* *There's* **enough food to go** *round.*

- **with: it + be + adjective (+ of + noun/pronoun).** *It was* **unkind of her to say** *that.*

- **with: so + adjective + as.** *Would you be* **so kind as to pass** *the sauce?*

- **with "only" to express an unsatisfactory result.** *He won in the lottery* **only to lose** *at the casino.*

- **after: be + the first/second etc/next/last/best etc.** *She was* **the first to congratulate** *him.*

- **in the expression: for + noun/pronoun + to -inf.** *For John to lend you his car was very unusual.*

- **in expressions such as: to tell you the truth, to begin with, to be honest etc.** *To be honest, I didn't know how to react.*

Note: If two infinitives are joined by "and" or "or", the "to" of the second infinitive can be omitted. *I'd prefer to go to a disco* **and dance or talk** *to my friends.*

The -ing form is used

- **as a noun.** *Smoking is harmful.*

- **after certain verbs (admit, anticipate, appreciate, avoid, consider, continue, delay, deny, discuss, enjoy, escape, excuse, fancy, finish, forgive, go (physical activities), imagine, involve, keep (= continue), mention, mind, miss, object to, postpone, practise, prevent, quit, recall, recollect, report, resent, resist, risk, save, stand, suggest, tolerate, understand etc).** *They have* **postponed moving** *house till next week.*

- **after: dislike, enjoy, hate, like, love, prefer to express general preference.** *I like swimming. (in general)* *** Note: like + to-inf** = it's a good idea *I like to help people.*

- **after: I'm busy, it's no use, it's (no) good, it's (not) worth, what's the use of, can't help, there's no point (in), can't stand, have difficulty (in), in addition to, as well as, have trouble, have a hard/difficult time.** *There's no point in arguing. What's the use of crying? It was your fault.*

- **after: spend/waste (time, money etc).** *You* **waste** *too much* **time watching** *TV.*

- **after prepositions.** *He became rich* **by working** *hard and* **without borrowing** *from anyone.*

- **after: look forward to, be/get used to, be/get accustomed to, object to, admit (to) etc** *I object to being told what to do with my life.*

- **after: hear, listen, notice, see, watch to express an incomplete action, an action in progress or a long action.** *I saw him throwing rubbish out of the window. (I saw part of the action. I didn't wait until he had finished. Perhaps he threw more rubbish.)* **BUT: hear, listen, see, watch + infinitive without "to"** express a complete action, something that one saw or heard from beginning to end. *I saw him throw rubbish out of the window. (I saw all of the rubbish being thrown out of the window.)*

The infinitive without to is used

- **after most modal verbs (can, could, may etc).** *He* **can go** *if he wants to.*
- **after had better/would rather/would sooner.** *You'd better go to bed.*
- **after make/let/see/hear/feel in the active.** *She* **made** *the baby* **eat** *all his soup.* **But in the passive: be made/be heard/be seen + to-inf.** *The baby* **was made to eat** *all his soup.* **Note that "let" turns into "was/were allowed to" in the passive.** *Her parents* **let** *her* **stay** *out till midnight. She* **was allowed to stay** *out till midnight.*

22 Write what each word is followed by: F.I. (full inf.), B.I. (bare inf.) or -ing form.

1	refuse	+ *F.I.*	**5**	would	+ B.I.	**9**	would like	+ F.I.	**13**	hear	+ B.I./ing. f
2	finish	+ ing.	**6**	object to	+ ing	**10**	it's no use	+ ing.	**14**	it's no good	+ ing. f.
3	dislike	+ ing.	**7**	promise	+ F.I.	**11**	admit	+ ing.f	**15**	decide	+ F.I.
4	would rather	+ B.I.	**8**	be known	+ F.I.	**12**	let	+ B.I.	**16**	deny	+ ing. f.

23 Fill in the blanks with the correct form of the infinitive or the -ing form. Mind the tenses.

1 The police made the bank robbers ...*give*... (give) themselves up.
2 He is not likely *to return / to have returned* (return) before five o'clock.
3 The criminals were forced *to surrender* (surrender).
4 They might not *have complained* (complain) about the meal if the service hadn't been so dreadful.
5 Man is said *to have invented* (invent) the wheel about ten thousand years ago.
6 You must *have been starving* (starve) to have eaten such a big dinner last night.
7 She'd better *have* (have) a good excuse for being so late.
8 They hope *to make* (make) a lot of money in their new business.
9 The wind tends *to increase* (increase) just before sunset.
10 He should *have told* (tell) his parents the truth when they asked him.
11 Imagine *living* (live) in a big house like that!
12 I'd rather not *visit* (visit) my parents this weekend.
13 She's too tired *to concentrate* (concentrate) on her work today.
14 You should *have seen* (see) his face when she told him the news.
15 It was such a shock *to hear* (hear) from her after all these years.
16 Ann would love *to be lying* (lie) on a beach now, instead of typing reports.
17 The doctor worked for fifteen hours without *taking* (take) a break.
18 John's father let him *borrow* (borrow) his car for the weekend.
19 There's no point *getting* (get) there early, because the gates don't open till 10 am.
20 Jim doesn't have enough patience *to be* (be) a teacher.

24 Fill in the blanks with the correct form of the infinitive or -ing form.

Whatever else Christmas may **1)** ...*stand for*...(stand for), one thing it still means is **2)** *eating* (eat). Christmas has traditionally been a time of the year when people have tried **3)** *to cheer* (cheer) themselves up during the cold months of winter. Last year more than 10 million turkeys were bought in Britain alone during the festive season **4)** *to satisfy* (satisfy) the nation's appetite. Health experts may continue **5)** *to complain* (complain) about all this self-indulgence, but they fail **6)** *to realise* (realise) that there is nothing new about celebratory feasting, particularly at this time of year. The Roman Saturnalia, which was supposedly a festival **7)** *to honour* (honour) the god of agriculture, started on 19 December. Among other things, the Saturnalia involved **8)** *lighting* (light) candles and **9)** *giving* (give) gifts. People who had spent the whole year **10)** *saving* (save) money suddenly became extravagant. In addition to **11)** *exchanging* (exchange) gifts, this time of year was also an occasion for masters and slaves alike **12)** *to eat* (eat) excessively. At one Saturnalia feast an emperor is reported **13)** *to have spent* (spend) the equivalent of £600,000 on a dinner for twelve guests which consisted of twenty courses and lasted all day. So, when mealtime comes round on 25 December, there's no point in **14)** *having* (have) a guilty conscience. In fact the occasional seasonal feast may promote good health and stop year-round **15)** *overeating* (overeat).

Christmas

2 *The Infinitive / -ing form / Participles*

25 Put the verbs in brackets into the -ing form or the infinitive with or without "to".

When Gilbert decided **1)** ...*to give up*... (give up) his job and **2)** .... (sell) all his possessions, everyone thought he was mad. But, as it turned out, he was just the first of many of my friends **3)** .... (do) this. In fact, escaping the pressures of everyday working life has become a priority for many people these days. They can't stand the idea of **4)** .... (work) until they are 65, only **5)** .... (retire) to some boring country village and **6)** .... (waste) their time **7)** .... (dig) the garden or **8)** .... (gossip) with the neighbours. They would rather **9)** .... (live) life to the full now, before they are too old **10)** .... (enjoy) it. **11)** .... (buy) a motorcycle and **12)** .... (tour) the world is a popular option. Other, less adventurous types might prefer **13)** .... (buy) a small farmhouse and live off the land. Personally, I fancy **14)** .... (sail) around the world in a yacht. As for Gilbert, he bought a house in a little country village and spends his time **15)** .... (walk) around the village and **16)** .... (talk) with the neighbours.

26 Put the verbs in brackets into the -ing form or the infinitive without to.

1 I watched her ...*get up*... (get up) and walk slowly out of the room.
2 I heard the phone .... (ring) twice and then stop.
3 Tim saw Jill .... (stand) outside the butcher's as he was driving to work.
4 Jane stopped to watch the river .... (flow) down the mountainside.
5 Listen to the wind .... (blow) through the trees.
6 We heard the workmen .... (drill) in the road as we were eating breakfast.
7 The witness saw the burglar .... (break into) the house and steal the television.
8 Listen to her .... (sing) the song and then tell us what you think of it.

Verbs taking to-infinitive or -ing form without a change in meaning

- **begin, continue, intend, start + to-inf or -ing form.** We don't normally have two -ing forms together.
  *He began **speaking**/**to speak**. not: He is beginning speaking.*
- **advise, allow, encourage, permit, require + object + to-inf.** *She doesn't **allow them to talk** in class.*
- **advise, allow, encourage, permit, require + -ing form.** *She doesn't **allow talking** in class.*
- **be advised, be allowed, be encouraged, be permitted, be required + to-inf.** *They **aren't allowed to talk** in class.*
- **need, require, want + to-inf./-ing form/passive inf.** *You **need to wash** the car. Your car **needs washing**. Your car **needs to be washed**.*

---

27 Complete the sentences using the words in bold. Use two to five words.

1 We weren't advised to book in advance.
   advise   They ...*didn't advise us to*... book in advance.
2 You really need to renew your passport before you go on holiday.
   needs   Your passport .... before you go on holiday.
3 They require hotel guests to vacate their rooms by twelve noon.
   are   Hotel guests .... their rooms by twelve noon.
4 The dietician advised us not to eat between meals.
   eating   The dietician .... between meals.
5 They need to consider the proposals more carefully.
   considered The proposals .... more carefully.

Verbs taking to-infinitive or -ing form with a change in meaning

1 **forget + to-inf** (= forget to do sth)
*He **forgot to switch off** the TV.*
forget + -ing form (= forget a past event)
*I'll never **forget meeting** Jane for the first time.*

2 **remember + to-inf** (= remember to do sth)
*I hope you'll **remember to tidy** your room.*
remember + -ing form (= recall a past event)
*I don't **remember** him ever **tidying up** his room.*

3 **mean + to-inf** (= intend to) *She **means to start** a new life.*
mean + -ing form (= involve) *I won't take the job if it **means moving** to Scotland.*

4 **go on + to-inf** (= finish doing sth and start doing sth else; then; afterwards) *She finished one letter and **went on to write** another.*
go on + -ing form (= continue) *She **went on writing** till the early hours of the morning.*

5 **regret + to-inf** (= be sorry to) *I **regret to inform** you that your services are no longer required.*
regret + -ing form (= have second thoughts about sth already done) *He **regrets misbehaving**.*

6 **would prefer + to-inf** (specific preference)
*I'd **prefer to see** you in private.*
prefer + -ing form (in general)
*I **prefer working** on my own.*
prefer + to-inf + rather than + inf without to
*He **prefers to paint** the flat on his own **rather than hire** a professional.*

7 **try + to-inf** (= do one's best; attempt)
***Try to eat** less high-cholesterol food.*
try + -ing form (= do sth as an experiment)
***Try cutting down** on fat. You might get thinner.*

8 **want + to-inf** (= wish) *I **want to stop** smoking.*
want + -ing form (= sth needs to be done)
*This room **wants tidying up**.*

9 **stop + to-inf** (= pause temporarily) *He **stopped** at the garage **to have** the tank filled.*
stop + -ing form (= finish; cease)
*He **stopped behaving** foolishly.*

10 **be sorry + to-inf** (= regret) *I'**m sorry to tell** you your flight has been cancelled.*
be sorry for + -ing form (= apologise for)
*He was **sorry for hurting** her feelings.*

11 **hate + to-inf** (= hate what one is about to do)
*I **hate to cut in,** but you must see the manager.*
hate + -ing form (= feel sorry for what one is doing) *I **hate causing** you so much inconvenience.*

12 **be afraid + to-inf** (= be too frightened to do sth; hesitate) *She **was afraid to climb** the tree.*
be afraid of + -ing form (= be afraid that what is referred to by the -ing form may happen)
*When she goes swimming, she'**s always afraid of being** stung by jellyfish.*

---

28 *Put the verbs in brackets into the -ing form or the infinitive.*

1 A: Oh, Mum, this programme's nearly finished. Can't I go on ...*watching*... (watch) TV for a while?
   B: No, I want you to do your maths homework and then go on .... (write) your English essay. You haven't even started it yet and it's due in tomorrow.

2 A: Your dress is filthy. It wants .... (wash).
   B: I know. I wanted .... (take) it to the cleaner's yesterday, but they were closed.

3 A: Don't you hate .... (not/know) anyone here?
   B: Yes, I get very lonely, but I hate .... (worry) my parents so I tell them I've made lots of friends.

4 A: I'll never forget .... (visit) Thailand for the first time.
   B: Yes, it was such a wonderful holiday. If only I hadn't forgotten .... (take) my camera.

5 A: Why don't we stop .... (get) something to eat on the way home?
   B: OK, but we should really stop .... (spend) money on junk food.

6 A: I'm sorry for .... (spoil) your plans last weekend.
   B: That's OK. I was sorry .... (hear) you weren't feeling very well.

7 A: Jane doesn't know how to work the computer but she's afraid .... (ask) for help.
   B: But isn't she afraid of .... (get) into trouble if she breaks it?

8 A: Did you remember .... (tell) Tim about the party?
   B: I don't remember .... (tell) him, but I'm sure I did.
9 A: Do you regret .... (offer) him the job?
   B: Yes, I regret .... (say) he's not a reliable employee.
10 A: I think I'd prefer .... (go) on holiday to Greece this year and spend
      some time visiting ancient sites.
   B: Yes, I prefer .... (do) something interesting to just .... (sit) on a beach
      all day. And I'd prefer .... (go) somewhere warm rather than ....
      (stay) in England.
11 A: Did you mean .... (park) so far away?
   B: Yes. Otherwise, it would mean .... (pay) to get into a car park.
12 A: I've been trying .... (contact) Mr Isaacs all morning.
   B: Why don't you try .... (phone) his club?

29 *Complete the sentences using the infinitive or the -ing form of an appropriate verb.*

1 His lawyer advised him ...*to take*... the journalist to court.
2 I wouldn't advise .... that dog - it might bite you.
3 The boss doesn't encourage .... in the office. He's a non-smoker.
4 Why do you keep .... me such stupid questions?
5 I would offer .... you with the housework but I'm rather busy.
6 Students are not allowed .... during the exam.
7 They don't allow .... in this park because some boys used to ride around too fast.
8 I really hate .... caught in the rain.
9 Your childish behaviour is beginning .... me.
10 She is afraid .... the lift so she uses the stairs.
11 Remember .... the cat or she'll starve to death.
12 It's hot in here. Do you mind .... the window?
13 The bank manager agreed .... me £5,000.
14 She put off .... her bags until a few hours before her flight.
15 Our dog Timmy loves .... with his ball in the garden.
16 She wrote him a note to remind him .... his laundry at 2 o'clock.
17 Steven is exhausted because he isn't used to .... so much exercise.
18 She looked so funny in her new hat we couldn't help ....
19 You should practise .... this tune on the piano until you perfect it.
20 I regret .... you that your bank account is overdrawn.

Participles

Present participles (verb + ing) describe what somebody or something is.	Past participles (verb + ed) describe how someone feels.
*It was a **boring** lecture. (What kind of lecture? Boring.)*	*They were **bored** by the lecture. (How did they feel during the lecture? Bored.)*

30 *Underline the correct participle.*

1 He was encouraging/encouraged towards his children.
2 They found the film very excited/exciting.
3 He was exhausting/exhausted after the marathon.
4 They were worrying/worried that they would be late.
5 Her behaviour is extremely annoying/annoyed.
6 We were shocking/shocked by his behaviour.
7 She told us a very entertaining/entertained story.
8 They were all surprising/surprised when he turned up at the party.
9 That book is really interested/interesting.
10 They were fascinated/fascinating by the view.

31 *Put the verbs in brackets into the infinitive or -ing form.*

Scotland was the perfect place **1)** ...*to grow up*... (grow up). My parents had spent years **2)** .... (save up) because they wanted **3)** .... (buy) a small farmhouse in the Scottish Highlands. Shortly after I was born their dream came true and our new life in the country began. To begin with, I was probably too young **4)** .... (appreciate) the fresh air and breathtaking views, but as I grew up I began **5)** .... (enjoy) exploring the unspoilt country-side. I soon got used to **6)** .... (have) to walk miles to the shops, and since it was too far **7)** .... (travel) to the nearest primary school, my parents did their best **8)** .... (educate) me at home. However, I never felt lonely and was usually too busy **9)** .... (help) my father on the land to worry about **10)** .... (not/have) any friends. My brothers and sisters were also starting **11)** .... (grow up) fast and we had no difficulty **12)** .... (amuse) ourselves for hours on end. When I reached the age of eleven, my parents decided it was time **13)** .... (send) me to secondary school as they didn't feel they were capable of **14)** .... (provide) me with the range of skills I would need for my future life. This would involve **15)** .... (travel) twenty miles to the nearest town and twenty miles back. I was sorry **16)** .... (say) goodbye to my old way of life, but at the same time I looked forward **17)** .... (mix) with new people. After **18)** .... (finish) school I was forced **19)** .... (move) to Edinburgh to look for work and I have now made the city my home. Although I love the cosmopolitan lifestyle, I sometimes can't help **20)** .... (wish) I was back in the Highlands.

▶ *In Other Words*

- It is exciting to watch a football match.
  Watching a football match is exciting.
- It's too cold for him to go swimming.
  It isn't warm enough for him to go swimming.
  It is so cold that he can't go swimming.
- They made her tell the truth.
  She was made to tell the truth.
- I prefer walking to riding a bike.
  I prefer to walk rather than ride a bike.
- Could you open the door?
  Would you mind opening the door?

- We were bored by the film.
  We found the film boring.
  The film bored us.
- He had difficulty (in) hearing the music.
  It was difficult for him to hear the music.
  He found it difficult to hear the music.
  He could hardly hear the music.
- They allowed him to attend the meeting.
  He was allowed to attend the meeting.
- It took her an hour to reach the station.
  She took an hour to reach the station.
  Reaching the station took her an hour.

32 *Complete the sentences using the words in bold. Use two to five words.*

1 He arrived too late to catch the 9.30 train.
    arrive   He ...*didn't arrive early enough*... to catch the 9.30 train.
2 Preparing the meal took her three hours.
    prepare   She .... the meal.

3 These trousers are too small for me.
enough These trousers .... for me.

4 Politicians found the results of the local election surprising.
were Politicians .... of the local election.

5 Could you pass me the cheese, please?
mind Would .... the cheese?

6 They made her pay £2,000 tax.
to She .... £2,000 tax.

7 She was allowed to stay at her friend's house.
her They .... at her friend's house.

8 He wasn't tall enough to become a policeman.
short He .... a policeman.

9 He had difficulty seeing in the dark room.
hardly He .... in the dark room.

10 It took her six months to learn how to drive.
took She .... how to drive.

11 I prefer going out to staying at home.
than I prefer to .... at home.

12 Would you mind keeping quiet while she's talking?
keep Could .... she's talking?

13 The runner could hardly keep up with the others.
had The runner .... up with the others.

14 I think it's interesting to visit other countries.
visiting I think .... interesting.

15 She prefers taking the train to travelling by coach.
take She prefers .... than travel by coach.

16 Could you run through the details once more?
mind Would .... the details once more?

17 They took ages to reach a decision.
them It .... a decision.

18 The police let the suspect make one phone call.
was The suspect .... one phone call.

19 The tourists found the carnival fascinating.
were The tourists .... the carnival.

20 It was difficult for the jury to reach a verdict.
difficulty The jury .... a verdict.

21 The 17-year-olds weren't old enough to get into the club.
too The 17-year-olds .... into the club.

22 She prefers speaking French to writing it.
than She prefers .... write it.

23 Learning about other cultures is important.
learn It .... about other cultures.

24 They made him work overtime.
was He .... overtime.

25 During the rush hour it takes me over an hour to get to work.
getting During the rush hour, ... over an hour.

26 The instructions were so complicated that I couldn't follow them.
too The instructions were .... follow.

27 It was difficult for me to hear what he was saying.
hardly I .... what he was saying.

28 Could you keep the noise down?
mind Would .... the noise down?

29 They made the passengers wait at the airport for hours.
were The passengers .... at the airport for hours.

30 I have difficulty in understanding his accent.
find I .... his accent.

33 *Find the word which should not be in the sentence.*

1   She went to the market for to do her weekly shopping.
2   I hope that to see you again some day.
3   Tim is not so experienced enough to take on such responsibilities.
4   Would you be so kind as that to help me carry those bags?
5   Drawing it is a relaxing hobby.
6   The Burtons enjoy to travelling abroad whenever they get the chance.
7   My sister made me to promise that I would never tell anyone her secret.
8   I don't mind that being asked to lend a hand.
9   We had quite an adventure when we went for climbing in the Swiss Alps.
10 Could you let me to use your dictionary, please?
11 I'll never forget about travelling by plane for the first time.
12 I heard John to tell her that he was leaving that Saturday.
13 You had better not to tell him that you have been fired again.
14 She went on to talking about her holidays until everyone was bored.
15 The sofa was too heavy for me to move it.
16 He suggested we waiting until Roger got back.
17 Children would love being told bedtime stories.
18 To entering the premises without permission is not allowed.
19 As well as he studying to become a doctor, Tom works part-time as a waiter.
20 The car needs being servicing.

1	*for*
2	
3	
4	
5	
6	
7	
8	
9	
10	
11	
12	
13	
14	
15	
16	
17	
18	
19	
20	

Oral Development 2

The Smiths went on an excursion last Sunday. Use the list below and your own ideas to say what happened using infinitives or -ing forms.
look forward to, enjoy, spend time, discuss, would rather, expect, decide, easy, involve, stop, surprised, want, see, too frightened, suggest

eg. The Smiths had been looking forward to having a day out for ages ...

Consolidation 2

Phrasal Verbs

bring about: cause to happen
bring back: 1) recall, 2) reintroduce
bring down: 1) cause to fall, 2) reduce prices
bring forward: suggest an idea
bring on: cause, usu sth unpleasant
bring out: publish
bring round: 1) help sb regain consciousness;
bring to, 2) persuade sb to change opinion
bring up: 1) raise a child, 2) vomit, 3) introduce a subject, 4) mention

• • • • • • • • • • • • •

be/get carried away: be/get excited
carry off: do sth successfully
carry on (with): continue esp despite difficulties
carry out: perform, complete
carry over: postpone
carry through: 1) complete despite difficulties, 2) help sb survive during troubled times

34 Fill in the correct particle(s).

1 The corruption scandal brought ...*down*... the government.
2 The cold weather probably brought .... her illness.
3 Stephen King's publisher is bringing .... his new book next month.
4 A wet cloth helped to bring the unconscious man ....
5 She's brought .... five children on her own.
6 My father didn't want to let me buy a car, but in the end I managed to bring him ....
7 Jane carried .... her part in the play without difficulty.
8 "Carry .... your work please," said the teacher.
9 Tom got carried .... by the music and wouldn't stop singing.
10 If we don't pay the ransom, the kidnappers will carry .... their threats.

35 Look at Appendix 1, then fill in the correct preposition.

1 They congratulated him ...*on*... getting his degree.
2 The airport was crowded ...... holidaymakers.
3 She keeps boasting .... her new house.
4 The Prime Minister refused to comment .... the rumours about his resignation.
5 He's very clever .... solving crosswords.
6 She's capable .... answering all the questions herself.
7 The cause ...... the fire was never discovered.
8 Don't put the blame .... him. It's not his fault.
9 He blamed John .... stealing the money.
10 They were astonished .... the number of candidates who had succeeded.
11 Which political party do you belong ....?
12 Concentrate .... what you're doing.

13 He charged me £10 .... the repairs.
14 She was charged .... murder.
15 The police are holding three suspects .... connection .... the bombing in Brighton last week.
16 Is there any connection .... sunbathing and skin cancer?
17 More money is needed to help care .... the homeless.
18 He cares deeply .... the welfare of his students.
19 Italian is frequently compared .... French as they are from the same language family.
20 The standard of education at Mount Carmel College compares favourably .... the standards elsewhere.

36 Complete the sentences using the words in bold. Use two to five words.

1 I'm sure he didn't steal the money.
   stolen   He ...*can't have stolen*... the money.
2 It is likely that he will travel to Europe.
   to   He .... to Europe.
3 It's a pity you didn't come to the disco with us.
   have   You .... to the disco with us.
4 It's too cold to go camping.
   warm   It .... to go camping.
5 The car was so expensive that we couldn't buy it.
   for   The car .... to buy.

6 Crying over spilt milk is useless.
  use   It .... spilt milk.
7 She tends to get very excited at office parties.
  carried She .... at office parties.

How to treat Multiple Choice Cloze Texts

- **Read the whole passage at least once to understand as much of the general meaning as possible.**
- **Look at the four choices given for each gap and try to reduce the choices you have to make by eliminating the obviously incorrect ones.**
  eg. He .... the world record for the long jump in 1992.
     A did   B broke   C made   D reached
  *The word "record" is not used with "do" or "make". Also we do not say "reach" a record - you "reach" a destination. Therefore **B: broke** is the correct answer.*
- **When you have finished, read the text again to see if it makes sense and is grammatically correct.**

37 *For questions 1 - 15, read the text below and decide which word A, B, C or D best fits each space. There's an example at the beginning (0).*

The lost art of old masters

The three blank spaces **(0)** ... the wall of the Frankfurt Schirn Gallery are probably more photographed than the old paintings which **(1)** ... there until last Thursday. That was the day when thieves **(2)** ... two paintings by JMW Turner, which were **(3)** ... loan from London's Tate Gallery. In fact, as theft increases, empty walls are **(4)** ... an increasingly familiar **(5)** ... in Europe's galleries. The thieves are usually **(6)** ... of professional gangs who study the layout of their target in **(7)** ... beforehand. They are becoming better at overcoming the tightest security. The thieves of Frankfurt waited **(8)** ... the gallery closed at 10 pm, overpowered the security guard before he could **(9)** ... on the alarm system and **(10)** ... with the paintings to a waiting car. The pictures are **(11)** ... at £37.7 million and, since they are **(12)** ... famous to sell, police suspect that the thieves will hold them to ransom. A £62,800 reward is being **(13)** ... for information. Unfortunately European Union policy has made it easier for thieves to **(14)** ... borders and harder for police to follow them. To discourage thieves, galleries may have to turn themselves **(15)** ... high security fortresses.

	A		B		C		D			A	B	C	D
0	A	in	B	over	C	on	D	along	**0**	☐	☐	▇	☐
1	A	hung	B	stayed	C	held	D	fixed	**1**	☐	☐	☐	☐
2	A	robbed	B	stole	C	burgled	D	borrowed	**2**	☐	☐	☐	☐
3	A	for	B	at	C	in	D	on	**3**	☐	☐	☐	☐
4	A	getting	B	becoming	C	having	D	growing	**4**	☐	☐	☐	☐
5	A	sight	B	scene	C	site	D	look	**5**	☐	☐	☐	☐
6	A	guests	B	members	C	partners	D	owners	**6**	☐	☐	☐	☐
7	A	fact	B	addition	C	detail	D	general	**7**	☐	☐	☐	☐
8	A	for	B	while	C	before	D	until	**8**	☐	☐	☐	☐
9	A	turn	B	go	C	rely	D	set	**9**	☐	☐	☐	☐
10	A	escaped	B	parted	C	got	D	hid	**10**	☐	☐	☐	☐
11	A	measured	B	charged	C	valued	D	appreciated	**11**	☐	☐	☐	☐
12	A	too	B	enough	C	very	D	quite	**12**	☐	☐	☐	☐
13	A	stated	B	offered	C	held	D	taken	**13**	☐	☐	☐	☐
14	A	swap	B	alter	C	change	D	cross	**14**	☐	☐	☐	☐
15	A	for	B	towards	C	into	D	over	**15**	☐	☐	☐	☐

Consilidation 2

38 Use the words in capitals to form a word that fits in the space in the same line.

Dangerous Work

The **(0)** ....of your being killed or injured at work determines how much life **(1)** .... you have to pay. An **(2)** ...., for example, has a fairly high life **(3)** .... - they are only at risk from the odd **(4)** .... cable - and are therefore in a low risk **(5)** .... . Higher premiums are paid by people who have more **(6)** .... jobs such as **(7)** .... workers. There were sixty-five deaths on building sites last year alone. **(8)** .... most accidents and deaths are caused by a **(9)** .... to ignore **(10)** .... regulations, when simple precautions and good sense can prevent fatalities.

PROBABLE	
INSURE	
ELECTRIC	
EXPECT	
FAULT	
CLASSIFY	
DANGER	
CONSTRUCT	
FORTUNATELY	
TEND	
SAFE	

0	probability
1	
2	
3	
4	
5	
6	
7	
8	
9	
10	

39 Read the text carefully. Some of the lines are correct and some have a word which should not be there. If a line is correct, put a tick (✔) in the space provided. If a line has a word which should not be there, write it in the space provided.

The surprising season

0	Throughout all history, spring weather conditions have
00	varied more than those of the other three seasons. In the
1	early spring of 1083 the River Thames it froze for over
2	14 weeks, while in spring 1412 it is dried up.
3	Spring flooding in 1092 meant to the year
4	was remembered for much poor crops. In fact,
5	through the centuries the most greatest number of
6	major droughts, floods, hurricanes and earthquakes
7	will have occurred during springtime. Indeed, looking
8	at agricultural records, 1660 is the only spring having
9	recorded as "very pleasant". Spring arrives at slightly
10	different times in different regions of the British Isles.
11	In lowland England it appears on around the middle
12	of March. In the west and south it arrives even at
13	earlier, while in the north and in hilly areas it does
14	not come until April. Here, when spring is mentioned about,
15	it means the average temperature which is over 6°C.

0	all
00	✓
1	
2	
3	
4	
5	
6	
7	
8	
9	
10	
11	
12	
13	
14	
15	

40 Fill in the following collocation grids.

	a bus	a sailing boat	a car	a horse	a camel	a bike	a yacht	a limo
drive	✔							
ride								
sail								

Practice test **1**

For questions 1 - 15, read the text below and decide which word A, B, C or D best fits each space. Mark your answers in the answer boxes provided.

Eccentric or mad?

Traditionally, the British have always been very fond **(0)** .... their eccentrics. Even today, British eccentrics are considered to be the strangest, **(1)** .... to American psychologist David Weeks. **(2)** .... the Leopard Man, for example. He lives alone in a cave on the Isle of Skye. He is tattooed from **(3)** .... to toe with leopard spots, and **(4)** .... a living selling seafood. But is this bizarre **(5)** .... a type of mental illness? It has long been believed that creativity and insanity are **(6)** .... In the last 30 years or so, psychologists have tried to find evidence to **(7)** .... this belief. One study found that creative people have a lot **(8)** .... common with eccentrics and also that they are more **(9)** .... to suffer from extreme depression, which is often associated with mental illness. But during David Weeks' detailed **(10)** .... into the personalities of eccentrics, he found that they are **(11)** .... the happiest and healthiest of people. Not **(12)** .... do they visit their doctors much less often than the **(13)** .... of us, but they are also usually **(14)** .... in several things at one time, so they always have a **(15)** .... in life.

0	**A** for	**B** about	**C** of	**D** with	0 A☐ B☐ C■ D☐
1	**A** concerning	**B** considering	**C** responding	**D** according	1 A☐ B☐ C☐ D☐
2	**A** Take	**B** See	**C** Watch	**D** Look	2 A☐ B☐ C☐ D☐
3	**A** head	**B** hair	**C** height	**D** peak	3 A☐ B☐ C☐ D☐
4	**A** creates	**B** makes	**C** gets	**D** has	4 A☐ B☐ C☐ D☐
5	**A** action	**B** treatment	**C** behaviour	**D** acting	5 A☐ B☐ C☐ D☐
6	**A** joined	**B** connected	**C** same	**D** attached	6 A☐ B☐ C☐ D☐
7	**A** support	**B** hold	**C** give	**D** bear	7 A☐ B☐ C☐ D☐
8	**A** on	**B** from	**C** in	**D** of	8 A☐ B☐ C☐ D☐
9	**A** likely	**B** probable	**C** possibly	**D** available	9 A☐ B☐ C☐ D☐
10	**A** search	**B** research	**C** check	**D** look	10 A☐ B☐ C☐ D☐
11	**A** among	**B** between	**C** by	**D** apart	11 A☐ B☐ C☐ D☐
12	**A** only	**B** just	**C** simply	**D** purely	12 A☐ B☐ C☐ D☐
13	**A** other	**B** most	**C** others	**D** rest	13 A☐ B☐ C☐ D☐
14	**A** interesting	**B** involving	**C** interested	**D** invested	14 A☐ B☐ C☐ D☐
15	**A** goal	**B** reason	**C** score	**D** want	15 A☐ B☐ C☐ D☐

For questions 16 - 30, read the text below and think of the word which best fits each space.
Use only one word in each space. Write your answers in the answer boxes provided.

Vegetables

We are frequently told these days that we should eat more vegetables **(0)** .... part of a healthy diet. However, a large **(16)** .... of people are still not taking this advice. One of the reasons could be that they **(17)** .... bad memories of the few vegetables they were forced to eat by **(18)** .... parents when they were children. **(19)** .... the other hand, potatoes are one **(20)** .... of vegetable which we are familiar **(21)** .... although we do not perhaps think of them **(22)** .... healthy food to eat. Of course, chips are not very good for us **(23)** .... of their high fat content, but potatoes can **(24)** .... cooked in many other interesting ways which do not harm our health. **(25)** .... vegetables which we will almost certainly **(26)** .... eaten are carrots, turnips and parsnips. Carrots can be eaten raw, while parsnips can be prepared **(27)** .... potatoes, and baby turnips are crisp and as sweet as apples when cooked. Alternatively, there are many different vegetables in the shops, **(28)** .... as celeriac, kohlrabi and salsify. These may **(29)** .... strange to us at the moment, but they are as easy to cook as **(30)** .... of the other vegetables mentioned and make a delicious change.

0	*as*	0
16		16
17		17
18		18
19		19
20		20
21		21
22		22
23		23
24		24
25		25
26		26
27		27
28		28
29		29
30		30

Part 3

For questions 31 - 40, complete the second sentence so that it has a similar meaning to the first sentence. Use the word given and other words to complete each sentence. You must use between two and five words. Do not change the word given. Write your answers in the answer boxes provided.

0 I'm sure they worked hard on the project.
   have
   They .... on the project.

| 0 | *must have worked hard* | ☐ 0 ▬ |

31 You'll have no difficulty getting out of the country.
   easy
   You'll find .... out of the country.

| 31 | | ☐ 31 ☐ |

32 The film was amusing.
   were
   We .... the film.

| 32 | | ☐ 32 ☐ |

33 He is like his father in many ways.
   takes
   He .... in many ways.

| 33 | | ☐ 33 ☐ |

34 I'm almost positive she spoke to Tom last night.
   must
   She .... last night.

| 34 | | ☐ 34 ☐ |

35 I'm afraid there's no milk left.
   run
   I'm afraid we .... milk.

| 35 | | ☐ 35 ☐ |

36 She spent hours planting the new flowers.
   took
   It .... the new flowers.

| 36 | | ☐ 36 ☐ |

37 I prefer watching westerns to watching romances.
   than
   I would prefer to watch .... romances.

| 37 | | ☐ 37 ☐ |

38 They made him work overtime.
   was
   He .... overtime.

| 38 | | ☐ 38 ☐ |

39 He hasn't finished cooking the meal yet.
   still
   He .... the meal.

| 39 | | ☐ 39 ☐ |

40 People say this is the best film ever made.
   supposed
   This .... the best film ever made.

| 40 | | ☐ 40 ☐ |

Part 4

For questions 41 - 55, read the text below and look carefully at each line. Some of the lines are correct and some have a word which should not be there. If a line is correct, put a tick (✔) by the number in the answer boxes provided. If a line has a word which should not be there, write the word in the answer boxes provided.

Electronic noses!

0	Smell is probably the most undervalued	**0**	✔	0
00	of the five senses, the others of which are as taste,	**00**	*as*	00
41	touch, sight and hearing. The perfume of roses either or	**41**		41
42	of a freshly-baked bread gives pleasure, but odours	**42**		42
43	can also be important in that checking the	**43**		43
44	quality of products coming off industrial production	**44**		44
45	lines or in detecting some disease. An electronic	**45**		45
46	nose has been developed so that has twelve sensors	**46**		46
47	to detect smells. They are very sensitive enough	**47**		47
48	to pick them up the difference between the	**48**		48
49	smell of two types of white wine. The electronic	**49**		49
50	nose is especially useful as well it can pick out "bad"	**50**		50
51	batches of, say, beer or perfume. Research it	**51**		51
52	suggests that people who suffer from certain	**52**		52
53	illnesses, such as the diabetes or lung cancer, give	**53**		53
54	off characteristic smells. Doctors will hope that, in	**54**		54
55	future, electronic noses might to help early diagnosis.	**55**		55

Part 5

For questions 56 - 65, read the text below. Use the word given in capitals at the end of each line to form a word that fits in the space in the same line. Write your word in the answer boxes provided.

Sleep

Scientists continually offer new **(0)** .... and make new **(56)** .... about the condition known as "sleep". People are paid to sleep with **(57)** .... machines attached to them. These monitor changes in eye **(58)** ...., heartbeat and body temperature, among other things. This information is fed into a computer and, after a few **(59)** ...., the scientist can establish the **(60)** .... and quality of sleep. It is still unclear how **(61)** .... these experiments are in establishing **(62)** .... what goes on between losing **(63)** .... and awakening. However, one's **(64)** .... the following day is dependent upon how **(65)** .... the previous night's sleep was.

INTERPRET	**0** *Interpretations*	0
DISCOVER	**56**	56
VARY	**57**	57
	58	58
MOVE	**59**	59
CALCULATE	**60**	60
DEEP	**61**	61
SUCCESS	**62**	62
EXACT	**63**	63
CONSCIOUS	**64**	64
BEHAVE	**65**	65
SATISFY		

3 Tense Forms

Present Forms

Present Simple	Present Continuous	Present Perfect	Present Perf. Continuous
permanent situations or states *She works in a bank.* **permanent truths or laws of nature** *The sun rises in the east.*	**temporary situations** *He is spending the week with his mother.* **changing or developing situations** *She is getting more and more impatient.*	**recently completed actions** *She has dyed her hair black. (The action is complete - her hair is now dyed black - evidence in the present)*	**actions started in the past and continuing up to the present.** *She has been doing her homework for an hour. (She started an hour ago and she's still doing it.)*
repeated/habitual actions (especially with frequency adverbs: often, usually, always etc) *He always goes to bed at 11 o'clock. (Here "always" means every day.)*	**frequently repeated actions with always, constantly, continually, expressing annoyance or criticism** *He's always getting into trouble. (Here "always" means constantly.)*	**complete past actions connected to the present with stated or unstated time reference** *He has bought a house. (Now he owns a house.) He has just returned from Paris. (stated time reference)*	**past actions of certain duration having visible results or effects in the present** *He has been running. That's why he's out of breath.*
reviews/sports commentaries/ dramatic narrative *Smythe serves the ball and Lanyon misses it ...*	**actions happening at or around the moment of speaking** *The sun is shining now. He is studying for the exams.*	**personal experiences/ changes which have happened** *I have lost weight recently.*	**to express anger, irritation, annoyance, explanation or criticism** *She has been using my make-up. (annoyance)*
timetables/programmes (future reference) *The train leaves at 8.00.* **in exclamatory sentences** *There goes the bus!*	**fixed arrangements in the near future** *I'm going to the theatre this evening.*	**emphasis on number** *He has seen three films this week. She has had four cups of coffee since she woke up.*	**Present Perfect Continuous is normally used with for, since or how long to put emphasis on duration** *He has been feeling unwell for days.*

Time expressions usually used with Present Forms

Present Simple	Present Continuous	Present Perfect & Present Perfect Continuous
every day/week/month/ year, usually, sometimes, always, rarely, never, often, in the morning/ evening/afternoon, at night, on Mondays etc	**now, at the moment, at present, nowadays, today, tonight, always, still etc**	**just, ever, never, already, yet (negations & questions), always, how long, so far, recently, since (= from a starting point in the past), for (= over a period of time), today, this week/month etc** For and since **are usually used with Present Perfect Continuous to emphasise the duration of an action.**

41 *Put the verbs in brackets into the correct present forms.*

"Well, I **1)** ...*have never won*... (never/win) anything like this before! I **2)** .... (only/enter) a few competitions in my life so this is a big surprise. Of course, I **3)** .... (watch) TV quiz shows for years, but now I **4)** .... (think) of taking part in more. The prize is wonderful. We **5)** .... (stay) here in Hawaii for ten days now and we **6)** .... (have) a great time. We **7)** .... (already/see) all the sights and my wife **8)** .... (buy) lots of souvenirs. We **9)** .... (send) postcards to all our friends to show them how we **10)** .... (spend) our time. Yes, we really **11)** .... (enjoy) ourselves. In fact, we **12)** .... (want) to stay forever."

3 Tense Forms

Stative verbs express a permanent state rather than an action and are not used in the continuous forms. These are: **verbs of the senses** used to express involuntary actions (feel, hear, see, smell, taste etc), **verbs of feelings and emotions** (adore, detest, dislike, enjoy, forgive, hate, like etc), **verbs of opinion** (agree, believe, suppose, understand etc) and **other verbs** (belong, concern, depend, know, mean, own, possess, need, prefer, want etc) *I see someone coming. She hates pop music. I don't agree with you. He knows a lot about computers.* **Note: feel** and **hurt** can be used in either continuous or simple forms. *She feels/is feeling better.* **Look, watch** and **listen** express deliberate actions and can be used in continuous forms. *He is listening to some records.*

Some stative verbs (be, love, see, smell, taste, think etc) have continuous forms but there is a difference in meaning.

STATE	ACTION
● I **see** them coming towards us. (= I have the ability)	● She**'s seeing** her doctor today. (= she's visiting)
● These flowers **smell** nice. (= they have a nice smell)	● Why **are you smelling** the food? Has it gone off? (= why are you checking the smell of)
● This soup **tastes** delicious. (= its flavour is good)	● She**'s tasting** the soup. (= she's testing the flavour)
● It **feels** like velvet. (= it has the texture of)	● He**'s feeling** the cloth. (= he's touching the cloth)
● He **has** a house. (= he possesses)	● We**'re having** a nice time. (= we're enjoying ourselves)
● **Do you like** his new car? (= Is it nice?)	● How **are they liking** the party? (= they are enjoying)
● I **think** he has left. (= I suppose)	● I**'m thinking** about his suggestion. (= I'm considering)
● Ann **is** polite. (= her character is)	● Tom **is being** very impolite. (= he is behaving impolitely)
● It **looks** as if it's going to snow. (= it appears)	● They **are looking** at the statue. (= they're viewing it)

42 Fill in with Present Simple or Continuous.

1 A: I **1)** ...*see*... (see) there's a great film on at the cinema tonight. Would you like to go?
   B: No, I **2)** .... (see) the dentist about my toothache.
2 A: I **1)** .... (think) about going on a picnic this afternoon.
   B: I wouldn't bother. I **2)** .... (think) it's going to rain.
3 A: Is John feeling OK? He **1)** .... (look) very red in the face.
   B: Yes, I know. I **2)** .... (look) for the doctor's telephone number now.
4 A: How **1)** .... (you/like) your stay in Budapest?
   B: I am really enjoying myself. I particularly **2)** .... (like) the Hungarian food.
5 A: Why **1)** .... (you/taste) the stew?
   B: I think you need to add some spices; it **2)** .... (taste) a bit bland.
6 A: Why **1)** .... (you/feel) the radiator, Dad?
   B: I don't think it's working; it **2)** .... (feel) very cold in here.
7 A: Tom **1)** .... (be) usually a very quiet boy.
   B: Yes, but he **2)** .... (be) very noisy today.
8 A: **1)** .... (you/have) a car?
   B: Yes, but I **2)** .... (have) some problems with it, so it's at the garage.
9 A: Why **1)** .... (you/smell) the roses?
   B: They always **2)** .... (smell) so wonderful at this time of year.

43 Put the verbs in brackets into the correct present forms.

Jane,
Thanks for agreeing to look after my flat while I'm away. I **1)** ...*have cleaned*... (clean) the flat thoroughly but as I **2)** .... (work) late all week, I **3)** .... (not/have) time to cook any food for you. My dog, Rover, **4)** .... (eat) a tin of dog food every night and the plants **5)** .... (need) watering once a week. Tonight I **6)** .... (stay) at the Hutton Hotel so you can contact me there if you need me.

Donna

Have gone to / Have been to / Have been in

He **has gone to** Scotland. *(He's on his way to Scotland or he's there now. He hasn't come back yet.)*
He **has been to** Munich once. *(He has visited Munich, but he isn't there now. He has come back.)*
He **has been in** Rotterdam for two years. *(He lives in Rotterdam now.)*

 Fill in "has/have been to/in", "has/have gone to".

1 Bertha's not here. She ...*has gone to*... the library.
2 I .... Madrid, but I only spent a few days there.
3 "How long ....you .... Birmingham?" "For nearly two years."
4 Tom is alone because his parents .... the seaside for the weekend.
5 Julia .... the supermarket - she'll be back in about an hour.

Since expresses a starting point. *I've been here* **since** *March.*
For expresses the duration of an action. *We've been here* **for** *three months.*

 Fill in "since" or "for".

Sue Wilson has been involved in sports **1)** ...*for*... more than 25 years. Her first interest was gymnastics, which she has been actively involved in **2)** .... she was ten, but she has also been interested in other forms of sport **3)** .... many years. She has been a keen cyclist **4)** .... 1980, when she made her first bicycle tour of Europe, and **5)** .... her marriage to all-round sportsman Tom Wilson in 1985, she has tried her hand at climbing, sailing and skydiving. Her talent as a writer has kept her busy **6)** .... the past ten years, and she has become familiar to TV viewers as a sports commentator **7)** .... her first TV appearance in 1988. Her plans for the future? "I've been interested in the role of women in sports ever **8)** .... I was a teenager. Now, after being so busy **9)** .... all these years, I've decided to take some time off so I can write a book about it." Since Sue has been part of the sporting world **10)** .... so long, her book should be fascinating.

 Look at the notes below, then write an article using the appropriate present forms.

For many years researchers - try - determine whether animals - share with humans the ability to use language/One particular researcher in America - spend - sixteen years exploring the degree to which a parrot - understand - what he - say/He - find that the bird - be able to - answer questions about objects and also - understand numbers/At the moment the researcher - try - to determine whether the bird actually - know what it - say - or whether it - simply imitate - a collection of sounds.

...*For many years researchers have been trying to determine whether animals* ....

47 *Put the verbs in brackets into the correct present forms.*

Dear John,

First of all, sorry I 1) ...**haven't written**... (not/write) for so long, but I was on holiday. 2) .... (you/get) your exam results yet? I'm sure you 3) .... (pass) them all since you always 4) .... (study) so hard. I 5) .... (wait) for mine at the moment and I 6) .... (try) not to worry! Well, I 7) .... (write) from my new flat. Yes, I 8) .... (move) house! Now we 9) .... (paint) and 10) .... (clean) the place to make it look nice. When it's finished, I am going to have a party and because I 11) .... (not/see) you for weeks I 12) .... (want) you to come. Write soon and let me know if I'll see you there.
Love,
Mary

3 Tense Forms

Put the verbs in brackets into the correct present forms.

1 Alan ...*is flying*... (fly) to Barcelona tonight. He ....
(already/pack) his suitcase but he .... (not/call) a taxi yet. His
plane .... (leave) at 8 pm.

2 Ann and Sally .... (be) flatmates. They sometimes .... (argue)
because Sally .... (always/make) a mess in the kitchen.

3 "Look over there! It's John Cooper." "Oh yes! But he .... (look) so
different! He .... (put on) at least 15 kilos and I .... (think)
he .... (wear) a toupée."

4 Ever since the accident Susan .... (be) afraid to drive. Next week she
.... (see) a psychologist who .... (specialise) in that
sort of problem.

5 "What a great match! Johnson ...... (pass) the ball to Green, who .... (shoot) and .... (score)!"

6 "What on earth .... (you/do)? Your clothes are all dirty!" "Well, I .... (work) in the garden all day. Look! I .... (already/plant) a lot of flowers. I .... (plan) to cut the grass now.

La Sagrada Familia

Past Forms

Past Simple	Past Continuous	Past Perfect	Past Perf. Continuous
past actions which happened one immediately after the other *She* **woke** *up,* **got** *out of bed and* **made** *a cup of tea.*	**action in the middle of happening at a stated past time** *This time last week* **I was travelling** *across Africa.*	**past action which occurred before another action or before a stated past time** *By his second day at camp he* **had made** *several friends.*	**action continuing over a period up to a specific time in the past** *She* **had been saving** *for a whole year before she bought her ticket to Australia.*
past habit or state *He* **rode** *his bike to school every day when he was a child.* **complete action or event which happened at a stated past time** *She* **sold** *her car last week. ("When?" "Last week." - stated past time)*	**past action in progress interrupted by another past action. The longer action is in the Past Continuous, the shorter action is in the Past Simple.** *I* **was taking** *a shower when I heard the telephone ring.*	**complete past action which had visible results in the past** *She felt much safer after she* **had locked** *all the doors.*	**past action of certain duration which had visible results in the past** *He* **had been shouting** *so loudly that he had a sore throat.*
complete past actions not connected to the present with a stated or implied time reference *Shakespeare* **wrote** *at least 36 plays. (Shakespeare is dead - he won't write any more.)*	**two or more simultaneous past actions of certain duration** *I* **was washing** *up while he* **was drying** *the dishes.* **background description to events in a story/narration** *I* **was walking** *along ...*	**the Past Perfect is the past equivalent of the Present Perfect** *The room was empty - everyone* **had gone** *out. (Present Perfect: The room is empty - everyone has gone out.)*	**the Past Perfect Cont. is the past equivalent of the Present Perfect Cont.** *The party was a great success because he* **had been preparing** *for it all week. (Present Perfect: The party is a great success because he has been preparing for it all week.)*

Time expressions usually used with Past Forms

Past Simple	Past Continuous	Past Perfect	Past Perf. Continuous
yesterday, last week etc, (how long) ago, then, just now, when, in 1992 etc	while, when, as, the moment that etc	for, since, already, after, just, never, yet, before, by, by the time etc	for, since

49 *Put the verbs in brackets into the correct past forms.*

Last year, Tom and Fiona **1)** ...*decided*... (decide) to buy a house. They **2)** .... (save up) for ages, and by the end of May they **3)** .... (put by) enough for the deposit on a house. They **4)** .... (live) in a tiny flat at the time and Fiona **5)** .... (insist) that she **6)** .... (want) a house with a big garden. They **7)** .... (search) for only a few days when they found exactly what they **8)** .... (look for) - a two-bedroomed house in nearly an acre of garden. Unfortunately the owner **9)** .... (ask) much more than they **10)** .... (be) willing to pay, and when they **11)** .... (look) more closely at the interior, they **12)** .... (see) that whoever **13)** .... (live) there before, **14)** .... (make) an absolute mess of the walls and floors. Still, Fiona **15)** .... (like) the garden and the location so much that she **16)** .... (manage) to convince Tom that, despite the price, it **17)** .... (be) the perfect house for them.

50 *Put the verbs in brackets into the correct past forms.*

Last summer some friends and I **1)** ...*arranged*... (arrange) to go camping. We **2)** .... (look) forward to going for weeks when finally the date of departure **3)** .... (arrive). We **4)** .... (load) the car with our luggage and **5)** .... (set off) early in the morning. The weather was perfect, the sun **6)** .... (shine) brightly and the wind **7)** .... (blow) gently. There **8)** .... (not/be) a cloud in the sky! Shortly afterwards, while we **9)** .... (travel) along the motorway, we **10)** .... (notice) that the car **11)** .... (make) a strange noise. Pete, who **12)** .... (drive) very fast, suddenly **13)** .... (stop) the car. Everyone **14)** .... (get out) and **15)** .... (go) round to the back of the car. To our surprise the boot was wide open - whoever **16)** .... (load) the luggage **17)** .... (not/close) it properly, and everything **18)** .... (fall out)!

Present Perfect	Past Simple
• He **has left.** *(unstated time; we don't know when he left)*	• He **left** a minute ago. *(stated time - When? A minute ago.)*
• She **has been** in Rome for two months. *(she's still in Rome - action connected to the present)*	• She **was** in Rome for two months. *(she isn't in Rome any more - action not connected to the present)*
• He**'s been** to the cinema five times this month. *(it's still the same month - action connected to the present)*	• He **went** to the cinema five times last month. *(action not connected to the present - it's the following month now)*
• I**'ve seen** Matt Dillon. *(action connected to the present - he's still alive)*	• I **saw** Sir Lawrence Olivier. *(action not connected to the present - he's dead)*
• The Queen **has decided** to give up the throne. *(announcing news)*	• She **announced** her decision this morning. *(giving details of the news - stated time in past)*

51 *Fill in with Present Perfect or Past Simple.*

1 A: "Is Paul there, please?"
   B: "Sorry, he **1)** ...*left*... (leave) about 10 minutes ago". I think he **2)** .... (go) to the library.
2 A: I **1)** .... (live) in Lisbon for two years now.
   B: Really? What a coincidence! I **2)** .... (live) there for a year before moving to America.
3 A: I need a holiday. I **1)** .... (only/have) two days off this year.
   B: Yes, but last year you **2)** .... (go) on holiday four times!
4 A: My father once **1)** .... (see) Elvis Presley in Las Vegas.
   B: Well, I **2)** .... (see) his daughter, Lisa, many times. She lives near me.

3 Tense Forms

5 A: The chairman **1)** .... (decide) to retire.
   B: Yes, actually he **2)** .... (inform) the managing director of his decision this morning.

Used to - Be used to + ing form/noun/pronoun - Would - Was going to

● **Used to** expresses past habitual actions and permanent states. (Note that stative verbs are not used with "would".)	*When I was young, I **used to go** climbing once a month. (also: would go)* *He **used to live** in Paris. (not: ~~would~~ - state)*
● **Would** expresses past repeated actions and routines - not states.	*When I was a child, I **would go** to the cinema every Sunday. (also: I used to go ...)*
● **Be used to** means "be accustomed to", "be in the habit of".	*Little children **are used to going to bed** early in the evening.*
● **Was going to** expresses actions one intended to do but didn't do.	*He **was going to buy** a house but he lost all his money at the racetrack.*

52 *Complete the sentences using the words in bold. Use two to five words.*

1 Sally went to ballet classes three times a week.
   go   Sally ...*used to go to*... ballet classes three times a week.
2 It was my intention to phone you last night, but I forgot.
   going   I .... you last night, but I forgot.
3 Lying on the beach all day is an unusual experience for me.
   used   I .... on the beach all day.
4 When I was young, I used to visit my grandmother every day after school.
   would   When I was young, ... every day after school.

53 *Read the notes, then write the story of Beatrix Potter using appropriate past forms.*

When she - grow up Beatrix Potter - be - very fond of animals and - always draw - pictures of her pet rabbit/She - earn a living as an illustrator for several years before her dream of becoming an author come true/It - be the result of a letter - she - send to a sick child describing the adventures of four rabbits/She - later publish it - as "The Tale of Peter Rabbit"/It - become - an instant success and more tales - follow/By the time Beatrix - die - she - write over twenty-five tales and - achieve recognition as one of the greatest children's writers.

When she was growing up Beatrix Potter was very fond of animals... ....

54 *Put the verbs in brackets into the appropriate past forms.*

1 Bill ...*was painting*... (paint) his front door when the telephone .... (start) ringing. He .... (answer) the phone and .... (speak) to his friend. Later he .... (notice) that he .... (leave) red fingerprints all over the phone.
2 "..................... (Tony/ring) you last night?" "Yes. He .... (wait) for days for you to phone him but since you .... (not/phone) he .... (sell) his motorbike to someone else."
3 "Your hair .... (look) different last night." "I know - I .... (want) to dye it red, but I .... (not/pay) attention when I .... (buy) the dye and I .... (not/realise) until it .... (be) too late that I .... (buy) the wrong colour."
4 One day my sister .... (call) me. She .... (not/know) what to cook for a dinner party she .... (give) that evening and she .... (want) some advice. I .... (give) her some simple recipes but I .... (be) surprised that she .... (not/contact) our mother. When I .... (ask) why, she .... (reply), "She's one of the guests."

5 Last Friday I .... (walk) to work when I .... (see) an old friend I .... (not/see) for a long time. I .... (throw) my arms around him. He .... (stare) at me with an open mouth. To my horror I .... (realise) I .... (mistake) him for my friend.

Future Forms

Future Simple	Be going to	Future Continuous	Future Perfect
decisions taken at the moment of speaking (on-the-spot decisions) *I'm hungry. I'll cook something to eat.*	**actions intended to be performed in the near future** *I'm going to join a gym on Saturday.*	**actions in progress at a stated future time** *This time next year she'll be running her own business.*	**actions finished before a stated future time** *They will have emigrated to Canada by Christmas.*
hopes, fears, threats, offers, promises, warnings, predictions, requests, comments etc, esp. with: expect, hope, believe, I'm sure, I'm afraid, probably etc *I promise I'll be on time.*	**planned actions or intentions** *Now that she's passed her exams she's going to train to be a solicitor.*	**actions which are the result of a routine (instead of the Present Continuous)** *I'll be playing tennis on Sunday. (I play tennis every Sunday - it's part of my routine.)*	**Note:** **by** or **not ... until/till** are used with Future Perf. **Until/till** are normally used with Future Perfect only in negative sentences. *He will have completed his studies by the end of the year. (not: till/until) He won't have arrived until tonight.*
actions or predictions which may (not) happen in the future *He'll probably pass his driving test.* **or actions which we cannot control and will inevitably happen** *Summer will be here soon.*	**evidence that something will definitely happen in the near future** *Those dark clouds mean it's going to rain soon.* *It's so hot - I'm going to faint.*	**when we ask politely about people's arrangements to see if they can do sth for us or because we want to offer to do sth for them** *Will you be going shopping at the supermarket today? Can you buy me some milk?*	**Future Perfect Cont.** **duration of an action up to a certain time in the future** *By his sixtieth birthday he will have been teaching for 35 years.*
things we are not yet sure about or we haven't decided to do yet *Perhaps I'll move house.*	**things we are sure about or we have already decided to do in the near future** *They are going to operate on his leg. (It has been decided.)*	**Present Simple (with future meaning)** timetables/programmes *The play begins at 7 o'clock this evening.*	**Present Continuous (with future meaning)** fixed arrangement in the near future *She's meeting her aunt this weekend.*

Shall is used:

with I/we in questions, suggestions, offers or when asking for advice.
Shall we go home now?
What shall I wear?

Will is used:

to express offers, threats, promises, predictions, warnings, requests, hopes, fears, on-the-spot decisions, comments (mainly with: think, expect, believe, I'm sure, hope, know, suppose and probably).
I hope you will keep in touch with me.

Time expressions used with:

Future Simple & Be going to	Future Perfect	Future Perfect Continuous
tomorrow, tonight, next week/month, in two/three etc days, the day after tomorrow, soon, in a week/month etc	before, by, by then, by the time, (until is used only in negative sentences with this tense)	by ... for

3 Tense Forms

Fill in the correct future forms.

Technology has made such dramatic advances in
the past decade that by the year 2005 who knows
what changes **1)** *...will have taken...* (take) place. It
is quite likely that by 2005 we **2)** ....
(use up) most of the earth's natural resources and
so we **3)** .... (rely) on wind power and
hydropower for our energy needs. As a result of
this shortage of energy, it is quite probable that scientists **4)** .... (find) a way for us to live
outside the earth. By the next century it's possible
that people **5)** .... (live) in cities on the
Moon or perhaps in cities on the seabed. It is to be
hoped that scientists **6)** .... (discover)
cures for fatal diseases such as Aids and, due to
the advancement of genetic engineering, hereditary
diseases passed down from generation to gener-

ation **7)** .... (exist) no longer. It is quite possible that by 2005 life expectancy **8)** ....
.... (increase) to 100 and that we **9)** .... (be able to) enjoy a healthier existence
than is now possible. Another area likely to have been further affected by technology in the year 2005 is
education. In schools, computers **10)** .... (replace) teachers and many students **11)** ....
.... (stay) at home to complete their education. We **12)** .... (see) changes in the work-
place too. The two main areas of employment **13)** .... (be) the so-called creative and caring professions, and the disappearance of jobs in manufacturing **14)** .... (result) in massive unemployment.

- **We never use future forms after: as long as, as soon as, after, before, by the time, if (conditional), unless, in case, until/till, when (time conjunction), whenever, while, once,
  suppose/supposing, on condition that etc.** *Let's buy some extra food in case they* **call** *round.
  (not: in case they will call round)*
- **When** used as a question word and **if** meaning "whether" (especially after I don't know, I
  doubt, I wonder etc) can be used with future forms. ***When will he bring*** *the books back? We
  don't know* ***if he will be appointed*** *to the post or not. (= whether)*

Fill in the correct present or future forms.

When you **1)** *...take...* (take) a holiday with Activity Wales, you **2)** .... (have) the time of your
life. As soon as you **3)** .... (arrive), you **4)** .... (feel) as if you **5)** .... (be) in a
different world. While you **6)** .... (stay) with us, we **7)** .... (do) our best to ensure
that your holiday **8)** .... (run) smoothly and you **9)** .... (not/get) bored. Activity
Wales **10)** .... (have) something to offer for all ages and tastes. If you **11)** ....
(want) to play golf, ride, sail or fish, our staff **12)** .... (be) happy to make the necessary arrangements, or if you simply **13)** .... (want) to relax and enjoy the breathtaking
scenery we **14)** .... (be) delighted to organise some guided walks. Before your holiday
15) .... (be) over, you **16)** .... (already/plan) your next visit.

Fill in "will" or "be going to".

1 A: Why do you need so much sugar?
   B: I *...'m going to...* make a cake.
2 A: Oh no! I've left my purse at home and I haven't got any money on me!
   B: Don't worry. I .... lend you some.
3 A: I don't know how to use this mixer.
   B: That's OK. I .... show you.

4   A: Why are all these people gathered here?
     B: The Prime Minister .... open the new hospital ward.
5   A: Did you remember to buy the magazine I asked for?
     B: Sorry, I didn't. I .... buy it when I go out again.
6   A: What's that on your curtains?
     B: It's a stain. I .... take them to the dry cleaner's tomorrow.
7   A: These bags are very heavy. I can't lift them.
     B: I ....carry them for you.
8   A: I hear you're going to Leeds University in September.
     B: Yes, I .... study French and German.
9   A: Why don't you tidy your room?
     B: I .... play football in ten minutes, so I haven't got time.
10 A: How can we get all this home?
     B: I .... ask James to come and help.

58   *Put the verbs in brackets into the appropriate future forms.*

A.   From 14 - 20 June, Liverpool **1)** ...*will be holding/is holding*... (hold) its International Garden Festival. Tickets **2)** .... (be) on sale to the public from Saturday 1 May and this year we **3)** .... (offer) special family tickets at the discount price of £15. The gates **4)** .... (open) at 9 am and the first event **5)** .... (start) at 9.30.

B.   Kenwhite's one-day sale **1)** .... (start) this Monday. The store **2)** .... (open) at 8 am and early morning shoppers **3)** .... (be able to) enjoy shopping in peace and quiet before the crowds **4)** .... (arrive). We **5)** .... (offer) substantial discounts on ladieswear and you **6)** .... (come across) some real bargains in our menswear range. By the end of the day we are sure that all of our customers **7)** .... (find) what they are looking for.

C.   Anne Mayton's latest book "The S-Plan Diet" **1)** .... (be) available in bookshops next week. The new S-plan diet **2)** .... (help) you lose weight safely and quickly. You **3)** .... (not/need) to miss meals and you **4)** .... (not/have to) spend hours measuring out portions of food. By the end of the diet the author guarantees you **5)** ... . (lose) at least 7 kilos or she **6)** .... (give) you your money back.

Time Words

● **Ago**: back in time from now (used with Past Simple)   *Ann left an hour **ago**.*
● **Before**: back in time from then. *Tony told me that Ann had left an hour **before**.* **Before** is also used with present or past forms to show that an action preceded another. *He'll come **before** you leave. He had cooked dinner **before** she came home.*
● **Already** is used with Perfect tenses in mid or end position in statements or questions. *He had **already** fixed the tap when the plumber arrived. Have you got dressed **already**?*
● **Yet** is used with Perfect tenses in negative sentences after a contracted auxiliary verb or at the end of the sentence. *He **hasn't yet** called. He hasn't called **yet**.* It can also be used at the end of questions. *Have they arrived **yet**?*
● **Still** is used in statements and questions after the auxiliary verb or before the main verb. *She can **still** dance well.* **Still** comes before the auxiliary verb in negations. *She **still hasn't** replied to my letter.*

59   *Underline the correct item.*

1   I'm sorry, I'm not ready to go out - I haven't finished doing the washing-up already/yet.
2   I don't think I've ever met her yet/before.
3   He's still/yet got a good memory even though he's almost eighty.
4   I used to live here six years before/ago.
5   He's lived in Rome all his life and he yet/still lives there.
6   I've before/already read this book - I don't want to read it again.

3 Tense Forms

7 The last time I fed the goldfish was two days before/ago.
8 I can't believe I've been here nearly a year yet/already.
9 I'm afraid the plumber hasn't arrived still/yet.
10 He can still/already speak and he's only one year old.

60 *Put the verbs in brackets into a correct tense.*

A. Last summer I 1) ...*visited*... (visit) the United States. I
2) .... (look forward) to the trip for ages, and I
3) .... (enjoy) myself very much. On the 4th of
July a friend 4) .... (suggest) we go and watch
the fireworks. I 5) .... (see) fireworks before, but I
6) .... (never/experience) anything like the
spectacle we 7) .... (witness) that night.

B. Sarah 1) .... (leave) school two years ago and for
the last year she 2) .... (look) for a decent job.
She 3) .... (hope) to find work as a secretary but
as she 4) .... (never/do) a secretarial course
before, I think she 5) .... (have) some difficulty
in finding such a job.

C. A: "Where 1) .... (you/be) lately? The last
time I 2) .... (see) you 3)..................... (be)
two years ago."
B: "I 4) .... (move) to London 18 months ago - I
5) .... (work) as a nurse there since then."
A: "Oh really! How 6) .... (it/go)?"
B: "Great! I 7) .... (enjoy) it very much at the moment, although at first it 8) .... (be) very hard."

D. A: "I 1) .... (have) a party tonight. Would you like to come?"
B: "I'd love to but unfortunately I 2) .... (already/arrange) to go out for dinner.
A: "What 3) .... (you/do) tomorrow?"
B: "Not much. I think a friend 4) .... (come) to visit me in the morning, but I 5) ....
.... (not/have) any plans for later in the day. 6) .... (you/fancy) going
for a drive?"

E. Peter 1) .... (drive) to work yesterday when a dog 2) .... (run) into
the middle of the road. Peter 3) .... (manage) to stop in time but the car which
4) .... (follow) behind him 5) .... (crash) into the back of his car.
Then the two cars 6) .... (collide) with a police car which 7) ....
(travel) in the opposite direction.

F. Some thieves 1) .... (break into) my house yesterday. Apparently, I 2) ....
(leave) the window open. This is the first time anything like this 3) .... (happen) to
me. The thieves 4) .... (get in) through the window and 5) ....
(steal) all my jewellery. None of the neighbours 6) .... (see) anything happen.

G. A: "What 1) .... (you/do) tonight?"
B: "I 2) .... (study) for my exams."
A: "What time 3) .... (you/finish) studying?"
B: "I 4) .... (finish) by 8 o'clock, I hope."
A: "Good - let's go to the cinema then. The film 5) .... (start) at 8.30."

H. A: "1) .... (you/see) "The Cure" concert last night?"
B: "No, but I 2) .... (see) them before. I 3) .... (go) to one of their
concerts five years ago."
A: "They 4) .... (improve) a lot since then."
B: "5) .... (they/still/make) records?"
A: "Oh yes, they 6) .... (just/release) a new one."

I. This time next week I 1) .... (be) on my honeymoon and I 2) ....
(forget) all about my problems at work. My husband and I 3) .... (relax) by the pool
and we 4) .... (look forward) to spending romantic evenings together.

61 *Complete the sentences. Mind the correct use of tense forms.*

1 I can't see you tonight because ...*I always go to the gym*... on Mondays.
2 Simon looks happy - he .... his test.
3 I'm sorry, Mum can't come to the phone because .... at the moment.
4 I wonder where Jim is; I .... since this morning.
5 By the time we arrived at the restaurant they .... eating.
6 You .... fatter every day - you really should go on a diet.
7 Tim .... while Pam was watching TV.
8 By the end of next year he .... in Madrid for three years.
9 She .... in Liverpool before she came to London.
10 She locked up the house, ... and drove away.
11 She's angry with her son because .... money from her purse.
12 I promise .... as soon as I get paid.
13 I wish they'd be quiet - they .... for hours.
14 By this time next week we .... in Lisbon.
15 He hasn't finished the work yet, but he .... by this evening.
16 Before ...., make sure you read the passage carefully.
17 The president .... Ohio in a week's time.
18 She .... on the project for two days before she finished it.
19 I .... tonight; would you like to join us?
20 He hasn't driven a car since .... that accident.

> ## In Other Words

- I've never met such a charming girl.
  She's the most charming girl I've ever met.
- It's a long time since she wrote to me.
  She hasn't written to me for a long time.
- She started learning French two years ago.
  She's been learning French for two years.
- When did he buy the flat?
  How long ago did he buy the flat?
  How long is it since he bought the flat?
- She hasn't returned yet.
  She still hasn't returned.

- I've never seen this film before.
  It's the first time I've ever seen this film.
- She came to London a year ago.
  She has been in London for a year.
- The last time I went out was a month ago.
  I haven't been out for a month.
- He started working as soon as she left.
  He didn't start working until she had left.
  He started working when she had left.
  He waited until she had left before he started working.

62 *Complete the sentences using the words in bold. Use two to five words.*

1 It's a week since I last saw him.
  seen I ...*haven't seen him for*... a week.
2 When did she move to France?
  since How long .... to France?
3 He has never seen this film before.
  ever It's the first time .... this film.
4 The last time he visited her was a week ago.
  for He ....a week.
5 They started eating as soon as the last guests arrived.
  had They waited until the .... they started eating.
6 They started learning computing two months ago.
  been They .... two months.
7 It's the fastest car I've ever driven.
  never I .... fast car.

8 They haven't come back yet.
  still   They .... back.
9 How long is it since he broke his leg?
  break   When .... his leg?
10 It's the first time he's ever seen a skyscraper.
  never   He .... before.
11 She started writing a novel a year ago.
  been   She .... for a year.
12 That's the smallest car I've ever seen.
  small   I have .... car.
13 They didn't go to bed until the programme had finished.
  when   They .... the programme finished.
14 I haven't called Ted for a long time.
  since   It's a long time .... Ted.
15 She hasn't sold the house yet.
  still   She .... house.
16 This is the most delicious meal I have ever eaten.
  such   I have .... meal.
17 I've never read that book before.
  first   It's the .... that book.
18 She started cooking when he arrived.
  until   She .... she started cooking.
19 I haven't been swimming for a week.
  was   The last .... a week ago.
20 He has been learning Russian for six months.
  started   He .... ago.

Oral Development 3

Below are pictures of two people - Jack, a professional skier and Alice, a studio model. Say what they're doing now, then imagine what their lives were like 5 years ago, what their lives are like now and what their lives will be like in 5 years' time. Try to use a variety of tenses.

Jack is a professional skier. He has been training for more than ten years.   etc

Consolidation 3

Phrasal Verbs

come across: meet/find by chance
come by: obtain
come down with: become ill from
come into: inherit
come off: 1) happen, 2) succeed
come out: 1) be published, 2) bloom
come round: 1) visit casually, 2) regain consciousness; come to, 3) be persuaded to change opinion
come on: come along; hurry up
come through: survive
come up: be mentioned
come up to: equal
come up with: find (an answer, solution etc)

• • • • • • • • • • • •

cut across: take a shorter route
cut back (on): reduce (production)
cut down: reduce length of sth
cut down (on): reduce amount consumed
cut in/into: interrupt (conversation)
cut off: disconnect
be cut off: be isolated
cut out: 1) leave out; remove, 2) (for) (passive) be suited for
cut up: cut into small pieces

63 Fill in the correct particle(s).

1 Tim's work failed to come ...*up to*... his boss's high standards.
2 Sue came .... her favourite doll while she was clearing out the attic.
3 She'll come .... to the idea of buying a bigger house if we explain all the advantages.
4 Lovely yellow daffodils come .... in the spring.
5 The question of expanding the company came .... at the meeting.
6 He stayed in bed after he had come .... the measles.
7 He came ..... a large fortune when his uncle died.
8 Her latest book has just come ....
9 The village was cut .... by the flood.
10 I don't think she's cut .... this kind of work.
11 Our electricity was cut .... after we forgot to pay the bill.
12 If you cut .... the field, you'll save time.
13 We are advised to cut .... our smoking.
14 You need to cut your summary .... - it's fifty words too long.
15 She cut .... the conversation to remind Bob it was time to go.

64 Complete the sentences using the words in bold. Use two to five words.

1 I'm sure it wasn't Jim who phoned.
   have   It ...*can't have been*... Jim who phoned.
2 They say he was the best footballer of the decade.
   said   He .... the best footballer of the decade.
3 It wasn't necessary for us to get a visa to visit Spain.
   need   We .... a visa to visit Spain.
4 I'm sure she has already left the office.
   have   She .... the office.
5 When did you get a letter from him?
   since   How long .... a letter from him?
6 Mr Pearce didn't take up golf until he retired.
   took   It wasn't until Mr Pearce .... golf.
7 He advises people on buying and selling houses.
   advice   He .... buying and selling houses.
8 It might snow this Christmas.
   possibility   There .... this Christmas.
9 The accident wasn't my fault.
   blame   I .... the accident.
10 January was the last time I saw him.
   since   I .... January.
11 The book was so difficult that I couldn't understand it.
   for   The book was .... understand.
12 Tom didn't feel like going out.
   mood   Tom wasn't .... out.

Consolidation 3

65 Look at Appendix 1, then fill in the correct preposition.

1 Success depends ...on... good organisation.
2 The old woman died .... pneumonia.
3 He had difficulty .... understanding her.
4 The helicopter crashed .... a hill.
5 She's very fond .... her grandchildren.
6 He doesn't care .... his appearance.
7 She was very disappointed .... her rise.
8 Tom is envious .... his friends.
9 He was delighted .... his presents.
10 They decided .... a quiet wedding.
11 Pisa is famous .... its Leaning Tower.
12 She was furious .... him ...... being late.
13 We are grateful .... you .... your help.
14 Have you heard .... Aunt Sheila?
15 Did you hear .... the robbery?
16 Have you heard .... this singer?

17 Smoking is harmful .... one's health.
18 He was found guilty .... six robberies.
19 There's no excuse ...... his terrible behaviour.
20 He's an expert ...... Middle-Eastern mythology.
21 The plumber was an expert .... unblocking drains.
22 If there's a delay .... claiming the money, you'll never get it back.
23 He's experienced .... archaeology.
24 The little girl dreams .... the same fearsome monster every night.
25 I would never dream .... leaving you.
26 His failure .... appear in court led to his being fined.
27 Her failure .... the exams disappointed her.
28 She's efficient .... typing.

66 Think of the word which best fits each space. Use only one word in each space.

Since the Channel Tunnel opened, getting to France has never been (0) ...so... easy. The fastest train arrives (1) .... Calais thirty-five minutes after (2) .... departure from England, and from there travellers can easily (3) .... some of the (4) .... picturesque towns in France (5) .... Le Touquet and Honfleur. The former is a pleasant resort (6) .... was originally created for rich cosmopolitan Britons (7) .... the turn of the century. As a (8) ...., it still retains an air of faded, fashionable beauty. The town (9) .... has numerous boutiques selling the latest designer clothes from Paris. In (10) ...., there is a beautiful beach which makes a good place for a walk or a swim (11) .... the weather is hot enough. Honfleur is another port which is becoming a popular destination (12) .... the British. Tourists are attracted (13) .... it because of its quaint atmosphere. The small commercial area is surrounded (14) .... tall narrow houses and outdoor cafés which spread onto the cobbled quays. Honfleur also boasts some of the best restaurants in (15) .... north of France, which is another of its attractions.

Expressions with "Do"	Expressions with "Make"
one's best/worst, business with sb, a crossword, damage to, one's duty, an exercise, an experiment, somebody a favour, good, one's hair, harm, homework, housework, a job, lessons, sth for a living, miracles (for), research, right/wrong, a service, the shopping, a good turn, a translation, the washing-up, wonders, work etc	allowances for, an appointment, an acquaintance, an arrangement, a bargain, the beds, the best of, a cake, certain, changes, coffee, a deal with sb, a decision, a difference, a discovery, an effort, an enemy of, ends meet, an excuse, friends with, a fortune, haste, fun of, a fool of somebody, an impression, improvements, a joke, a mess, a mistake, money, a note, a nuisance, a noise, an offer, peace, preparations, a profit, progress, sure, a translation, trouble, war, a will etc

67 Fill in "do" or "make" in the correct form.

1 Have you ...done... the washing-up yet?
2 Will you .... me a favour?
3 She tried to .... a soufflé but it was a complete failure.

4 Don't .... such a fuss about unimportant things.
5 She .... a very good impression at the interview yesterday.

6 They've already .... all the preparations for the party.

7 I promise I'll .... my best to make it work.

8 I don't think this .... any sense.

9 Don't take so many pills. They won't .... you any good.

10 I'm not feeling well. I'd better .... an appointment with the doctor.

11 She .... a fortune selling cosmetics.

12 After eight years of war, both countries agreed to .... peace.

13 He .... a very good job mending my roof.

14 I can't believe this is my old house. You .... wonders with it!

15 The oil-producing companies ....an agreement to keep the prices low this year.

68 *Use the words in capitals to form a word that fits in the space in the same line.*

Choosing a Car

There comes a time when not having a car becomes **(0)** .... . Choosing your first car is an **1)** .... experience. Most men's **(2)** .... is so vivid that they see themselves speeding along in a **(3)** .... sports car, attracting **(4)** .... looks from those they pass. In **(5)** .... this does not happen that often. More practical and **(6)** .... aspects have to be considered when choosing a car. The **(7)** .... is normally between a small city car which is **(8)** .... to run and easy to park and a larger family car which would be more **(9)** .... and probably be fitted with more **(10)** .... features.

PRACTICAL	0	*impractical*
EXCITE	1	
IMAGINE	2	
POWER	3	
ENVY	4	
REAL	5	
FINANCE	6	
CHOOSE	7	
ECONOMY	8	
	9	
COMFORT	9	
SAFE	10	

69 *Read the text carefully. Some of the lines are correct and some have a word which should not be there. If a line is correct, put a tick (✔) in the space provided. If a line has a word which should not be there, write it in the space provided.*

Mecca

0 Mecca is a city of about 200,000 inhabitants	0	✔
00 in the Saudi Arabia, and lies about 40 miles	00	*the*
1 east of Jeddah, which it is its port on the Red Sea.	1	
2 It is the birthplace of Muhammad and the most greatest	2	
3 place of pilgrimage in whole the Islamic world. It is	3	
4 estimated that on each year more than 100,000	4	
5 pilgrims go to Mecca, so that increasing its tourist industry.	5	
6 This also encourages and the development of the	6	
7 numerous of small industries and craftsmen's workshops that	7	
8 produce leather goods and silverware to sell to the	8	
9 pilgrims. Mecca has always been an important crossroads	9	
10 for trade and although too it was a religious centre before	10	
11 the rise of Islam, both its religious and economic	11	
12 importance grew as if a result of the new faith.The	12	
13 town is an impressively constructed and extends down the valley	13	
14 along roads which are unusually wide for an Arab city. Its	14	
15 religious life is main centred in the Great Mosque.	15	

4 Clauses / Linking Words

Sentences can consist of main and subordinate clauses. Subordinate clauses can be:
- **noun clauses:** *I know **that he'll be a little late.***
- **relative clauses:** *Show me the pictures **which you took.***
- **adverbial clauses** (clauses of time, place, manner, reason, concession, purpose, result, comparison, condition) *He left early **so as not to miss the bus.***

Relative Clauses

Relative clauses are introduced by: a) relative pronouns, i.e. **who, whom, whose, which** or **that** or b) relative adverbs i.e. **when, where** or **why**.

Relative Pronouns

	Subject of the verb of the relative clause (cannot be omitted)	Object of the verb of the relative clause (can be omitted)	Possession (cannot be omitted)
used for people	**who/that** *That's the man **who/that** stole the money.*	**whom/who/that** *The man **(who/whom/that)** you saw last night was my uncle.*	**whose** *That's the girl **whose** brother is a singer.*
used for things/ animals	**which/that** *I read a book **which/that** was written by Samuel Johnson.*	**which/that** *The cat **(which/that)** you saw lying on the sofa is my favourite one.*	**whose/of which** *That's the coat the sleeves **of which/whose** sleeves are made of velvet.*

- **Whom, which, whose can be used in expressions of quantity with of** (some of, many of, half of etc)
  *She received a lot of postcards. Most of them were from her friends. She received a lot of postcards, **most of which** were from her friends.*
- **That can be used instead of who, whom or which but it is never used after commas or prepositions.**
  *She's the actress **who/that** was awarded first prize. The man in the corner, **who** is sitting next to Jane, is my uncle. ("that" is not possible.)*

Relative Adverbs

Time Place Reason	**when** (= in/on/at which) **where** (= in/at/on/to which) **why** (= for which)	*1982 was the year **(when)** I moved to Wales.* *That's the hotel **where** we spent our honeymoon.* *That's the reason **(why)** they were celebrating.*

Prepositions in Relative Clauses

We do not normally use prepositions before relative pronouns.
*The house **in which** she lives is in the suburbs. (formal - not usual)*
*The house **which** she lives **in** is in the suburbs. (usual)*
*The house she lives **in** is in the suburbs. (more usual)*

 70 *Fill in: where, whose, who, which, why or when.*

Having visited a few countries **1)** ...*where*.... the climate is different to yours, you will appreciate how important it is to plan carefully before travelling. Not planning well enough is the reason **2)** .... some holidays can go wrong. A holiday **3)** .... involves a lot of walking, for example, means you need to go at a time **4)** .... it is neither too hot nor too cold. It also means you need to plan to go with someone **5)** .... enjoys walking and **6)** .... stamina is equal to yours. A travel companion **7)** .... likes the same things as you is ideal, but it's very difficult to meet someone **8)** .... likes and dislikes are exactly the same as yours. In any case, you need to decide on a holiday **9)** .... suits both of you and a country **10)** .... climate is not uncomfortable for either of you.

71 *Rewrite the sentences in as many ways as possible.*

1 That's the zoo where they took the tiger.
  ...That's the zoo to which they took the tiger.
  That's the zoo they took the tiger to....
2 The place where you went is my home town.
  ....
3 That's the girl he gave the present to.
  ....
4 He's the one person on whom she can depend.
  ....
5 This is the park where the village fair is held.
  ....

Defining / Non-defining Relative Clauses

- A **defining relative clause** gives necessary information and is essential to the meaning of the main clause. It is not put between commas. *People **who hunt illegally** should be punished.*
- A **non-defining relative clause** gives extra information which is not essential to the meaning of the main clause. It is put between commas. *Her mother, **who is a kind woman**, has helped her a lot.* **Note how the commas change the meaning of the sentence.** *The players, who were involved in the fight, were sent off the pitch. (all the players were sent off.) The players who were involved in the fight were sent off the pitch. (only the players who were involved in the fight were sent off)*

72 *Fill in the relative pronoun adding commas where necessary. Write (D) for defining, (ND) for non-defining and whether the relative pronoun can be omitted or not.*

1 That's the man ...*who/that*... I was talking about.   .D.   ....*omitted*........
2 Her school .... is very old is closing down.   ....
3 Have you seen the pencil .... I bought yesterday?   ....
4 Ann .... contract expires next week is looking for another job.   ....
5 This house .... he inherited from his parents is worth a fortune. ....
6 The company .... I set up last year is expanding.   ....
7 She is the singer .... latest record reached the top of the charts. ....
8 I've never met anyone before .... was quite so rude.   ....
9 This jumper .... my grandmother knitted for me is too small.   ....
10 The necklace .... I bought in Egypt is very old.   ....
11 They are the friends .... invited us to their daughter's wedding.   ....
12 The documentary .... I saw last night was very informative. ....
13 Elephants .... are hunted for ivory are becoming extinct.   ....
14 The girl .... speaks four languages is in my class.   ....
15 This is the hospital .... was built in 1920.   ....
16 The police are looking for a man .... car was found abandoned in Newcastle last night.   ....
17 That man .... name is Bill stole my purse.   ....
18 She is a person .... I shall always be grateful to.   ....
19 He's the man .... she's going to marry.   ....
20 This book .... is about Vietnam is fascinating.   ....
21 I know few people .... are as considerate as she is.   ....
22 His group .... is touring Europe is called "Blunt".   ....
23 The woman .... dog was stolen is offering a reward.   ....
24 I met a really interesting man .... name I have since forgotten.   ....
25 She's the girl .... I'm sharing my flat with.   ....
26 My team .... won the cup are going to tour America.   ....
27 "Macbeth" is a play .... was written by Shakespeare.   ....

4 Clauses / Linking Words

73 **Use relatives to combine the following sentences as in the example:**

1 That's the hotel. We stayed there last summer. ...*That's the hotel where we stayed last summer.*....
2 This is the car. He drives to work in it every day. ....
3 That's the actor. He was in the film you mentioned. ....
4 She bought a brooch. It once belonged to a duchess. ....
5 That's the house. It was damaged in the earthquake. ....
6 They met a man. His fortune is believed to be around £3,000,000. ....
7 That's the mansion. The Queen's youngest son lives there. ....
8 They called a woman. She was a psychic. ....
9 We went back to the café. I'd left my purse there. ....
10 That's the painting. It is a Picasso masterpiece. ....

In Other Words

- That's the town I was born in.
  That's the town where I was born.
  That's the town which I was born in.
- They let us stay, which was kind of them.
  It was kind of them to let us stay.
- This is Mr Foster; his son is a famous pianist.
  This is Mr Foster whose son is a famous pianist.
- Sunday is the day when she got married.
  Sunday is the day on which she got married.

- I bought a fridge which was faulty.
  The fridge I bought was faulty.
- That man gave my brother a job.
  That's the man who gave my brother a job.
- She brought some letters but none of them were for me.
  She brought some letters, none of which were for me.
- They arrested six men; two of them are Swiss.
  They arrested six men, two of whom are Swiss.

74 **Complete the sentences using the words in bold. Use two to five words.**

1 He lost his passport, which was silly of him.
   lose   It was ...*silly of him to lose*... his passport.
2 That's the hotel we are staying in.
   where   That's .... staying.
3 That woman complained to the manager.
   who   That's .... to the manager.
4 We met several people from Portsmouth, but none of them knew Dr Irons.
   whom   We met several people from Portsmouth, ... Dr Irons.
5 The car we rented was very unreliable.
   which   We .... very unreliable.
6 Clare Spender is the author; her book became a bestseller overnight.
   whose   Clare Spender is .... a bestseller overnight.
7 We bought a kilo of apples; some of them were bruised.
   which   We bought a kilo of apples, ... bruised.
8 August is the month when most people take their holidays.
   which   August .... most people take their holidays.
9 She has a class of twenty students; half of them are of Canadian origin.
   whom   She has a class of twenty students, ... are of Canadian origin.
10 Sue tried on some shoes but none of them fitted.
   which   Sue tried on some shoes, ... fitted.
11 At the film festival we saw many people; some were famous actors.
   whom   At the film festival we saw many people, ... famous actors.

Clauses of Time

- Clauses of time are introduced by: **after, as, as long as, as soon as, just as, once, since, when, before, by the time** (= before, not later than), **while, until/till** (= up to the time when), **the moment (that), whenever, every time, immediately** etc. *He bought a villa* **as soon as** *he got the money.*
- Time clauses follow the rule of the sequence of tenses; that is, when the verb of the main clause is in a present or future form, the verb of the time clause is in a present form, and when the verb of the main clause is in a past form, the verb of the time clause is in a past form too. Note that **will** is never used in clauses of time. *I'll give it to you* **when** *you* **tell** *me why you want it. (not:* when you will tell me*) She* **had finished** *reading* **before** *they* **came** *home. (not:* before they come home*)*
- When the time clause precedes the main clause, a comma is used. When the time clause follows, no comma is used. *When he finishes, he can go home. He can go home when he finishes.*
- **when** (time conjunction) + present tense   *When he* **comes**, *he'll tell you.*
  when (question word) + will/would   *When* **will he come**?
- **If** is used for things which may happen. *Wait for me* **if** *I'm late.* **When** is used for things which are sure to happen. *I'll be back* **when** *I finish shopping.*

---

75 *Underline the appropriate time phrase and put the verbs into the correct tense.*

New research offers proof that global warming is a direct consequence of man's activity on earth and not a result of some unidentified natural phenomenon. **1)** (After/As soon as) noting climate changes on a computer, researchers **2)** .... (show) that the Earth's average temperature has risen by 0.7° C **3)** (before/since) the Industrial Revolution. **4)** (While/As soon as) the results were published, climate changes once again **5)** .... (become) headline news. Other research predicts that **6)** (by/by the time) the end of the century average rainfall will be 30% higher than today as a result of a warmer climate. Air pollution is blamed for the sharp rise in the Earth's temperature and **7)** (until/whenever) strict laws **8)** .... (be/introduced), the problem will continue to get worse. Something needs to be done **9)** (the moment/before) it **10)** .... (be) too late. **11)** (When/Whenever) E.U. countries **12)** .... (meet) last month, they agreed to cut down on pollution levels. **13)** (Just as/Once) clean sources of power **14)** .... (be/developed), we will have taken the first steps towards stopping global warming.

---

76 *Fill in "if" or "when" and put the verbs into the correct tense.*

1 Tom will phone you ...*when*... he ...*wakes up*... (wake up).
2 .... do you think you .... (finish) the project?
3 .... there .... (be) any problems, I will phone you.
4 .... the exams .... (be) over, we will have a party.
5 .... Ted .... (apply) for the job, I'm sure he will get it.
6 .... we .... (arrive) late at the theatre, there will be no tickets left.
7 I have no idea .... he .... (return) from his trip to Paris.
8 .... (you/stop) interfering in my life?
9 Please let me know .... you .... (hear) from them, will you?
10 .... we .... (have) nothing else to discuss, we can all leave now.

77 *Complete the sentences in any meaningful way using an appropriate time word.*

1 They had finished packing ...*before/by the time we returned from work.* ...
2 A door-to-door salesman turned up ....
3 She came across her childhood diary ....
4 .... the baby had already been born.
5 .... he realised he was being followed.
6 .... the report, I will have it typed.

4 Clauses / Linking Words

Clauses of Reason

- **Clauses of reason are introduced by:** as, since, because, for, the reason for, the reason (why), on the grounds that **etc.** *As he was late for work, he got a taxi.*
- **Because** usually answers a why-question. *"Why did you lie to him?" "Because I was afraid of being punished."* **For** always comes after a comma in written speech or a pause in oral speech. *I didn't tell him anything, for I don't trust him.*
- **Other ways of expressing reason:**
  Because of/Due to + noun/-ing form *She was late because of/due to heavy traffic.*
  Because of/Due to + the fact that ... *Because of the fact that/Due to the fact that it had been snowing for four days, all roads were closed.*

Clauses of Result

- **Clauses of result are introduced by:** that (after such/so...), (and) as a result, (and) as a consequence, consequently, so **etc.** *The sea is so cold that they can't swim.*

such a(n) + (adjective) + singular countable	*It was such a nice dress that she bought it.*
such + (adjective) + uncountable /plural noun	*It was such bad weather that we stayed indoors.*
such + a lot of + noun	*There were such a lot of people on the bus that there were no seats left.*
so + adjective/adverb	*He speaks so quickly that hardly anyone can understand him.*
so + much/many/little/few + noun	*She won so much money in the lottery that she bought a mansion.*
so + adjective + a(n) + noun	*It was so delicious a cake that we ate it all. (not usual)*
as a result/therefore/consequently/so + clause	*He didn't have a visa and as a result he couldn't enter the country.*

78 *Fill in so, such or such a(n).*

Mandy was getting **1)** ...so.... bored one afternoon that she decided to go shopping. She always took **2)** .... pleasure in buying things for herself that she would often spend lots of money in just one day. She set out feeling really excited. After two hours she had bought **3)** .... many things that she could hardly carry them. The shops were closing and there was **4)** .... lot of traffic in the streets that she couldn't find a taxi. She started feeling frustrated as the parcels and bags she was carrying were getting in everyone's way. She was **5)** .... anxious to get back home that she decided to take the underground. She took **6)** .... long time to find her purse among her things that people waiting behind her in the queue started muttering. When she finally found it, there was **7)** .... little money in it that she didn't have enough to buy a ticket. Mandy was **8)** .... embarrassed that she just wanted to disappear. She left the station and was in **9)** .... desperate state that she didn't know what to do. "I've spent **10)** .... much money," she thought, "that I've made a fool of myself in front of complete strangers." Mandy eventually got home with all her shopping after getting a lift in a pizza delivery van!

79 *Join the sentences using the words in brackets.*

1 It was a hard job. We were exhausted by the time we had finished. (such...that) ...*It was such a hard job that we were exhausted by the time we had finished.* ...

2 He'd forgotten to bring the report with him. He had to go home and get it. (because)

....

3 The food was bad. We complained to the manager. (Since ...)

....

4 It was a long journey. They packed some food to take with them. (due to the fact)

....

5 I hate sailing. I get seasick. (the reason)

....

6 Their house is too small. They are going to look for a larger one. (consequently)

....

7 Sharon is busy this weekend. She can't come to the seaside with us. (Since)

....

8 The exam was difficult. Many students failed. (such...that)

....

9 They fell behind with the project. They had to work overtime. (as a result)

....

10 Their flight was delayed. They spent the night in a hotel. (as)

....

▶ ## In Other Words

- He was so busy that he couldn't talk to me.
  He was too busy to talk to me.
- It's such an expensive dress that I can't buy it.
  The dress is too expensive for me to buy.
- No one knows the reason for his absence.
  No one knows (the reason) why he is absent.
- It was such a nice day that we went out.
  It was so nice a day that we went out.

- The flight was cancelled because there was a strike.
  The flight was cancelled due to/because of a strike.
- He lost his ticket so he couldn't board the plane.
  He lost his ticket and as a result/consequently/therefore he couldn't board the plane.

80 *Complete the sentences using the words in bold. Use two to five words.*

1 The team were so good that we couldn't beat them.
   such   They were ...*such a good team that*... we couldn't beat them.
2 It was such a boring film that we left in the middle.
   so   It was .... we left in the middle.
3 No one knows why they are emigrating.
   for   No one knows .... emigrating.
4 Our car broke down so we were very late.
   consequently Our car broke down .... very late.
5 She was so insistent that we couldn't ignore her.
   too   She was .... ignore.
6 They couldn't go to the post office because of a snowstorm.
   as   They couldn't go to the post office .... snowstorm.
7 She had a very bad night's sleep, so she was exhausted.
   result   She had a very bad night's sleep .... she was exhausted.
8 Do you know the reason for her leaving her job?
   why   Do .... her job?
9 The coffee was so strong that I couldn't drink it.
   such   It .... that I couldn't drink it.
10 He was such a skilful player that he seldom lost a game.
   so   He was .... he seldom lost a game.
11 He didn't get the job because he was inexperienced.
   to   He didn't get the job .... experience.

Oral Development 4

Use the notes below and your own ideas to talk about Clare Harvard. Try to link your ideas together using relative pronouns/adverbs, time words, and words introducing clauses of reason or result.

Clare Harvard from Portsmouth

- wanted a career in management
- studied hard - got a place at university
- worked extremely hard at university - passed all her exams
- got a Management degree
- graduated - was offered a job in a large multinational company
- ambitious and was promoted within a year
- well-respected by her colleagues for her hard work and dedication

S1: Clare, who comes from Portsmouth, wanted a career in management. She studied hard so that she could get a place at university ...

81 *Complete the sentences using the words in bold. Use two to five words.*

1 She gave us a lift, which was kind of her.
   of   It was ...*kind of her to give*... us a lift.
2 That's the college my son got his degree from.
   where   That's .... got his degree.
3 I bought several dictionaries but none of them are really up to date.
   which   I bought .... are really up to date.
4 This is Emma Thompson; her husband is an Oscar nominee.
   whose   This is Emma Thompson, ... nominee.
5 The reason for his resignation is strictly personal.
   why   The reason .... strictly personal.
6 It was such an appalling event that we'd rather forget about it.
   so   It was .... we'd rather forget about it.
7 It was so late that I couldn't get to the meeting.
   too   It was .... get to the meeting.
8 He forgot to post his application so he didn't get called for an interview.
   result   He forgot to post his application .... he didn't get called for an interview.
9 He came into his inheritance and immediately after he bought a Ferrari.
   soon   He bought a Ferrari .... into his inheritance.
10 The children were so polite that everyone took to them.
   such   They were .... everyone took to them.
11 When he got the phone call, he left the house immediately.
   moment   He left the house .... the phone call.
12 The last time I saw Peter was 14 February.
   since   I .... 14 February.
13 Careless drivers should be punished.
   carelessly People .... should be punished.
14 One of the five students he interviewed was Spanish.
   whom   He interviewed .... was Spanish.

Expressing Purpose - Clauses of Purpose

Purpose is expressed with:

● to/in order to/so as to + inf	*I'll leave home early **to get** to work on time. (informal)* *She's studying **so as to qualify** as a lawyer. (formal)*
● so that + can/will (present/future reference)	*She works hard **so that** she **will** have better career prospects.*
● so that + could/would (past reference)	*He gave me directions **so that** I **could** find his house easily.*
● with a view to/with the aim of + -ing form	*He did a Master's degree **with the aim of applying** for a managerial post when he had finished.*
● for + noun/-ing form	*This is a knife **for cutting** bread.*
● in case + Present (present/future reference) ● in case + Past (past reference)	*I'll write it down **in case** I **forget** it.* *He took an umbrella **in case** it **rained.***

Negative Purpose is normally expressed with:

● so as not/in order not + to -inf	*She studied hard **so as not**/**in order not to fail** her test. (not: She studied hard ~~not to fail~~ her test.)*
● so that + can't/won't (present/future reference) so that + couldn't/wouldn't (past reference)	*Tie up the dog **so that** it **won't** get out of the garden.* *She locked the door **so that** burglars **couldn't** get in.*
● for fear/lest + might/should for fear of sth/doing sth	*He didn't say where he was going **for fear** he **might** be followed.* *He gave them all his money **for fear of being** shot.*
● prevent + noun/pronoun + (from) + -ing form	*She put on her raincoat to **prevent herself (from) getting** soaked.*
● avoid + -ing form	*He took a taxi to work to **avoid being** late.*

● **Clauses of Purpose follow the rule of the sequence of tenses.** *She's going to buy a dictionary **so that** her spelling **will improve**. They **tied** him up **so that** he **wouldn't escape**.*

82 *Rephrase the following sentences in as many ways possible as in the example:*

1 I brought her a present. I wanted to cheer her up. ...*I brought her a present so as to cheer her up. I brought her a present in order to cheer her up. I brought her a present to cheer her up. I brought her a present so that I could cheer her up. I brought her a present with the aim of cheering her up*.... etc

2 She didn't answer the phone. She didn't want to have to talk to anyone. ....

....

....

3 They bought a bigger house. They wanted to have more room. ....

....

....

4 He always kept a spare tyre in the boot. He might have a puncture. ....

....

....

5 The hospital staff went on strike. They wanted to protest about working conditions. ....

....

....

6 Pauline didn't go to the party. She didn't want to bump into Ian. ....

....

....

83 *Use the notes below to write the letter. Use purpose words where possible.*

Dear Mr Bowes,

1 I write/invite you/attend/interview/27th May/Edge Hill College.

....

2 We hold interviews/view/appoint/Senior Lecturer/English Department.

....

3 If you be unable/attend/please phone/college as soon as possible/we arrange/alternative date.

....

4 You/be requested/read/enclosed information/avoid waste time on the day of the interview.

....

5 The day last/9 am to 3.30 pm/give interviewees time/familiarise themselves/college.

....

6 When you arrive/college/please report/reception/you be shown/staff common room.

....

I look forward to meeting you shortly.

Yours sincerely,
M. Davies
(Head of English Dept.)

84 *Complete the sentences using the words in bold. Use two to five words.*

1 I didn't tell her the bad news. I didn't want to upset her.
 avoid I didn't tell her the bad news ...*to avoid upsetting*... her.
2 Mary wrote out a shopping list. She didn't want to forget anything.
 that Mary wrote out a shopping list .... forget anything.
3 Paul trained hard every day. He wanted to be the best.
 as Paul trained hard every day .... the best.
4 Lee gave up her job. She planned to continue her education.
 view Lee gave up her job .... her education.
5 She turned the oven down. She didn't want to burn the cakes.
 might She turned the oven down .... burn the cakes.
6 He was saving all his money. He intended to buy a house.
 aim He was saving all his money .... a house.
7 Peter left the office early. He wanted to be at the cinema on time.
 in Peter left the office early .... at the cinema on time.
8 This is a pencil sharpener. You use it to sharpen pencils.
 for This is a pencil sharpener. It is used .... pencils.
9 I'll bring a pack of cards. We might want to play later.
 case I'll bring a pack of cards .... play later.
10 We didn't want to get stuck in a traffic jam so we bypassed the city centre.
 avoid We bypassed the city centre .... in a traffic jam.

11 Before we went to Africa we had injections so we wouldn't get malaria.
   prevent   Before we went to Africa we had injections .... malaria.

12 He's taking his camera on holiday. He might want to take some photos of the wildlife.
   case   He's taking his camera on holiday .... to take some photos of the wildlife.

13 Peter goes to night school. He wants to learn French.
   order   Peter goes to night school .... French.

14 If you want him to remember to phone the bank, leave a note on his desk.
   that   Leave a note on his desk .... to phone the bank.

15 She tries her best. She wants to stand out in her field.
   as   She tries her best .... in her field.

Oral Development 5

Peter has decided to go on a mountaineering holiday. Look at the list below then decide, in order of importance, which things he should take with him and why. You can mention items which are not in the list. Use words of purpose to link your ideas together.
map, compass, rope, thick jacket, sleeping bag, climbing boots, warm clothes, insect repellent, swimming trunks, evening suit, suntan lotion, thick socks, suitcase, waterproof

eg. Peter should take a map and a compass in case he gets lost.

Expressing Concession - Clauses of Concession

Concession is expressed with:

- **although/even though/though + clause**
- **despite/in spite of + noun/-ing form**
- **despite/in spite of the fact + that-clause**
- **while/whereas/but/on the other hand/yet + clause**
- **nevertheless/however + clause**
- **however/no matter how + adj/adv + subject (+ may) + verb**
- **whatever/no matter what + clause**
- **adj/adv + though + subject + verb/(may + bare inf)**
- **adj/adv + as + subject + verb**

Although it was expensive, she bought it.
Despite his wealth/being rich, he never lends money.
In spite of the fact that he's rich, he never lends money.
*She swam fast, **yet she finished third.***
*He is bright; **however, he is rather lazy.***
***However clever you are,** you won't solve this puzzle.*
***However fast he runs,** he won't catch the robbers.*
***Whatever you do,** you won't succeed.*
***Loudly though he knocked** on the door, nobody heard.*
***Exhausted as she was,** she went to the party.*

- **Note that a comma is used when the clause of concession either precedes or follows the main clause.** *Whatever she says, he won't believe her. He won't believe her, whatever she says.*

4 Clauses / Linking Words

85 **Underline the correct item.**

1 However/<u>Despite</u> the great danger, we decided to attempt the rescue.
2 In spite of the fact that/Despite she is disabled, she plays a lot of sports.
3 He decided not to do the computer course, although/whereas it would have been useful to him.
4 He knows he is damaging his health, despite/yet he continues to smoke.
5 Even though/In spite of strong opposition from the public, the company went ahead with its plans.
6 Brilliant though/although the cook may be, he knows nothing about French sauces.
7 Although/However he ate a lot of spicy food at the reception, he didn't suffer from indigestion.
8 I can't agree with you on this subject, however/whatever hard you may try to convince me.
9 I arrived late at the cinema, but/as I still got a good seat.
10 No matter how/No matter what measures the government takes against hooliganism, there will still be fans who overreact.

86 **Rephrase the sentences in as many ways as possible in order to express concession.**

1 He prepared the meal very quickly. Everyone enjoyed it. *...Although/Even though he prepared the meal very quickly, everyone enjoyed it. Despite/In spite of his having prepared the meal very quickly, everyone enjoyed it. etc...*
2 She disliked the book. She read all of it. ....
....
3 He has a good income. He only rents a small flat. ....
....
4 She's been having French lessons for years. She doesn't speak French very well. ....
....
5 She went shopping yesterday. The cupboards are already bare. ....
....
6 He set his alarm for 6 am. He was still late for work. ....
....
7 They took their costumes with them. They didn't go swimming. ....
....
....

87 **Fill the gaps with the following words:**

whatever, no matter how, although, nevertheless, in spite of, whereas

1) *...Although....* Christmas is one of the great Christian festivals, nowadays it has more than a religious aspect. It is an occasion celebrated all over the world 2) .... people's religious beliefs. 3) .... Christmas is still a time of peace and goodwill towards others. 4) .... its religious origins Christmas falls at the same time of year as the great pagan festivals. Christmas presents, in fact, are of pagan origin. Some countries exchange gifts on 25 December 5) .... others wait until 6 January. Children's presents are traditionally left for them by Father Christmas, a jolly character with a white beard and a red suit. 6) .... old you are, Christmas continues to hold a special magic for young and old alike.

88 *Complete the sentences using the words in bold. Use two to five words.*

1 She tried hard, but she couldn't solve the problem.
   as   Hard ...*as she tried*...,she couldn't solve the problem.
2 However much you complain, they won't give you a refund.
   how   No .... complain, they won't give you a refund.
3 He's a writer but he often makes spelling mistakes.
   being   In .... a writer, he often makes spelling mistakes.
4 Although she exercises a lot, she's not very strong.
   fact   Despite .... a lot, she's not very strong.
5 In spite of his leaving home early, he was late for the appointment.
   though   Even .... early, he was late for the appointment.
6 The plot was complicated, but I enjoyed the film a lot.
   though   Complicated ...., I enjoyed the film a lot.
7 John works as a travel agent, but he's never been abroad.
   of   In .... a travel agent, John has never been abroad.
8 However hard he tried, he didn't succeed.
   matter   He didn't succeed, ... he tried.
9 In spite of having a good voice, he could never be a professional singer.
   has   Although ...., he could never be a professional singer.
10 She did her best. She failed the exam.
   yet   She .... failed the exam.

Oral Development 6

Look at the pictures below and the information given. Talk about each of the women using words expressing concession as in the example. You may also use your own ideas.

Mary

housewife/used to teach before her children were born
children have now grown up/decided not to go back to work
enjoys gardening/garden is too big to look after on her own
would like to become more involved in community life/not have much free time

Jane

managing director/doesn't find work very stressful
lives alone/doesn't feel lonely
loves cooking/not much time to spend in the kitchen
quite enjoys entertaining clients in the evenings/prefers spending time on her own

eg. *Although Mary's a housewife now, she used to teach before her children were born ...*

4 Clauses / Linking Words

Clauses of Manner

- **Clauses of manner are introduced by: as if/as though** (after the verbs act, appear, be, behave, feel, look, seem, smell, sound, taste), **as, how, (in) the way, (in) the way that, the way in which, (in) the same way, (in) the same way as.** *It* **smells as if** *they are frying chicken. Do* **as** *you like.*
- **Were can be used instead of was in formal English in all persons in clauses introduced with as if/as though.** *She behaves* **as if** *she* **were/was** *the Queen.*
- **The tense forms used after as if/as though depend on whether the ideas are true or untrue.**

---

as if/as though + any tense form (expressing similarity/probability - how sb/sth seemed)
She sounds **as if** *she* **is** *Italian. (She may be Italian.)*
She looked **as if** *she* **was** *tired. (She may have been tired.)*

as if/as though + Past Simple/Past Continuous (unreal in the present)
She treats me **as if** *she* **were** *my mother. (but she isn't)*

as if/as though + Past Perfect (unreal in the past)
She talked about Marilyn Monroe **as if** *they* **had been** *close friends. (but they hadn't been)*

---

89 *Put the verbs in brackets into the correct tense.*

1 Does he ever have a holiday? It seems as though he ...*works*... (works) seven days a week!
2 My father is so proud of his cooking - he behaves as though he .... (be) a trained chef.
3 The boy was staring at the motorbike as if he .... (never/see) one before.
4 She is so skinny! She looks as though she .... (never/eat) a proper meal in her life!
5 He slept for ten hours last night but today he's acting as though he .... (not/have) any sleep at all.
6 She isn't a member of the aristocracy but she acts as though she .... (be).
7 My brother isn't rich but he spends money as if he .... (be) a millionaire.
8 He talked about Hawaii as if he .... (be) there, but we knew he hadn't.
9 The boy was so hungry that he ate the food as though he .... (not/eat) for a week.
10 The hand-painted bowl was quite cheap but it looked as though it .... (be) expensive.
11 You look as though you .... (have) some good news recently.
12 It seems as if the burglar .... (break in) through the study window.
13 As Mansell rounds the last corner, it looks as if he .... (win) the race easily.
14 I talked to him on the phone and he sounded as though he .... (just/wake up).
15 The baby seems as if it .... (have) a temperature; why don't you get the thermometer?

90 *Complete the sentences using the words in bold. Use two to five words.*

1 He was hungry. He felt like he could eat a horse.
   as   He was so hungry he ...*felt as though he could*... eat a horse.
2 Someone must have added too much salt to the soup.
   though   The soup tasted .... too much salt.
3 He seems to have put on weight since I last saw him.
   if   He looks .... on weight since I last saw him.
4 She had a feeling that she had been in that house before.
   if   She felt.. in that house before.
5 I installed the computer as he had instructed me.
   way   I installed the computer .... instructed me.
6 He isn't a rock star but he behaves like one.
   though   He behaves .... a rock star.
7 She seemed to need a rest.
   if   She looked .... a rest.

Exclamations

- Exclamations are used to express anger, fear, shock, surprise etc. They always take an exclamation mark (!). Some exclamations are: Oh dear!, Ah!, Oh!, Good gracious! etc.

- **What + a(n) + (adjective) + singular countable noun**   *What a nice day!*
- **What + (adjective) + uncountable/plural noun**   *What awful weather!* ***What** nice manners!*
- **How + adjective/adverb**   ***How** clever he is!* ***How** slowly he speaks!*
- **You + (adjective) + noun**   *You (filthy) **liar**!*
- **such (a/an) + (adjective) + noun**   *It's **such an** old car!*
- **so + adjective/adverb**   *He's **so nice** to us!*
- **adverb/adverbial particle + subject + verb of movement**   ***Off** he went!*
- **Here/There + subject + verb**   ***There** she goes! but: **There** goes Mary! (when the subject is a noun, it follows the verb)*
- **Interrogative - negative question at the beginning of the sentence**   ***Isn't it** awful!*

---

91   *Rephrase the following as in the example:*

1   What fantastic photos! ...
Aren't these photos fantastic! /
These photos are so fantastic! / How fantastic these
photos are! / There are such fantastic photos!...

2 This beach is so crowded!	6 This is such a beautiful view!	10 What a helpful assistant!
3 He has such an expensive car!	7 The exam was so difficult!	11 She's so conscientious!
4 How polite they are!	8 It's been such a hot summer!	12 This is such nice weather!
5 What a spoilt boy!	9 Don't they look angry!	13 How talented you are!

92   *Fill in: what (a/an), how, so or such (a/an).*

1   ...*What a*... wonderful opportunity!
2   .... funny he is!
3   This is .... healthy meal!
4   .... friendly staff!
5   He has .... expensive taste!
6   .... miserable he looks!
7   She works .... hard!
8   .... terrible liar!
9   It's .... tragedy!
10 She's .... easy to talk to!
11 .... fantastic costume!

12 .... sad music!
13 .... enthusiastic she is!
14 He's .... imaginative artist!
15 They're .... helpful!
16 .... lucky man!
17 .... wonderfully she sings!
18 .... tasteful decorations you've got!
19 He's .... irresponsible employee!
20 .... amazing achievement!
21 They have .... much money.
22 .... ridiculous hairstyle!

93   *Fill in: what (a/an), how, so or such (a/an).*

Don: Have you seen the new drama teacher?
John: Yes. She is **1)** ...*so*...beautiful!
Don: She certainly is. She's got **2)** .... lovely eyes!
John: And **3)** .... gracefully she moves!
Don: Have you heard her speak? She has **4)** .... soft voice!
John: **5)** .... pity we don't do drama!
Don: Yes, we're **6)** .... unlucky!

4 Clauses / Linking Words

Linking Words

Linking words show the logical relationship between sentences or parts of a sentence.

94 *Rewrite the sentences from the table in as many ways as possible. Whenever this is not possible, make up a new sentence so that other linking words can be used.*

eg. *She is both young and successful. She's not only young but she's also successful. etc*

Positive Addition	and, both...and, not only...(but also/as well), too, moreover, in addition to, furthermore, further, also, not to mention the fact that, besides	She is young **and** successful.
Negative Addition	neither...nor, nor, neither, either	**Neither** Jane **nor** Paula has any desire to meet him again. Jane has no desire to meet him again. **Nor** does Paula.
Contrast	but, not...but, although, while, whereas, despite, even if, even though, on the other hand, in contrast, however, (and) yet, at the same time	She can speak Russian fluently; **however**, she is unable to read or write it.
Similarity	similarly, likewise, in the same way, equally	When you move house, you must notify the post office of your change of address. **Similarly,** you must register with the local county council.
Concession	but, even so, however, (and) still, (and) yet, nevertheless, on the other hand, although, even though, despite/in spite of, regardless of, admittedly, considering, whereas, while, nonetheless	She applied for the job **even though** she wasn't suitably qualified.
Alternative	or, on the other hand, either...or, alternatively	They could take a holiday now **or/on the other hand/alternatively** they could wait until the summer.
Emphasis	besides, not only this but...also, as well, what is more, in fact, as a matter of fact, to tell you the truth, actually, indeed, let alone	I find him pushy and demanding and, **what is more**, he is self-centred.
Exemplification	as, such as, like, for example, for instance, particularly, especially, in particular	I enjoyed all the books you lent me but **in particular** I liked "Wild Swans".
Clarification	that is to say, specifically, in other words, to put it another way, I mean	He needs to concentrate more on his schoolwork. **Specifically,** he has to pay more attention in the classroom.
Cause / Reason	as, because, because of, since, on the grounds that, seeing that, due to, in view of, owing to, for, now that, so	The company has decided to take on more staff **now that** sales are increasing.

Manner	as, (in) the way, how, the way in which, (in) the same way (as), as if, as though	*The manager explained* **how** *the organisation could increase productivity.*
Condition	if, in case, assuming (that), on condition (that), provided (that), providing (that), unless, in the event (that), in the event of, as/so long as, granted/granting (that), whether, whether...or (alternative condition), only if, even if, otherwise, or (else), in case of	*Please notify us* **in the event that/in case** *you are unable to attend the meeting.*
Consequence of a condition	consequently, then, under those circumstances, if so, if not, so, therefore, in that case, otherwise, thus	*I may take a long lunch break tomorrow.* **If so**, *I can go to the hairdresser's then.*
Purpose	so that, so as (not) to, in order (not) to, in order that, for fear (that), in case	*I took plenty of magazines with me* **in case** *I got bored during the flight.*
Effect / Result	such/so...that, consequently, for this reason, as a consequence, thus, therefore, so	*The room at The Ritz was double-booked and,* **as a consequence,** *we were moved to another hotel.*
Comparison	as...as, than, half as...as, nothing like, the...the, twice as...as, less...than	*You look* **nothing like** *your sister.*
Time	when, whenever, as, while, now (that), before, until, till, after, since	*As a freelance writer she can choose to work* **whenever** *she wants.*
Place	where, wherever	*She makes friends* **wherever** *she goes.*
Exception	but (for), except (for), apart from	*We have sent invitations to everyone* **apart from** *the Fords.*
Relative	who, whom, whose, which, what, that	*Let me introduce you to the man* **whose** *ideas have revolutionised the workplace.*
Chronological	**beginning:** initially, first..., at first, to start/begin with, first of all **continuing:** secondly ..., after this/that, second.., afterwards, then, next, before this **concluding:** finally, at last, in the end, eventually, lastly, last but not least	**First of all,** *we need to decide what the problem is.* **Then,** *we need to consider all possible solutions.* **Finally,** *we must decide on the best alternative.*
Reference	considering, concerning, regarding, with respect/regard/reference to, in respect/regard/reference to this/to the fact that	**Considering** *the length of time he took to write the report, it is not up to standard.* **With reference to** *what we agreed last week, I would like to remind you that the deadline has been brought forward to 1 June.*
Summarising	in conclusion, in summary, to sum up, as I have said, as (it) was previously stated, on the whole, in all, all in all, altogether, in short, briefly, to put it briefly	**To sum up,** *the film was a complete waste of time.*

4 Clauses / Linking Words

95 **Join the sentences, then identify the functions of the linking words in brackets.**

1 You could leave now. You could wait and ride with us. (either ... or) ...*You could either leave now or wait and ride with us. (alternative)*...

2 He's not a very good tennis player. He practises all the time. (considering)
....

3 He decided to change jobs. He wanted a chance to be more creative. (on the grounds that)
....

4 I don't feel like going out tonight. I never enjoy myself at discos. (besides)
....

5 He's afraid of heights. He wants to go rock climbing. (and yet)
....

6 You should write down your appointments. You won't forget them. (so that)
....

7 We're going to go on with the project. They say it's no longer necessary. (even if)
....

8 This house is exactly what we are looking for. It's a real bargain. (moreover)
....

9 She hardly ever practises the piano. She plays very well. (even though)
....

10 It was an interesting conference. There was one speaker who was boring. (in spite of)
....

11 She always gives money to poor people. She's extremely generous. (in other words)
....

12 I enjoy her company. She's been a great help to me. (not only ... but also)
....

13 She sings like an opera star. She isn't a star though. (as if)
....

14 Exercising will help you feel better. Eating less will improve your health. (likewise)
....

15 He isn't qualified for the job. He hasn't had much practical experience. (what is more)
....

16 You can play tennis for free here. You have to book in advance though. (provided)
....

17 I received a letter today. It was about my insurance policy. (regarding)
....

18 You should always wear a seatbelt. You may have an accident. (in case)
....

96 **Replace the underlined words with synonymous ones.**

Attention all staff: 1) First of all complaints have been made to the management by the company chairman concerning the making of personal phone calls. **2)** In view of the fact that this year's bill is double last year's, some action has to be taken. **3)** Consequently, no members of staff **4)** except for senior management may use the phone for such purposes. **5)** Secondly, we have received complaints from the contract cleaners claiming that staff preparing coffee are making too much mess. **6)** Concerning this matter we kindly request that staff clean the coffee area after use, **7)** in other words, wipe away any stains and dispose of paper cups in the bins provided. **8)** Finally, it has come to our attention that certain employees persist in smoking in the designated no-smoking areas. This must stop, **9)** otherwise there will be a total ban on smoking in all areas. Thank you for your cooperation in these matters.

▶ Oral Development 7

Students look at the picture, then one after the other continue the story using the following linking words:
To begin with, consequently, then, not only ... but also, in order to, which, only if, on the other hand, because, what is more, since etc

Harry is a man in his early thirties who seems to be in trouble. It all started when ...

97 *Complete the sentences using the words in bold. Use two to five words.*

1 I was born in that hospital.
   was   That's ...*the hospital where I was*... born.
2 He has decided to emigrate to Australia; we can't stop him.
   prevent   We can't .... to Australia.
3 I didn't tell her the news because I didn't want to upset her.
   so   I didn't tell her the news .... her.
4 He couldn't get a credit card because he owed the bank money.
   result   He owed the bank money .... he couldn't get a credit card.
5 It was such a rude remark that we all felt insulted.
   so   It was .... we all felt insulted.
6 He bought a computer as he intended to work from home.
   view   He bought a computer .... from home.
7 She seldom left the house because she was afraid of being attacked.
   fear   She seldom left the house .... attacked.
8 Whatever you say, I will never trust that man.
   what   I will never trust that man .... you say.
9 That's the shop where he used to work when he was young.
   in   That's the shop .... when he was young.
10 You must phone work if you are ill.
   event   You must phone work .... you are ill.
11 She was tall but she couldn't reach the top shelf.
   though   Tall .... not reach the top shelf.
12 There was heavy traffic on the motorway so we arrived late.
   due   We arrived late .... on the motorway.
13 I like all my dresses but the red one is my favourite.
   particular I like all my dresses but the red one .... favourite.
14 Once they all arrived, she began the seminar.
   had   She waited .... before she began the seminar.

15 Gary was the only one who didn't enjoy the meal.
   except   Everyone .... Gary.
16 What a slow worker you are!
   slowly   How .... work!
17 I'm not going to work today because I've got a cold.
   owing   I'm not going to work today .... I've got a cold.
18 His second film is very different to his first.
   like   His second film .... his first.
19 I'm writing concerning the advertised position.
   reference   I'm writing .... the advertised position.
20 This is Mr Jones; you will be seeing him tomorrow.
   who   This is Mr Jones .... tomorrow.
21 It looked like it was going to rain.
   if   It looked .... to rain.
22 Although he knew it was rude, he couldn't help laughing.
   prevent   Although he knew it was rude .... from laughing.
23 The holiday was too expensive; we couldn't afford it.
   such   It was .... we couldn't afford it.
24 Take your book; you may get bored.
   case   Take your book .... bored.
25 Always check the dictionary if you don't want to make spelling mistakes.
   avoid   Always check the dictionary .... spelling mistakes.

98 *Find the word which should not be in the sentence.*

1 Please call us the moment you will have any news from him.
2 The twins can go out after they will have finished cleaning their room.
3 She called her parents so to let them know she was going to be late.
4 Tim's promised to help in case we will need someone to organise the reception.
5 When you will contact your lawyer, he'll give you all the details.
6 They held a charity ball in order that to raise money for the homeless.
7 He sent them a letter for to complain about the poor service.
8 He gave me such a useful advice that I was grateful.
9 She left her keys in the office and as consequently she couldn't get into her flat.
10 We were having such a good time at the party as that we were reluctant to leave.
11 As he came late because he missed the beginning of the film.
12 Despite of his lack of qualifications, he was able to get a good job.
13 However how hard he tried, he wasn't able to make us change our minds.
14 No matter how much fast he drives, he will never win the race.
15 Rich though he may as be, he never gives money to charity.
16 Gerry behaves as if he were been the owner of the house.
17 What a nice furniture this is!
18 The man who I was talking to him is the owner of the company.
19 That's the girl whose her mother is a well-known author.
20 I've always wanted to visit the city where Mozart was born there.
21 Elaine, whom you met her last week, is my best friend.
22 The doctor told me to avoid from eating fatty foods.
23 He has so little of spare time that he can't take up a hobby.
24 As a result of his being stupidity he lost every penny.
25 It was such a lovely weather that we went swimming.

1	will
2	
3	
4	
5	
6	
7	
8	
9	
10	
11	
12	
13	
14	
15	
16	
17	
18	
19	
20	
21	
22	
23	
24	
25	

Consolidation 4

▶ Phrasal Verbs

do away with: abolish
do down: speak badly of sb
do in: kill
do out: clean
do up: 1) fasten; tie, 2) redecorate
do with: 1) need; want, 2) have a connection with
do without: manage to live or continue without

• • • • • • • • • • • • •

fall back: move back; retreat
fall back on: use sth in the absence of sth else; turn to
fall behind: 1) fail to keep up with, 2) be late with payment
fall for: 1) be tricked, 2) fall in love with sb
fall in with: accept sb's plans, ideas
fall off: decrease
fall on: 1) attack, 2) eat (food) hungrily
fall out (with): quarrel
fall through: fail to be completed

99 Fill in the correct particle(s).

1 No one can do ...*without*... water for more than two days.
2 The death penalty was done .... in Britain many years ago.
3 You'd better do your shoes .... or you'll trip over your laces.
4 He was arrested for doing .... a woman with a gun.
5 It's so hot, I could do .... a nice cool drink.
6 Theatre attendance has fallen .... because of the rise in ticket prices.
7 Our holiday plans fell .... when all the airlines went on strike.
8 After some disagreement, they finally fell .... our suggestions.
9 Once we'd spent all our money, we fell .... our credit card.
10 John fell .... the rest of the class after being ill for three weeks.
11 George always falls .... girls with blonde hair.
12 I fell .... one of my friends and haven't spoken to her for weeks.

100 Look at Appendix 1, then fill in the correct preposition.

1 If you insist ...*on*... going against their orders, you must be prepared to face the consequences.
2 There has been a noticeable increase .... staff turnover.
3 She bought a house with a garden as she's very keen .... gardening.
4 George is very keen .... start university.
5 His openness and sincerity are the key .... his political success.
6 Factories have a negative impact .... the environment.
7 When I was at university, I lived .... a student grant.
8 I am always being mistaken .... my cousin.
9 Julie has been married .... Bill for nearly ten years.
10 She's notorious .... telling incredible lies.
11 I didn't expect so many people to object .... the scheme.
12 We hoped you would be more obedient .... the rules.
13 Most people are indifferent .... the welfare of the homeless.
14 He asked her to write him a cheque .... £75.
15 Poor working conditions are believed to have caused a decrease .... production.
16 Don't disturb him as he's busy .... his assignment.
17 The criminal was assured .... a fair trial.
18 Christine got engaged .... her boyfriend Ted.
19 The class is engaged .... a discussion about politics.
20 The interviewee made a good impression .... the manager.
21 What we lack .... our flat is enough storage space.
22 They were very impressed .... his ability.
23 The workers were protesting .... the wage cuts.
24 Gary prides himself .... his honesty.
25 Do you take pride .... your work?
26 I've never had the pleasure .... meeting her before.
27 He is jealous .... his younger brother's success.
28 He was nervous .... the forthcoming exams.
29 The hostess was pleasant .... each of her guests.
30 I'm really pleased .... your performance.
31 We always take pleasure .... their company.

101 For questions 1 - 15, read the text below and decide which word A, B, C or D best fits each space. There's an example at the beginning (0).

Anorexia

Anorexia is a comparatively new illness and seems to be **(0)** .... to the society we live in which increasingly **(1)** .... us on our appearance. The media encourages us to try to be **(2)** .... and beautiful. Falling short of these criteria can put enormous **(3)** .... on the majority of us who are less than **(4)** .... Each year there are estimated to be at **(5)** .... 2,000 new cases of anorexia. About one sufferer in ten is male, but most anorexics are females in their teens and twenties who suffer **(6)** .... a distorted self image, feeling fat and ugly, **(7)** ..... slim and attractive they may appear to others. Though constantly hungry, anorexics attempt to gain **(8)** .... of their lives by **(9)** .... to eat. The problem commonly **(10)** .... in teenage years, when responsibilities increase. In **(11)** .... cases, it can **(12)** .... anaemia, heart and kidney problems and, in almost a fifth of the cases, death by starvation or secondary infection. Treatment **(13)** .... encouraging patients to **(14)** .... weight by providing counselling and therapy which, in essence, guides the sufferers **(15)** .... a normal life.

0	**A** resulted	**B** linked	**C** caused	**D** developed
1	**A** watches	**B** judges	**C** measures	**D** criticises
2	**A** narrow	**B** slight	**C** light	**D** slim
3	**A** pressure	**B** tension	**C** weight	**D** force
4	**A** exact	**B** perfect	**C** excellent	**D** good
5	**A** minimum	**B** less	**C** least	**D** more
6	**A** by	**B** from	**C** of	**D** for
7	**A** whether	**B** either	**C** moreover	**D** however
8	**A** control	**B** direction	**C** power	**D** authority
9	**A** forbidding	**B** refusing	**C** rejecting	**D** denying
10	**A** develops	**B** delivers	**C** turns	**D** takes
11	**A** enlarged	**B** extended	**C** prolonged	**D** expanded
12	**A** lead	**B** catch	**C** cause	**D** give
13	**A** considers	**B** involves	**C** concerns	**D** deals
14	**A** put	**B** win	**C** earn	**D** regain
15	**A** in	**B** from	**C** at	**D** towards

Answer grid:

	A	B	C	D
0		■		
1				
2				
3				
4				
5				
6				
7				
8				
9				
10				
11				
12				
13				
14				
15				

102 Complete the sentences using the words in bold. Use two to five words.

1 Are you likely to see him again?
   chance   Is there ...*any chance of your seeing*... him again?
2 He was late because there was an accident on the motorway.
   due   He was .... on the motorway.

3 He definitely won't pass his driving test.
   hope   There's .... his driving test.
4 I am disappointed with your exam results.
   let   You .... with your exam results.
5 I left home early so as to be on time for work.
   would   I left home early .... on time for work.
6 In Austria we visited Mozart's birthplace.
   where   We saw the .... while we were in Austria.

103 *Use the words in capitals to form a word that fits in the space in the same line.*

Idioms

A high **(0)** .... of the English language consists of idioms which a **(1)** .... will have to acquire in order to achieve complete **(2)** .... . However, good **(3)** .... is not based on the quantity of idioms used, but on their appropriate usage. Students of English can **(4)** .... make themselves understood using a minimal amount of **(5)** .... language, but some feel it is a **(6)** .... to learn them and then use them as often as possible to make a good **(7)** .... and show how good their language is. However, using them **(8)** .... can sound worse than not using them at all. Thankfully, there are many **(9)** .... teachers who can provide clear **(10)** .... and help with practice.

PERCENT	0
LEARN	1
FLUENT	2
COMMUNICATE	3
EASE	4
IDIOM	5
NECESSARY	6
IMPRESS	7
CORRECTLY	8
QUALIFY	9
EXPLAIN	10

0	*percentage*
1	
2	
3	
4	
5	
6	
7	
8	
9	
10	

104 *Read the text carefully. Some of the lines are correct and some have a word which should not be there. If a line is correct, put a tick (✔) in the space provided. If a line has a word which should not be there, write it in the space provided.*

Marketing Interview

0	After searching out the jobs page of "The Times" I came	*out*
00	across an advertisement that really excited me. It	✓
1	was for a trainee marketing assistant with a large	
2	food company. After applying, I was invited me for	
3	an interview almost straightaway. Following from a	
4	brief private interview, I was led into a room which containing	
5	twenty or so other candidates in. We	
6	were put into groups of four and given off three new	
7	products to launch: a soft drink, an ice cream	
8	and some chocolates. We have had two hours	
9	to discuss and choose on names, packaging	
10	and advertising plans before we presenting our	
11	ideas to the other groups. I really enjoyed it and	
12	forgot it I was in an interview. Fortunately,	
13	the interviewers must have thought I had a something	
14	as they asked me back for a second interview, after	
15	which I was offered to work with them.	

Practice test 2

For questions 1 - 15, read the text below and decide which word A, B, C or D best fits each space. Mark your answers in the answer boxes provided.

Alternative Therapy

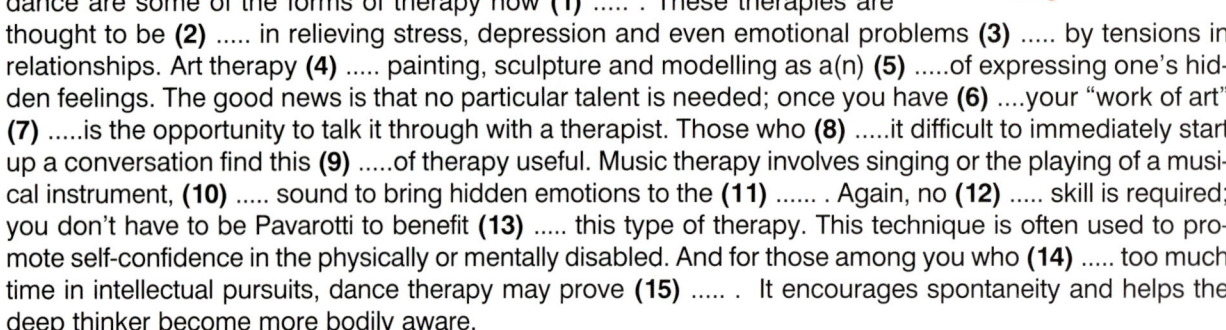

Creative therapy is now regarded **(0)** ..... a worthy alternative to the more conventional forms of treatment such as psychoanalysis. Art, music and dance are some of the forms of therapy now **(1)** ..... . These therapies are thought to be **(2)** ..... in relieving stress, depression and even emotional problems **(3)** ..... by tensions in relationships. Art therapy **(4)** ..... painting, sculpture and modelling as a(n) **(5)** .....of expressing one's hidden feelings. The good news is that no particular talent is needed; once you have **(6)** ....your "work of art" **(7)** .....is the opportunity to talk it through with a therapist. Those who **(8)** .....it difficult to immediately start up a conversation find this **(9)** .....of therapy useful. Music therapy involves singing or the playing of a musical instrument, **(10)** ..... sound to bring hidden emotions to the **(11)** .... Again, no **(12)** ..... skill is required; you don't have to be Pavarotti to benefit **(13)** ..... this type of therapy. This technique is often used to promote self-confidence in the physically or mentally disabled. And for those among you who **(14)** ..... too much time in intellectual pursuits, dance therapy may prove **(15)** ..... . It encourages spontaneity and helps the deep thinker become more bodily aware.

0 A as	**B** like	**C** by	**D** to
1 A visible	**B** available	**C** handy	**D** ready
2 A likely	**B** capable	**C** possible	**D** effective
3 A directed	**B** caused	**C** occurred	**D** happened
4 A contains	**B** has	**C** involves	**D** needs
5 A means	**B** attempt	**C** type	**D** effort
6 A completed	**B** worked	**C** been	**D** added
7 A it	**B** there	**C** that	**D** here
8 A have	**B** make	**C** seem	**D** find
9 A condition	**B** shape	**C** pattern	**D** form
10 A consisting	**B** having	**C** using	**D** trying
11 A surface	**B** top	**C** front	**D** side
12 A strange	**B** typical	**C** peculiar	**D** special
13 A in	**B** by	**C** of	**D** from
14 A have	**B** spend	**C** use	**D** spare
15 A invaluable	**B** priceless	**C** precious	**D** worthy

	A	B	C	D
0	▬	☐	☐	☐
1	☐	☐	☐	☐
2	☐	☐	☐	☐
3	☐	☐	☐	☐
4	☐	☐	☐	☐
5	☐	☐	☐	☐
6	☐	☐	☐	☐
7	☐	☐	☐	☐
8	☐	☐	☐	☐
9	☐	☐	☐	☐
10	☐	☐	☐	☐
11	☐	☐	☐	☐
12	☐	☐	☐	☐
13	☐	☐	☐	☐
14	☐	☐	☐	☐
15	☐	☐	☐	☐

Part 2

For questions 16 - 30, read the text below and think of the word which best fits each space. Use only one word in each space. Write your answers in the answer boxes provided.

Mountain Biking

Mountain biking is becoming an increasingly popular sport, as people become **(0)** .... interested in keeping **(16)** .... and doing activities which take them out of their homes.

It is not only a pleasurable way of improving your fitness, but **(17)** .... one of the most rewarding ways to explore the countryside. However, it is important to follow a **(18)** .... simple rules, otherwise you could **(19)** .... the environment and spoil **(20)** .... people's enjoyment.

Cyclists can use any road but they must **(21)** .... attention to the type of path they are on. Some paths **(22)** .... only designed for people who are **(23)** .... foot, so if you are cycling **(24)** .... these, you could cause inconvenience to walkers as **(25)** .... as ending up being taken to court **(26)** .... the owner of the land you are on.

On any other path, you should still respect walkers and be careful **(27)** .... you are passing horse riders. Other things which you are asked to do are to close gates behind you, so **(28)** .... farm animals cannot escape, and to take your rubbish home with you. Always **(29)** .... someone know where you are going and carry the right equipment and clothing for unexpected conditions,

(30) .... you could be creating unnecessary problems for yourself.

0	*more*	0
16		16
17		17
18		18
19		19
20		20
21		21
22		22
23		23
24		24
25		25
26		26
27		27
28		28
29		29
30		30

For questions 31 - 40, complete the second sentence so that it has a similar meaning to the first sentence. Use the word given and other words to complete each sentence. You must use between two and five words. Do not change the word given. Write your answers in the answer boxes provided.

0   I'm sure they worked hard on the project.
have
They .... on the project.

| 0 | *must have worked hard* | 0 |

31 It takes four hours to drive from London to Swansea.
drive
It's .... from London to Swansea.

| 31 | | 31 |

32 I can't decide where to go on holiday.
mind
I can't .... where to go on holiday.

| 32 | | 32 |

33 I think he was lying about the money.
have
He .... about the money.

| 33 | | 33 |

34 If you work faster, you'll finish sooner.
the
The .... you'll finish.

| 34 | | 34 |

35 Ann doesn't want to stay in this hotel.
rather
Ann .... in this hotel.

| 35 | | 35 |

36 Although he is a doctor, he doesn't earn much.
being
Despite ...., he doesn't earn much.

| 36 | | 36 |

37 You shouldn't say bad things about your friends.
run
You .... your friends.

| 37 | | 37 |

38 I'm sure she wasn't promoted.
have
She .... promoted.

| 38 | | 38 |

39 They enjoyed themselves a lot at the party.
time
They .... at the party.

| 39 | | 39 |

40 I've never spoken to such a rude person.
the
He is .... ever spoken to.

| 40 | | 40 |

Part 4

For questions 41 - 55, read the text below and look carefully at each line. Some of the lines are correct and some have a word which should not be there. If a line is correct, put a tick (✔) by the number in the answer boxes provided. If a line has a word which should not be there, write the word in the answer boxes provided.

Flying the Flag

0	How does it the American flag fly on the moon	**0**	*it*
00	when there is no air or wind? Like everything	**00**	✓
41	else in the Apollo programme, the flag, which that was	**41**	
42	planted on the moon by astronaut Neil Armstrong	**42**	
43	on 20 July 1969, was in the outcome of some	**43**	
44	serious planning. Since the moon is without no	**44**	
45	atmosphere, there can be no winds, and a	**45**	
46	conventional flag would have to hung over	**46**	
47	the pole. Such an arrangement was being considered	**47**	
48	perfectly satisfactory for US courtrooms, but	**48**	
49	NASA managers were felt that Americans	**49**	
50	would be like to see a proper flag "flying"	**50**	
51	on the moon's surface. It is almost	**51**	
52	certainly the very most expensive American	**52**	
53	flag to ever made and the most expensive	**53**	
54	to raise. It is still there today, and is likely that to	**54**	
55	remain in the place for the forseeable future.	**55**	

Part 5

For questions 56 - 65, read the text below. Use the word given in capitals at the end of each line to form a word that fits in the space in the same line. Write your word in the answer boxes provided.

The Power of the Mind

Scientists have recently become interested in strange **(0)** .... powers. A professor at Edinburgh University is leading an **(56)** .... into the most **(57)** .... aspect of the brain's **(58)** .... . He has chosen a controversial and **(59)** .... subject - telepathy. Direct mind-to-mind **(60)** .... is when one person knows what another is thinking. Many people have doubts that this is really a **(61)** .... subject, and the professor's work has only recently received **(62)** .... . He believes that telepathy is a **(63)** .... talent, but that some people are more **(64)** .... than others. However, most people still believe that it involves some kind of **(65)** .... or trickery.

PSYCHOLOGY	**0**	*psychological*	0
INVESTIGATE	**56**		56
MYSTERY	**57**		57
ABLE	**58**		58
SURPRISE	**59**		59
COMMUNICATE	**60**		60
SCIENCE	**61**		61
RECOGNISE	**62**		62
NATURE	**63**		63
SENSE	**64**		64
HONESTY	**65**		65

Pre - test **1**

A *Choose the correct item.*

1 I am sorry .... you that you're suspended.
   A informing   **B** inform
   C to inform   **D** have informed

2 I'll .... some research before writing my essay.
   A do   **B** make
   C work   **D** have

3 She's been working at Supersave .... 1990.
   A for   **B** ago
   C since   **D** before

4 Can you .... me a favour and babysit tonight?
   A make   **B** do
   C create   **D** have

5 Please stop .... I can't concentrate.
   A talk   **B** to talk
   C to talking   **D** talking

6 Take a drink in case you .... thirsty.
   A get   **B** will get
   C would get   **D** got

7 He's used .... with children.
   A to coping   **B** cope
   C coping   **D** to cope

8 .... he lives in Italy, he can't speak Italian.
   A As   **B** Despite
   C In spite of   **D** Although

9 He objects to people .... in his house.
   A smoked   **B** smoke
   C smoking   **D** had smoked

10 Most children prefer to play .... do their homework.
   A from   **B** rather than
   C to   **D** rather

11 He .... an excuse to avoid helping us.
   A made   **B** did
   C claimed   **D** worked

12 .... its high price, she bought the Porsche.
   A As   **B** Although
   C Though   **D** Despite

13 We spent two weeks .... on the project.
   A to working   **B** work
   C working   **D** to work

14 If you .... an effort, you will succeed.
   A try   **B** have
   C do   **D** make

15 We .... haven't finished painting the house.
   A still   **B** before
   C already   **D** yet

16 We heard him .... the whole sonata.
   A play   **B** to playing
   C to play   **D** played

17 He gave us .... useful information!
   A too   **B** so
   C such   **D** such a

18 I really appreciate your .... me in hospital.
   A visiting   **B** visit
   C to visit   **D** to visiting

19 The management does not allow ....
   A to smoking   **B** smoke
   C to smoke   **D** smoking

20 Louisa has .... learnt to ride a bike.
   A yet   **B** still
   C already   **D** before

21 Will you remember .... the tickets?
   A to collect   **B** collect
   C to collecting   **D** collecting

22 The dog made .... much noise that we couldn't sleep.
   A such   **B** such a
   C too   **D** so

23 School groups are permitted .... the museum free.
   A visiting   **B** to visiting
   C visit   **D** to visit

24 The suspect was seen .... the house at 2 am and drive away.
   A to leave   **B** leave
   C left   **D** to leaving

B **Put the verbs in brackets into the correct tense.**

Last summer Gordon **1)** .... (start) university. He **2)** .... (apply) to various institutions for months and **3)** .... (begin) to wonder if he would ever succeed. He **4)** .... (study) hard every day since he started and, for that reason, he still **5)** .... (not/make) many friends. However, he **6)** .... (begin) to feel more at home now and he thinks he **7)** .... (be) quite happy here. Next week he **8)** .... (start) revising for the end-of-term tests.

C **Put the verbs in brackets into the correct tense.**

Janet and John **1)** .... (just/get) married. They **2)** .... (go out) with each other for three years before they **3)** .... (decide) to get engaged. John **4)** .... (buy) her a ring last week. At the moment, they **5)** .... (travel) around Europe on a motorcycle. They both **6)** .... (love) motorcycles. When the honeymoon is over they **7)** .... (buy) a house in Oxford. I think they **8)** .... (be) very happy.

D **Complete the sentences using the words in bold. Use two to five words.**

1 She didn't start typing until her boss asked her.
   started   She waited until her boss asked her .... typing.
2 It would be a good idea to lock the door before you leave.
   had   You .... before you leave.
3 He's the most intelligent person I've ever met.
   never   I .... intelligent person.
4 The exercise was so difficult that we couldn't finish it.
   too   The exercise was .... finish.
5 Going on trips abroad alone is sometimes boring.
   go   It is sometimes boring .... abroad alone.
6 Mike prefers going by train to flying.
   than   Mike prefers to .... fly.
7 My grandmother is too ill to make the journey.
   enough   My grandmother .... make the journey.
8 He made me promise that I would keep it a secret.
   to   I .... that I would keep it a secret.
9 How long is it since you found out about it?
   find   When .... about it?
10 I've never seen this picture before.
   first   It's the .... this picture.
11 It's ages since we went out.
   been   We .... ages.
12 I'm sure Louise didn't lose her temper.
   have   Louise .... her temper.
13 I didn't call her because I didn't want to upset her.
   avoid   I didn't call her .... her.
14 Helen's been dieting for three weeks.
   started   Helen .... ago.
15 Perhaps they will give us their new address.
   give   They .... their new address.
16 He isn't the boss but he acts like he is.
   were   He acts .... the boss.
17 It was difficult for them to find a flight.
   had   They .... a flight.
18 He'll probably get to Paris before we do.
   likely   He .... Paris before we do.

19 She found his reaction surprising.
   was   She .... reaction.
20 He wore sunglasses to avoid being recognised.
   that   He wore sunglasses .... be recognised.

E *Fill in the blanks with the correct particle(s).*

1 He came .... a fortune on his father's death.
2 He came .... his car through dishonest means.
3 He brought .... his child alone.
4 The village was cut .... for weeks because of the snow.
5 John and Sue broke .... after their argument.
6 I took the bus because my car broke ....
7 We fell .... our neighbours because of their constant noise.
8 I'm thirsty. I could do .... a drink.

F *Fill in the blanks with the correct preposition(s).*

1 She's very attached .... her pet hamster.
2 You're jealous .... me because I won the prize.
3 She was charged .... assault.
4 The beaches were crowded .... people.
5 It's so noisy I can't concentrate ...... my work.
6 The President congratulated the diplomat .... his work.
7 Is June well? I haven't heard .... her for months.
8 Catwalk models take a lot of pride .... their appearance.

G *Correct the following sentences by taking out the inappropriate word.*

1 Jane will be late so as we'll meet her later.
2 I have found out gardening to be relaxing.
3 The supermarket doesn't charge an extra for deliveries.
4 On Saturday mornings I enjoy going for shopping.
5 I have been read all of Agatha Christie's novels.
6 In the summer I drink so lots of water.
7 My parents they say I must study hard.
8 I can't decide where to go out on holiday this year.
9 I always find that what I want at the market.
10 Fiona is so more friendly than Jill.
11 Which of university can I go to?
12 Next year I want to learn me to speak French.

1	
2	
3	
4	
5	
6	
7	
8	
9	
10	
11	
12	

H *Fill in the correct word derived from the words in bold.*

1 The pop star wore sunglasses and a wig to avoid .... by adoring fans.
2 Sunbathing is my favourite form of ....
3 This book is so ....; I just can't put it down.
4 The circumstances surrounding the crime were very ....
5 The .... of gold in California made lots of people rich.
6 Most countries in Europe are presently going through a period of .... decline.
7 He was a superb politician and soon won the .... of the voters.
8 Porsches usually have very fast and .... engines.
9 She arrived for her interview .... on time.
10 I was amazed at her .... to cope under so much stress.
11 My new sofa is so .... I could sit and relax on it for hours.
12 For .... reasons, you should always wear a crash helmet when on a motorbike.

RECOGNISE
RELAX
EXCITE
MYSTERY
DISCOVER
ECONOMY
POPULAR
POWER
EXACT
ABLE
COMFORT
SAFE

- **Adjectives** describe nouns and are the same in singular and plural. *They are close friends. (What kind of friends? Close.)* They can be **factual** *(small, round, yellow etc)* or **opinion** *(awful, ugly etc).* Note that after **appear, be, become, get, feel, look, seem, smell, sound, stay, taste** we use adjectives, not adverbs. *It tastes awful. (not: ~~awfully~~)*

- Most common adjectives (long, late etc) do not have a particular ending. However, there are certain common endings for **adjectives which are formed from nouns and verbs**. These are:

-able	*fashionable*	**-ent**	*persistent*	**-ical**	*mechanical*	**-like**	*woman-like*
-al	*magical*	**-esque**	*picturesque*	**-ious**	*rebellious*	**-ly**	*deathly*
-ant	*hesitant*	**-ful**	*successful*	**-ish**	*stylish*	**-ory**	*sensory*
-ar	*spectacular*	**-ian**	*Iranian*	**-ist**	*racist*	**-ous**	*humorous*
-ary	*disciplinary*	**-ible**	*terrible*	**-ive**	*selective*	**-some**	*bothersome*
-ate	*considerate*	**-ic**	*melodic*	**-less**	*faultless*	**-y**	*sandy*
-ial	*artificial*						

- The most common prefixes used with adjectives are:

a	-	*asexual*	**im**	-	*immoral*	**pre**	- *prearranged*
ab	-	*abnormal*	**in**	-	*inactive*	**pro**	- *pro-war*
anti	-	*antisocial*	**ir**	-	*irresponsible*	**sub**	- *sub-zero*
dis	-	*disinterested*	**mal**	-	*maladjusted*	**super**	- *superhuman*
hyper	-	*hyperactive*	**non**	-	*non-existent*	**un**	- *unavailable*
il	-	*illegible*	**over**	-	*overweight*	**under**	- *understaffed*

- **Compound adjectives** are formed with:
  1 **present participles.** *a long-playing record, a fee-paying student*
  2 **past participles.** *cut-off jeans, undercooked meat, a rolled-up carpet*
  3 **cardinal numbers + nouns.** *a three-year contract, a ten-minute journey, a two-week course*
  4 **prefixes and suffixes.** *a modern-day costume, an open-ended discussion*
  5 **well, badly, ill, poorly + past participle.** *a poorly-kept garden, a well-timed joke, a badly-furnished room*

- **Present** and **past participles** can be used as adjectives. *The lecture was boring. We were exhausted.*

 105 *Use the words in capitals to form a word that fits in the space in the same line.*

The Benefits of Exercise

Working full-time can be a very **(0)** .... experience for most people; long hours and the pressure to be **(1)** .... in a **(2)** .... society both contribute to the build-up of anxiety. If you're feeling **(3)** ...., there's no better way to relax than to exercise. However, many people return from work too **(4)** .... to move. People are criticised for being lazy and **(5)** ...., and for watching too much television which is not **(6)** .... to our health. Taking regular exercise can be both relaxing and **(7)** .... and people who feel healthy often also feel more **(8)** .... . You don't need to be especially **(9)** .... to take up a sport; simply choose one that is **(10)** .... to your character.

STRESS	0	*stressful*
SUCCESS	1	
COMPETE	2	
NERVE	3	
EXHAUST	4	
ACTIVE	5	
BENEFIT	6	
	7	
PLEASURE	8	
CONFIDENCE	9	
ENERGY		
SUIT	10	

5 Adjectives / Adverbs / Comparisons

106 Use the words in capitals to form a word that fits in the space in the same line.

For an **(0)** .... holiday destination, few cities can compare to New York. From **(1)** .... Fifth Avenue to the run-down and **(2)** .... ghettos of the Bronx, New York is a city of **(3)** .... contrasts. However **(4)** .... it may seem, it is worthwhile wandering the streets on your own to get a feeling for the **(5)** .... areas of the city. Of course it is **(6)** .... to use your common sense. You should be **(7)** .... when approached by strangers, and always keep in mind that violence is **(8)** .... and that acting **(9)** .... is the best protection against attack. Keeping this in mind, you can be assured of having a **(10)** .... time.

EXCITE	0	*exciting*
FASHION	1	
FRIGHT	2	
SPECTACLE	3	
ALARM	4	
CHARACTERISE	5	
ADVISE	6	
CAUTION	7	
PREVAIL	8	
AFRAID	9	
MARVEL	10	

107 Write the opposites of the following adjectives.

1 active ...*inactive*...
2 existent ....
3 well-adjusted ....
4 legible ....
5 religious ....
6 moral ....
7 available ....
8 responsible ....
9 respectful ....

108 Make compound adjectives to describe the following:

1 An award that is well deserved. ...*a well-deserved award*...
2 A product that lasts a long time. ....
3 A suit that isn't made well. ....
4 A story that never ends. ....
5 A meal that has three courses. ....
6 An employee who isn't paid well. ....
7 A house that has two storeys. ....
8 An office that isn't organised well. ....

● Certain adjectives are used with **the** as nouns to talk about groups of people in general. These are: the elderly, the middle-aged, the old, the young, the blind, the deaf, the disabled, the living, the sick, the poor, the rich, the homeless, the hungry, the strong, the weak, the unemployed etc.
Young people are full of curiosity./*The young* are full of curiosity. (refers to young people in general)
The young people in our town are planning a concert. (refers to a specific group of young people)

109 Fill in "the" where necessary.

1 The Government is cutting benefits for ...*the*... unemployed and .... unemployed people all over the country are organising protest marches.
2 .... homeless in our town are being helped by .... young people, who are organising a sale to raise money for .... needy people in general.
3 A friend of mine works in a school for .... deaf, where she teaches .... deaf children.
4 .... middle-aged people tend to criticise .... young for their disrespectful attitude.
5 After the earthquake, ... dead were buried in mass graves while .... living tried to make shelters for .... injured.

5 Adjectives / Adverbs / Comparisons

Order of Adjectives

- **When there are two or more adjectives, they normally go in the following order:**

	Opinion	Fact Adjectives							
	adjectives	size	age	shape	colour	origin	material	used for/ be about	noun
It's a	beautiful	big	old	round	brown	Italian	oak	dining	table.

- **Afraid, alike, alive, alone, ashamed, asleep, content, ill, glad etc are never followed by a noun.** *The baby is asleep. (not: ~~the asleep baby~~)*
- **Nouns of material, purpose or substance can be used as adjectives.** *a cotton skirt, a winter dress, a shopping bag.* **However, certain adjectives derived from such nouns are used metaphorically.** *silky hair (hair like silk) but a silk scarf (a scarf made of silk), a stony expression (cold expression) but a stone cottage (a cottage made of stone), golden hair (hair like gold) but a gold pen (a pen made of gold), feathery leaves (leaves which look like feathers) but a feather duster (a duster made of feathers), metallic colour (colour that looks like metal) but a metal chair (a chair made of metal), leathery skin (skin looking/feeling like leather) but a leather wallet (a wallet made of leather), a leaden feeling (an unpleasant feeling) but lead pipes (pipes made of lead), a steely look (a strong, determined look) but steel framework (framework made of steel)*

110 *Rewrite the sentences putting the adjectives into the correct place. Identify what kind of adjectives they are.*

1. He was carrying a briefcase. (leather, nice, black, new) ...*He was carrying a nice new black leather briefcase. (opinion/age/colour/material)*...
2. He gave her a scarf. (silk, fantastic, French, red) ....
3. I bought chairs from an antique shop. (American, three, oak, old) ....
4. She is an actress. (English, intelligent, young, dramatic) ....
5. The table lamp was broken by the children. (metal, white, small) ....
6. She bought a carpet. (expensive, Persian, antique, woollen) ....
7. He crashed his car yesterday. (sports, brand new, yellow) ....
8. It was a dress. (hand-made, gorgeous, wedding, lace) ....
9. I saw a film on TV last night. (Italian, exciting, detective) ....
10. They live in a house. (big, lovely, country, old-fashioned, brick)...
11. She is a salesperson. (young, computer, successful) ....
12. I bought a book. (old, poetry, Latin) ....
13. We watched a programme. (short, English, interesting, educational) ....
14. She bought a raincoat. (plastic, long, cheap) ....
15. They found a trunk. (wooden, rectangular, antique, interesting) ....
16. He bought a yacht. (Swedish, second-hand, huge) ....

111 *Underline the correct adjective.*

1. She gave him a stone / stony look when he criticised her daughter.
2. These metal / metallic chairs are suitable for outdoor use as they are weatherproof.
3. The sky was full of light feather / feathery clouds.
4. She is admired for her gold / golden hair and metal/metallic blue eyes.
5. The old farmer had dark leather / leathery skin.
6. This new body milk gives you smooth, silk / silky skin in a matter of days.
7. She had a lead / leaden expression on her face.
8. The gold / golden candlesticks were very expensive so we bought some silver / silvery ones instead.
9. He wears woolly / woollen suits and expensive leather/leathery shoes.
10. She has a steel / steely manner towards her colleagues.

5 Adjectives / Adverbs / Comparisons

112 Put the adjectives in the correct order.

Dear Louisa,

We've nearly finished furnishing the cottage, and I must say I'm very pleased with it. Yesterday they delivered an 1) ...**antique French oak**... (oak, antique, French) cupboard which Peter had bought as a surprise for me. It looks lovely in the 2) .... (upstairs, front, big) bedroom. We've put up 3) .... (plain, linen, off-white) curtains and I found two 4) .... (woollen, old, beautiful, flower-patterned) carpets for the sitting room. We've made friends with our 5) .... (new, charming, next-door) neighbours. He is a 6) .... (well-known, fiction, popular) writer, and she is a garden designer. I'm hoping she'll help us with our 7) .... (old, overgrown, big) garden. There's a 8) .... (thirty-year old, beautiful, cherry) tree at the bottom of the garden and we're planning to build a 9) .... (stone, small, square) patio so we can sit outside in the summer. You must come over soon and enjoy a 10) .... (home-made, delicious) meal in our new home.

Best wishes,
Natalie

- **Adverbs normally describe verbs, adjectives, other adverbs or whole sentences**. *She dances* **well**. *(How does she dance? Well.)* **They say how** (adverbs of manner - *slowly*), **when** (adverbs of time - *yesterday*), **where** (adverbs of place - *next door*), **how often** (adverbs of frequency - *usually*) or **to what extent** (adverbs of degree - *absolutely*) **something happens. There are also sentence adverbs** *(possibly etc)* **and relative adverbs** *(where, why, when).*

Formation of Adverbs from Adjectives

Adverbs are formed from adjectives + -ly. *quick ➡ quickly, calm ➡ calmly*
- **adjectives ending in consonant + -y ➡ -ily**. *sleepy ➡ sleepily, weary ➡ wearily, weepy ➡ weepily*
- **adjectives ending in -ic add -ally**. *tragic ➡ tragically, frantic ➡ frantically*
- **adjectives ending in -le drop -le and add -ly**. *irritable ➡ irritably, reliable ➡ reliably*
- **adjectives ending in -e add -ly**. *false ➡ falsely, but: whole ➡ wholly, true ➡ truly*
- **adjectives ending in -ly** (**elderly, fatherly, friendly, lively, lonely, lovely, motherly, silly, ugly etc**) **form their adverb with in a(n) ... way/manner**. *in a motherly manner, in a lively way etc.*

Adjectives and Adverbs which have the same form

best, better, big, cheap*, clean*, clear*, close*, cold, daily, dead, dear*, deep, direct, dirty, early, easy, extra, far, fast, fine*, free, further, hard, high, hourly, inside, kindly, last, late, long, loud*, low, monthly, past, quick*, quiet*, right, slow, straight, sure, thin*, thick, tight, weekly, well, wide, wrong, yearly etc
*Ann was our **last** guest. She came in **last**.* **Those adverbs with an asterisk (*) can be found with -ly ending without a difference in meaning, but then they are more formal.** *Walk slow! (informal) ALSO Walk slowly! (formal)*

113 Identify the underlined words as adjectives or adverbs.

1 He felt uncomfortable because his jeans were too <u>tight</u>.   ....*adjective*.........
2 I buy Time Magazine <u>weekly</u> whereas he subscribes to it on a <u>yearly</u> basis.   ....
3 I couldn't get the book down from the top shelf because it was so <u>high</u>.   ....
4 If you want to find the post office, go <u>straight</u> down the high street and
   you'll see it on your left.   ....
5 Tom constantly arrives <u>late</u> for work.   ....
6 The <u>late</u> Prime Minister was a collector of antiques.   ....
7 The walls were so <u>thin</u> you could hear the next-door neighbours.   ....
8 He worked <u>hard</u> all day to finish painting the house.   ....

9 She bought this rug <u>cheap</u> from the market. ....
10 He kicked the ball <u>high</u> into the air. ....

Adverbs with two forms and differences in meaning

deep = a long way down
deeply = greatly
direct = by the shortest route
directly = immediately
easy = gently and slowly
easily = without difficulty
free = without cost
freely = willingly

full = exactly; very
fully = completely
hard = intently; with effort
hardly = scarcely
high = at / to a high level
highly = very much
last = after all others
lastly = finally

late = not early
lately = recently
near = close
nearly = almost
pretty = fairly
prettily = in a pretty way
short = suddenly
shortly = soon

sure = certainly
surely = without a doubt
wide = off-target
widely = to a large extent
wrong = incorrectly
wrongly = unjustly (wrongly goes before verbs/past part. - wrong/wrongly go after verbs)

114 *Underline the correct item.*

1 Lately / Late there has been a rise in the price of vegetables; they are not near / nearly as cheap as they used to be.
2 I can hard / hardly believe that he has gone. Surely / Sure he wouldn't have left without me!
3 It is wide / widely believed among scientists that we will short / shortly run out of natural resources.
4 He is very high / highly thought of at the office because he works so hardly / hard; that's why he full / fully deserves promotion.
5 You wrong / wrongly accused him of stealing the pen without hearing his explanation first - now he is deep / deeply offended.
6 He managed to get to Lisbon easily / easy by flying there direct / directly.
7 It is not wide / widely known that students can get medication free / freely.
8 She was prettily / pretty embarrassed when she realised that she had arrived lastly / last at the party.
9 He hard / hardly ever studies, yet he always produces a high / highly standard of work.
10 I fully / full understand your concern.

Quite - Fairly - Rather - Pretty

● **Quite** (fairly, to some degree) is used in **favourable comments**. *She's **quite** good at painting.* **Quite** meaning "completely" is used with adverbs, some verbs and adjectives such as: alone, amazing, brilliant, certain, dead, dreadful, different, exhausted, extraordinary, false, horrible, impossible, perfect, ridiculous, right, sure, true, useless etc. *I'm **quite** sure he stole the money.* **Quite** is used before **a/an**. *She's **quite** a good dancer. I **quite** enjoyed the film.*
Rather is used: a) in **unfavourable comments**. *He's **rather** mean with money.* b) in **favourable comments** meaning "to an unusual degree". *The lecture was **rather** informative. (It was more informative than we expected)* and c) with **comparative degree**. *It's **rather** sunnier today than yesterday.* **Rather** is used before or after **a/an**. *He's **a rather** rude person. He's **rather a** rude person.*
● **Fairly** and **pretty** are synonymous with **quite** and **rather**. **They can be used after a.** *He's **a fairly/pretty** well-behaved person.*

115 *Complete the sentences using quite, fairly, rather or pretty.*

1 It's ...*quite*... wet out today. You'd better wear your boots.
2 The party on Saturday was .... enjoyable. I'm glad I went.
3 The food in this restaurant is .... good although it's .... expensive.
4 His new film is .... interesting but it's .... a long one.
5 That exercise may be .... difficult but it will be .... good for your vocabulary.
6 Although his speech was .... short it was still .... boring.
7 We .... enjoyed our holiday in Finland though the weather was .... cold.
8 John is .... a short man but he's .... good looking.
9 She's a .... intelligent girl but she is .... difficult to get to know.
10 We wanted to walk but it was .... a long way to go on foot.

5 Adjectives / Adverbs / Comparisons

Word Order of Adverbs

- Adverbs can be used in front, mid or end position in a sentence. **Front position** is at the beginning of a sentence. **Mid position** is normally before the main verb or after the auxiliary. **End position** is at the end of a sentence.

Front	Mid		End
At university I	*often*	*saw her walking around*	*confidently.*

- Adverbs of manner can go in any position. When placed in front position, they give emphasis.
  He climbed up the stairs **quickly**. **Quickly** *he climbed up the stairs. (emphasis)*

- When there is more than one adverb in the sentence, their usual order is manner-place-time.

subject	verb	manner	place	time
She	*was studying*	*hard*	*in her room*	*all night.*

- When there is a verb of movement, then the order is place - manner - time.

subject	verb	place	manner	time
He	*goes*	*to school*	*on foot*	*every day.*

- Time adverbs go in end position. They also go in front position to emphasise the time.

subject + verb	place	manner	time	time	subject+ verb	place	manner
He goes	*to the park*	*on his bike*	*every day.*	*Every day*	*he goes*	*to the park*	*on his bike.*

- **Adverbs of frequency** (sometimes, always, usually, never, often, seldom, rarely etc) go after an auxiliary but before the main verb. *You* **are always** *late. He* **usually comes** *late.* They go before the auxiliary in short answers. *"Does he help you clean the house?" "Yes, he* **always does.***"*

- **Adverbs of degree** (hardly, almost, nearly etc) go before the words they modify. *She works* **quite** *hard.*

116 *Rewrite the sentences putting the adverbs in the right place.*

1 He eats his sandwiches. (at break time/always/quickly).
   ...*He always eats his sandwiches quickly at break time*....
2 Birds migrate. (to warmer countries/usually/in winter)
   ....
3 The plane crashed. (into the sea/suddenly/an hour ago)
   ....
4 Politicians prepare their speeches. (thoroughly/at home/generally/in advance)
   ....
5 The thief crept into the house. (silently/at midnight)
   ....
6 Newspapers are delivered. (only/weekly/in remote areas)
   ....
7 Hundreds of people are imprisoned. (in Britain/each year/wrongly)
   ....
8 People who sunbathe can get burnt. (badly/on the beach/frequently)
   ....
9 Hotplan's new washing machine has been designed to save you money. (cleverly/now/in the home)
   ....
10 Staff have been made aware of the consequences of a shrinking market. (rapidly/recently/fully)
   ....

117 *Rewrite the text putting the adverbs into the correct place.*

Hotel Miramar

Our hotel is located in the fashionable resort of Praia da Rocha in Portugal's Algarve region. (conveniently) The Hotel Miramar sits on top of the cliffs overlooking the beach below. (picturesquely) The service we offer is exceptional - the hotel staff work to make your visit memorable. (all day / hard) Each room is designed to enable you to rest and each has its own bathroom. (specially / comfortably) The rooms have been decorated to help you to relax and feel at home. (tastefully / completely) Sample the local dishes prepared in our hotel restaurant. (traditionally /every evening) We are proud of our chef who selects only the freshest fruit and vegetables and then prepares each dish for your pleasure. (expertly / particularly / daily) So don't delay! Reserve your rooms and spend your holiday with us. (this summer / at once)

...Our hotel is conveniently located in the fashionable resort...

Regular Comparative and Superlative Forms

Adjectives	Positive	Comparative	Superlative
of one syllable add **-(e)r/-(e)st** to form their comparative and superlative forms	short simple big	short**er** (than) simpl**er** (than) bigg**er** (than)	**the** short**est** (of/in) **the** simpl**est** (of/in) **the** bigg**est** (of/in)
of two syllables ending in **-ly, -y, -w** also add **-er/-est**	funny narrow	funn**ier** (than) narrow**er** (than)	**the** funn**iest** (of/in) **the** narrow**est** (of/in)
of two or more syllables take **more/most**	modern intelligent	**more** modern (than) **more** intelligent (than)	**the most** modern (of/in) **the most** intelligent (of/in)

- We normally use **than** with the **comparative** form. *Tim is **shorter than** Tony.* We normally use **the...of/in** ("in" refers to places, groups etc) with the **superlative** form. *She's **the smartest of** all.*
- Certain adjectives form their comparative and superlative either with **-er/-est** or **more/most**. These are: **clever, common, cruel, friendly, gentle, narrow, pleasant, polite, shallow, simple, stupid, quiet.** *quiet - quieter - quietest ALSO quiet - more quiet - most quiet*

118 *Put the adjectives in brackets into the correct form.*

Israel

Come and visit one of **1)** ...*the most interesting*... (interesting) countries in the world - Israel, where the people are **2)** .... (hospitable) than anywhere else. You will see some of **3)** .... (old) biblical sites in the world, as well as **4)** .... (modern) cities with **5)** .... (good) restaurants in the Middle East. To make travel arrangements **6)** .... (easy), our tour includes guided visits to some of **7)** .... (holy) and **8)** .... (important) sites for a number of different religions. You will also get the opportunity to float in the Dead Sea - **9)** .... (low) point on earth. The climate is **10)** ....(pleasant) than anything you will have experienced before. Even in **11)** .... (hot) of summers you will find places to cool off. Our company offers tailor-made tours for **12)** .... (small) groups than is usual on a package holiday. We provide accommodation in intimate hotels which offer **13)** .... (friendly) service than the larger, **14)** .... (impersonal) ones. Even **15)** .... (frequent) traveller will experience something new in this unique country. Book today!

5 Adjectives / Adverbs / Comparisons

Adverbs	Positive	Comparative	Superlative
adverbs having the same forms as their adjectives add -er/-est	fast	faster	the fastest
early drops **-y** and adds **-ier/-iest**	early	earlier	the earliest
two syllable or compound adverbs take **more/most** (Compound adverbs are adjectives + **-ly**. *thoughtful - thoughtfully*)	often patiently	**more** often **more** patiently	**the most** often **the most** patiently

Irregular Forms

Positive	Comparative	Superlative
good / well	better	best
bad / badly	worse	worst
much	more	most
many / a lot of	more	most
little	less	least
far	farther	farthest
far	further	furthest

Well is the adverb of good. *She is a good dancer. She dances **well**.*

a) **further/farther (adv) = longer (in distance)**
*His house is **further/farther** away than John's.*
further (adj) = more
*I need no **further** help from you.*

b) **very + positive degree** *I'm **very** happy in my job.*

c) **even/much/far/a bit + comparative degree**
*The weather's **even** less bearable today: it's **much** worse than last year.*

d) **most + adj/adv of positive degree = very**
*He was **most** helpful and answered all my questions.*

e) **any + comparative** (used in negatives and questions)
*Can you write **any** quicker, please?*

---

119 *Fill in the relevant adverbs in their comparative or superlative forms.*

Bicycles look set to become **1)** ...*the most commonly*... (common) used form of transport in Britain. Not only are bicycles better for the environment than cars, but they allow you to travel **2)** .... (convenient). You can get from point A to point B **3)** .... (quick) than by car and you can find somewhere to leave your bike much **4)** .... (easy). Many younger people now ride a bike to work because they find it **5)** .... (good) suits their lifestyle and enables them to get around **6)** .... (practical). In addition, they often arrive **7)** .... (early) than their colleagues who drive to work and who have to wait **8)** .... (long) in traffic jams than they do.

120 *Underline the correct word.*

1 She drove <u>very</u> / even quickly along the lane.
2 "We will give you further / farther news as we receive it," the newsreader said.
3 Her parents were more / most pleased when she won the prize.
4 Can't he speak any / much louder than that? No one can hear him.
5 She plays very / much more noisily than any child I've ever met.

121 *Put the adjectives in their comparative or superlative forms.*

If you want to own **1)** ...*the fastest*... (fast), **2)** .... (powerful) car on the road, you can't go wrong with a Tornado. You will not only have **3)** .... (comfortable) ride you've ever experienced, you'll also be **4)** .... (safe) than in any other car on the market. No other manufacturer is **5)** .... (careful) than we are to ensure that its safety features are of **6)** .... (high) possible standard. So if you want to be **7)** .... (proud) car owner in your neighbourhood, come and test drive the Tornado today!

Type of Comparisons

● as ... (positive degree) ... as not so/as ... (positive degree) ... as such a(n)/so ...as	*For hair **as soft as** silk try this new shampoo.* *The service isn't **as good as** it used to be.* *It's **not such a** long way **as** we thought.*
● twice/three times etc/half as ... (positive degree) ... as	*She earns **twice as much as** me.* *She's only **half as well-qualified as** her sister.*
● the same as	*The Orion costs **the same as** the Golf.*
● look, sound, smell, taste + like	*That **sounds like** a good idea.*
● less ... (positive degree) ... than the least ... (positive degree) ... of/in	*I have **less free** time **than** Cathy but Laura has **the least free** time **of** all.*
● the + comparative ..., the + comparative	***The busier** the roads are, **the longer** it will take to get there. **The less** you sleep, **the more** tired you get.*
● comparative + and + comparative	*Jobs are getting **harder and harder** to find.*
● prefer + -ing form or noun + to + -ing form or noun (general preference)	*She **prefers living** for the moment **to thinking** about the future. Most people **prefer summer to winter**.*
● would prefer + to-inf + rather than + inf without to (specific preference)	*I **would prefer to book** our tickets now **rather than wait** until the last minute.*
● would rather/sooner + inf without to + than + inf without to	*He'**d sooner go** alone **than go** with Edward.*
● clause + whereas/while + clause (comparison by contrast)	*Carole enjoys adventure **while/whereas** her sister prefers peace and quiet.*

122 *Complete the sentences using the words in bold. Use two to five words.*

1 Wouldn't you prefer to get a takeaway rather than have to cook tonight?
   sooner   Wouldn't you ...*sooner get a takeaway than*... have to cook tonight?
2 If we stay longer, we can spend more time sightseeing.
   the   The .... time we can spend sightseeing.
3 I'd rather go home than go to the cinema.
   than   I'd prefer .... go to the cinema.
4 In some countries men and women are paid the same.
   as   In some countries women .... men.
5 Crisps are not as nutritious as nuts.
   less   Crisps.. nuts.
6 No other job is as well-paid.
   best   It .... job.
7 John and I have received the same number of job offers.
   many   I have received .... John.
8 Last night I felt more tired than ever.
   as   I have .... I did last night.
9 Tony finds history easier than geography.
   not   Geography .... history for Tony.
10 As he gets older, he becomes less tolerant.
   the   The .... tolerant he becomes.

11 I love going to football matches but my sister prefers going to tennis tournaments.
    whereas   I love going to football matches .... to tennis tournaments.

12 Helen had twice as much work as Janet.
    half   Janet had .... Helen.

13 I like being self-employed. It's better than working for someone else.
    to   I prefer ....for someone else.

14 My grandfather is getting less and less patient as he gets older.
    impatient   My grandfather is getting .... as he gets older.

15 Laura is a less sensitive girl than her sister.
    such   Laura isn't .... her sister.

16 Airships are not as dangerous as they used to be.
    than   Airships .... they used to be.

17 My father is spending less time at the office now he's nearing retirement.
    as   My father is .... at the office now that he's nearing retirement.

18 Martha and Julie have the same views.
    as   Martha's views .... Julie's.

19 I think I would prefer to leave rather than wait until he comes.
    sooner   I think I .... until he comes.

20 If we climb higher, the view will be better.
    the   The .... the view will be.

Like is used	As is used
● **for similarities.** *He works **like** a mule. (He isn't a mule.)*	● **to say what sb or sth really is (jobs or roles)** *He works **as** a dentist. (He's a dentist.)*
● **after feel, look, smell, sound + noun.** *She looks **like** her mother.* *It smells **like** burnt toast.*	● **in certain expressions: as usual, as...as, as much, such as, the same as.** *She was late **as usual**.*
● **with nouns, pronouns or the -ing form to express similarity.** *Frogs' legs are supposed to taste just **like chicken**.* *Is that your Mum? You look **like her**.* *It's **like walking** on air.*	● **after: accept, be known, class, describe, refer to, regard, use.** *He's **regarded as** an expert on computers.*
	● **in clauses of manner to mean "in the way that".** *We must write the essay **as** they have shown us.*

123 *Fill in as or like.*

1   ...**As**... you mentioned, they are .... two peas in a pod. Jack looks exactly .... his twin brother Jim. They even have the same personality .... each other.

2   Ugh! This soup tastes just .... water. Didn't you make it .... I told you?

3   He treats his friends .... dirt. I detest people behaving .... that. He should treat people .... he'd like to be treated himself.

4   .... he didn't know what his relations looked ...., they sent him a photo so he would recognize them at the airport.

5   I have been working .... a tour guide for two years now, but I don't really regard it .... a serious career. It's time to do something different. I might even go back to college .... my sister has done.

6   .... usual it looks .... if it's going to rain. It's no wonder Lancashire is described .... the wettest county in Britain.

7   He drinks .... a fish and smokes .... a chimney and, ... we all keep telling him, he won't live long.

8   .... much .... I admire his work, I don't think he deserves to be known .... the greatest novelist of the century.

▶ In Other Words

- Jane is more beautiful than Mary.
  Mary isn't as beautiful as Jane (is).
  Mary is less beautiful than Jane.
- Can't you buy a cheaper coat than that?
  Is that the cheapest coat you can buy?
- Joe's got the same number of suits as Ted.
  Ted has got as many suits as Joe.
- He's the fastest driver of all.
  No one else drives as fast as he does.
  He's faster than any other driver.
  He is a faster driver than anyone else.
  He drives faster than anyone else.

- I've never seen such a tall man.
  He's the tallest man I've ever seen.
- He's a good tennis player.
  He plays tennis well.
- As he gets older, he becomes more sensible.
  The older he gets, the more sensible he becomes.
- That dress is similar to this one.
  That dress and this one are alike.
- Tom is very fatherly to his children.
  Tom behaves in a fatherly way to his children.

124 Complete the sentences using the words in bold. Use two to five words.

1 Unfortunately we couldn't find a better solution in the time available.
   best   Unfortunately it ...*was the best solution*... we could find in the time available.
2 Spanish and Portuguese are said to be alike.
   similar   Spanish is .... Portuguese.
3 I've never eaten such a hot curry.
   the   It's .... I've ever eaten.
4 She is extremely disrespectful to her colleagues.
   way   She behaves .... to her colleagues.
5 Sheila is not as talented as her sister.
   less   Sheila is .... her sister.
6 She was the best prepared of all the candidates.
   than   She was .... all the candidates.
7 As prices increase, the cost of living becomes higher.
   the   The .... the cost of living becomes.
8 She writes very creatively.
   creative She .... writer.
9 George made the same number of mistakes as Peter.
   as   George made .... Peter.
10 It's more expensive to live in London than in Liverpool.
   not   It's .... to live in Liverpool as in London.
11 MacMahon is the most skilful player in the team.
   as   No one else in the team .... MacMahon.
12 The seller wouldn't accept a lower offer.
   lowest   It was .... the seller would accept.
13 She's the most eccentric person I've ever met.
   never   I've .... eccentric person.
14 As she gets richer, she becomes more extravagant.
   the   The .... extravagant she becomes.
15 We've never had such a heated argument before.
   most   It .... we've ever had.
16 The boss is very friendly to her staff.
   way   The boss behaves .... to her staff.
17 She received the same number of gifts as her cousin on her birthday.
   many   She received .... her cousin on her birthday.
18 He speaks German fluently, because he was born in Germany.
   a   He ...., because he was born in Germany.

5 Adjectives / Adverbs / Comparisons

125 *Find the word which should not be in the sentence.*

1 She is more prettier than her sister.
2 This film is as more exciting than the one we saw last week.
3 This is the more best meal I've had in a long time.
4 As time went by he became so more and more restless.
5 The more earlier we leave, the sooner we'll get there.
6 We hardly not go anywhere these days.
7 This coat is very cheaper than the one Sue bought.
8 Sarah is the more polite than her sister.
9 This necklace is twice as more expensive as that one.
10 I'd rather do my homework tonight than to leave it for tomorrow.
11 It sounds as like a fire engine to me.
12 Very most people seem to be in favour of the decision.
13 No one else I know is as selfish as like Julia.
14 He is regarded as like the best film director of the decade.
15 No other secretary is as much efficient as she is.
16 You should treat people just so as you would like to be treated.
17 She invested the most of her money in shares.
18 This periodical has much interesting articles about wildlife conservation.
19 This play is similar as to his last one.
20 She'd sooner than forget about it.

1	*more*
2	
3	
4	
5	
6	
7	
8	
9	
10	
11	
12	
13	
14	
15	
16	
17	
18	
19	
20	

Oral Development 8

Look at the pictures below then talk about the professions using comparative and superlative forms. Use the adjectives given as well as your own ideas.
dirty, well-paid, exciting, interesting, boring, creative, challenging, stressful, dangerous, safe, hard, varied, repetitive, skilled, unskilled

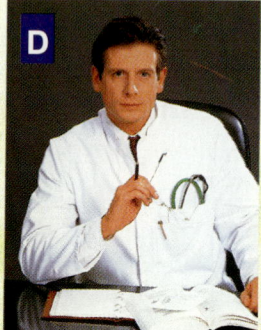

A firefighter's job is the most dangerous of all.

Consolidation 5

▶ *Phrasal Verbs*

get about: move around; spread
get sth across: make sth understood
get away (from): 1) escape, 2) leave
get along (with): have a friendly relationship
get at: 1) reach, 2) imply, suggest
get away with sth: avoid being punished for sth
get sb down: depress
get off: 1) to avoid punishment, 2) to descend from a bus etc
get on: 1) enter a bus etc, 2) manage
get on with: continue, often after interruption
get over: 1) return to usual state of health, happiness etc after sth bad, 2) overcome
get (a)round: coax; persuade sb by kindness
get through: 1) finish work, 2) reach sb by phone

• • • • • • • • • • • • •

give away: 1) give sth for free, 2) reveal
give off: emit
give back: return
give in: 1) surrender, 2) hand in
give out: distribute
give up: 1) stop (a habit etc), 2) surrender

126 *Fill in the correct particle(s).*

1   I can't get ...*through*... to Joan. I think there's a fault on the line.
2   He's a good speaker and gets his views .... very well.
3   It took Ted a long time to get .... the breakup of his marriage.
4   The young boys got .... with a caution because it was their first offence.
5   You must give .... smoking. It's ruining your health.
6   Please give .... your homework by next Friday.
7   The record shop has a promotion and is giving .... free CDs.
8   The milk is giving .... a horrible smell.
9   I want to get .... the city for a few days.
10 I'm afraid my father and I don't get ...... at all.
11 All this bad news really gets me ....
12 How are you getting .... without a cooker?
13 Stop talking and get .... your work.
14 You have to get .... your revision tonight.
15 She gave .... my secret so I'm terribly hurt.
16 He stopped resisting and gave himself .... to the police.

127 *Look at Appendix 1, then fill in the correct preposition.*

1   I don't know the result ...*of*... my exams yet.
2   He made a lot of mistakes resulting .... his inexperience.
3   Her arrogance resulted .... her losing all her friends.
4   I am obliged .... you .... all your invaluable assistance.
5   Was he really involved .... the incident?
6   You can lean .... me.
7   The ladder was leaning .... the wall.
8   The guest apologised .... the hostess .... staining the sofa with wine.
9   Some people are deliberately cruel .... stray animals.
10 There are big differences ...... the two cultures.
11 Claire is familiar .... the procedure.
12 That man seems familiar .... me; I must have seen him before.
13 You cannot deny there is a relationship .... crime and poverty.
14 She has a good relationship .... her children.
15 I find it hard to sympathise .... Denise.
16 She's not very sympathetic .... the poor.
17 James was suspected .... starting the riot.
18 Poor Jill suffers .... hay fever.
19 She spends a lot of money .... cosmetics.
20 I'm sorry .... forgetting our anniversary.
21 She's very sorry .... the state of the house.
22 The manager was not satisfied .... his staff.
23 That's the same car .... mine.
24 What are you so excited ....?
25 South Africa is a country rich .... gold.
26 Kindly refrain .... throwing litter in the park.
27 I am writing .... reference to your letter.
28 Don't refer .... his recent dismissal.
29 It's no use trying to reason .... her.
30 There was no reason .... him to shout like that.
31 He spends a lot of time .... updating his stamp collection.

128 *Complete the sentences using the words in bold. Use two to five words.*

1   Richard isn't too young to ride a motorbike.
    old   Richard ...*is old enough to ride*... a motorbike.

2 In general, women are shorter than men.
   as   In general, men .... women.
3 I can't wait to go on holiday.
   forward   I'm really .... on holiday.
4 Prices may go up next year, so you should buy now.
   case   You should buy now .... next year.
5 Mark does not run as fast as he did.
   used   Mark .... he does now.
6 They sunbathed all day long when they were on holiday.
   spent   They .... when they were on holiday.
7 Helen hasn't tried Japanese food before.
   time   It's the .... Japanese food.
8 She'd rather watch tennis than football.
   prefers   She .... football.
9 The police managed to catch the bank robbers after a three-day chase.
   catching   The police .... the bank robbers after a three-day chase.
10 Can't he do any better than this?
   the   Is .... he can do?
11 I don't know all the facts.
   aware   I .... all the facts.
12 Whose fault was the fire at the factory?
   blame   Who .... the fire at the factory?
13 He came here three months ago.
   been   He .... three months.
14 They decided to cancel the wedding.
   off   They .... the wedding.
15 He crossed the street because he didn't want to speak to her.
   speaking   He crossed the street .... to her.
16 His father doesn't want him to drink spirits.
   disapproves His father .... spirits.

129 *For questions 1 - 15, read the text below and think of the word which best fits each space.*
Use only one word in each space. Write your answers in the answer boxes provided.

Choose your Sport Carefully

Regular exercise such **(0)** ...*as*... jogging or swimming is good **(1)** .... the heart. It can also give you more energy to enjoy life. As a **(2)** .... of regular exercise, your body gets better **(3)** .... using oxygen. It becomes easier for your heart to pump blood **(4)** .... your body. After a while, the heart doesn't **(5)** .... to work quite as hard. Exercise is often thought to be an easy **(6)** .... of losing weight. But in **(7)** .... , exercise tends to increase your appetite. Many people discover they lose **(8)** .... weight with exercise alone. **(9)** .... diet and exercise are needed to achieve this. Some people exercise because they think it will help them to live longer. If that is your reason for exercising, then you **(10)** .... avoid short, intensive exercise. Squash, for example, **(11)** .... is a fast game, may be harmful **(12)** .... you're unfit or middle-aged. Other sports can be dangerous **(13)** .... Although both rugby and football are popular sports, a rugby player is three **(14)** .... more likely to be injured than a tennis player. It is advisable, **(15)** .... , to choose a sport that suits you and not one that is going to harm you.

130 Use the words in capitals to form a word that fits in the space in the same line.

Forests

One third of **(0)** .... Europe is covered by trees.
This sounds **(1)** .... , but most of these trees were planted
recently and are no **(2)** .... for the ancient natural
forests. Europe's ancient woods are **(3)** .... habitats for
a large number of **(4)** .... species. Fast-growing
modern forests, however, are dark and **(5)** .... to birds
and animals. The Worldwide Fund for Nature recently
held a seminar to increase **(6)** .... for a new campaign
called "Forests for Life". The **(7)** .... wants to introduce
bans on trade in **(8)** .... made from wood from these
forests. By the year 2000 they hope to have built
up a network to provide **(9)** .... for
(10) .... areas and help restore damaged forests.

WEST	0	*western* ▭ 0 ▬
IMPRESS	1	▭ 1 ▭
REPLACE	2	▭ 2 ▭
SUIT	3	▭ 3 ▭
ENDANGER	4	▭ 4 ▭
INVITING	5	▭ 5 ▭
PUBLIC	6	▭ 6 ▭
ORGANISE	7	▭ 7 ▭
PRODUCE	8	▭ 8 ▭
PROTECT	9	▭ 9 ▭
EXIST	10	▭ 10 ▭

131 Read the text carefully. Some of the lines are correct and some have a word which should not be there. If a line is correct, put a tick (✔) in the space provided. If a line has a word which should not be there, write it in the space provided.

Exam worries

0 There's a teaching exam I want to take next	0	✔ ▭ 0 ▬
00 year but I'm very cautious about applying it.	00	*it* ▭ 00 ▬
1 In the first place, the pass rate isn't high up;	1	▭ 1 ▭
2 in fact only a fifty percent of candidates actually	2	▭ 2 ▭
3 pass. Secondly, it's very expensive to do the	3	▭ 3 ▭
4 course and exam. It costs at £1,500 and	4	▭ 4 ▭
5 you need to take three months off the work.	5	▭ 5 ▭
6 Thirdly, it's quite so stressful. Before you can	6	▭ 6 ▭
7 sit the final practical and written exams you	7	▭ 7 ▭
8 must have been written ten compositions and	8	▭ 8 ▭
9 have had ten lessons observed which are	9	▭ 9 ▭
10 being considered to have been of a high enough	10	▭ 10 ▭
11 of standard. In addition to all these points,	11	▭ 11 ▭
12 I want to make certain I have enough of the	12	▭ 12 ▭
13 right kind of teaching experience to pass through	13	▭ 13 ▭
14 before I attempt the exam. It's lots of much	14	▭ 14 ▭
15 money to waste if you're not all sure of passing.	15	▭ 15 ▭

6 Passive Voice / Causative Form

Passive Voice

The **passive** is formed with the appropriate tense of the verb **to be + past participle**. Present Perfect Continuous, Future Continuous, Past Perfect Continuous are not normally used in the passive. Note that only transitive verbs (verbs which take an object) can be put into the passive.

	Active Voice	Passive Voice
Present Simple	They **restore** buildings.	Buildings **are restored**.
Present Continuous	They **are restoring** the building.	The building **is being restored**.
Past Simple	They **restored** the building.	The building **was restored**.
Past Continuous	They **were restoring** the building.	The building **was being restored**.
Future Simple	They **will restore** the building.	The building **will be restored**.
Present Perfect	They **have restored** the building.	The building **has been restored**.
Past Perfect	They **had restored** the building.	The building **had been restored**.
Future Perfect	They **will have restored** the building.	The building **will have been restored**.
Present infinitive	They should **restore** the building.	The building should **be restored**.
Perfect infinitive	They should **have restored** the building.	The building should **have been restored**.
-ing form	They like people **restoring** buildings.	They like buildings **being restored**.
Perfect -ing form	**Having restored** the building, ...	The building, **having been restored**, ...
Modal + be + p.p.	They **must restore** the building.	The building **must be restored**.

Note: **Get** is used in colloquial English instead of **be** to express something happening by accident. *He'll **get hurt** if he plays like that.*

The passive is used

- when the person performing the action (**agent**) is **unknown, unimportant** or **obvious from the context**. *The rooms **have been searched** thoroughly. (by the police - obvious agent)*
- to **emphasise** the agent. *The maths lesson was taken **by the English teacher** yesterday.*
- when we are interested more in the action than the agent, such as in **news reports, formal notices, instructions, processes, headlines, advertisements** etc. *"Crocodiles **have been set** free ..."*
- to make **statements** more **formal** or **polite**. *The vase **has been broken**. (more polite than saying "You have broken the vase.")*

132 Write sentences in the passive as in the example:

1 (Her hair/dye/at the moment) ...Her hair is being dyed at the moment....
2 (The Queen/not drive/to the embassy/yet) ....
3 (The Hay Wain/paint/Constable) ....
4 (Most olives/grow/the Mediterranean) ....
5 (The convict/take/to prison/now) ....
6 (His wound/not treat/yet) ....
7 (My car/break into/last night) ....
8 (The trees/prune/a tree surgeon/last week) ....
9 (Reservations/can/make/by dialling 001 now) ....
10 (Our house/clean/weekly) ....
11 (He/bring up/his grandparents) ....
12 (The book/not write/yet) ....
13 (The building/demolish/by next year) ....
14 (The new school/open/next week/the mayor) ....
15 (Sally's shoes/re-heel/last Saturday) ....
16 (The dustbins/empty/recently) ....

6 Passive Voice / Causative Form

133 *Put the verbs in brackets into the correct passive form.*

1 Polar bears ...*are hunted* ... (hunt) for their fur.
2 A lecture .... (give) in the main hall at the moment.
3 After ... (award) a medal for bravery, he became a local hero.
4 Her ankle .... (hurt) when she fell down.
5 She thinks her car .... (steal) by someone she knows.
6 The apartment .... (sell) last week.
7 I hate .... (lie to) by my friends.
8 Nurses really ought .... (pay) more than they are.
9 The music must .... (turn down) by 12 o'clock at the latest.
10 Your free gift .... (send) to you in the next few days.
11 I wish I .... (teach) how to use a computer when
I was at school.
12 Human bones .... (find) by archaeologists yesterday.
13 My car .... (repair) at the moment, so I can't give you a lift.
14 New York .... (say) to be one of the most dangerous cities in the world.
15 Hopefully, all forms of discrimination .... (wipe out) by the end of this century.

Changing from Active into Passive

- **The object of the active verb becomes the subject in the passive sentence. The active verb changes into a passive form and the subject of the active verb becomes the agent which is either introduced with "by" or is omitted.**

	Subject	Verb	Object	Agent
Active	*Kate*	*wrote*	*the story.*	
Passive	*The story*	*was written*		*by Kate.*

- **By + agent is omitted when the agent is unknown, unimportant, obvious from the context or words such as: someone, people, I, etc.** *They will give more information soon.* ➡ *More information will be given soon. ("by them" is omitted)*
- **By + agent is used to say who or what did the action.** *She was knocked down by a lorry.* **With + instrument or material is used to say what the agent used.** *The policeman was stabbed with a knife.*
- **Verbs followed by a preposition** (*look after, accuse of etc*) **take the preposition immediately after them when turned into the passive.** *She looks after her daughter well.* ➡ *Her daughter is looked after well.*
- **For verbs which take two objects, it is more usual to begin the sentence with the person.** *They gave her all the details.* ➡ *She was given all the details. (more usual than: All the details were given to her.)*
- **In passive questions with who, whom or which we do not omit by.** *Who offered her the job?* ➡ *Who was she offered the job by?*
- **Make, hear, help, see are followed by a to-infinitive in the passive.** *They saw him cross the street.* ➡ *He was seen to cross the street.* **Note that hear, see, watch can be followed by a present participle in the active and passive.** *We heard him playing the guitar.* ➡ *He was heard playing the guitar.*

134 *Change the sentences from the active into the passive. Omit the agent where it can be omitted.*

1 The British eat over thirty million hamburgers each year.
...*Over thirty million hamburgers are eaten by the British each year*....
2 Who wrote "One Hundred Years of Solitude?" ....
3 The bad weather has spoiled my holiday plans. ....
4 Do they always pay their workers on time? ....
5 The children picked the strawberries. ....
6 She saw them go out. ....
7 You should wash those walls before you paint them. ....

8 Penguin have translated all her books into English. ....

9 He objects to people telling him what to do. ....

10 Tesco are converting the old bank into a supermarket. ....

11 They told him not to say anything to her. ....

12 Did they give you a reward for finding their cat? ....

13 The nurses take very good care of the patients. ....

14 Everyone heard her shouting at the students. ....

15 Why have they given him a promotion? ....

16 I love people giving me presents. ....

17 When we got to the theatre, they had sold all the tickets. ....

18 The police have just arrested the man who broke into our house. ....

19 What did he tell you to do? ....

20 Oxfam will hold a fashion show next week. ....

21 They are holding the next World Cup in France. ....

22 When did they demolish that building? ....

23 The officers took the suspect in for questioning. ....

24 Will they hand out free T-shirts at the concert? ....

25 Does the school provide accommodation for all new teachers? ....

135 Change the sentences from the passive into the active.

1 Why was James asked to leave the club? ...*Why did they ask James to leave the club?*...

2 They love being invited to parties. ....

3 The best cream cakes are made by Sayers. ....

4 By the end of the party all the food had been eaten. ....

5 Sanchez was beaten by Graff in the Women's Tennis Final. ....

6 My glasses must have been thrown away by mistake. ....

7 The building is being examined by Health and Safety experts this week.

....

8 Who was the television invented by? ....

9 She was heard complaining about the new timetable. ....

10 She was sent a telegram by the Queen on her 100th birthday. ....

11 The English language is now spoken by over two billion people worldwide. ....

12 My overdraft is being extended by the bank tomorrow. ....

13 Hundreds of free gifts are being given away by Donels this Saturday. ....

14 Why haven't the beds been made yet? ....

15 I hate being taken for granted. ....

16 The tickets should have been booked weeks ago. ....

17 A new shopping centre is being built on the outskirts of town. ....

18 Why was I not told about the meeting? ....

19 Further information can be obtained from your local post office. ....

20 When will you be interviewed for the post? ....

21 Who was Gilbert interviewed by? ....

22 She hasn't been christened yet. ....

23 A new shampoo is being developed in the lab. ....

24 The awards will be presented by Tom Hanks. ....

25 Rainforests are being cut down in the Amazon. ....

136 Fill in "by" or "with".

1 This suit was designed ...*by*... Armani.

2 This cake is filled .... fresh cream.

3 Who was Australia discovered ....?

4 Ford cars are made .... experts.

5 The baby was covered .... a blanket.

6 "Carmen" was composed .... Bizet.

7 The coat was lined .... fur.

8 The food will be provided .... caterers.

9 The stew was flavoured .... garlic.

10 The Royal Wedding was watched .... millions.

137 *Change into the passive.*

Last month Samuel Block opened a restaurant in the centre of Macclesfield. He had planned it for over five years but he only completed it after local businessmen raised a large sum of money. A top hotelier has trained the waiters and they will wear specially designed uniforms to fit in with the restaurant's modern look. They have brought in a famous chef from France and they are going to give him complete control over the daily menu.

> The verbs **believe, expect, feel, hope, know, report, say, think** etc are used in the following passive patterns in personal and impersonal constructions.
>
> ● **subject (person) + passive verb + to -inf**
>   **(personal construction)**
>
> *Doctors expect he will recover soon.*
> **He is expected to** *recover soon.*
>
> ● **It + passive verb + that-clause**
>   **(impersonal construction)**
>
> **It is expected that** *he will recover soon.*

138 *Turn the following into the passive as in the example:*

1 They say he is a millionaire.
  He ...*is said to be a millionaire*....
  It ...*is said that he is a millionaire*....
2 They expect the plane will be landing soon.
  The plane ....
  It ....
3 They believe he was working illegally.
  He ....
  It ....
4 They say he is feeling better.
  He ....
  It ....
5 They thought he had been brave to do so.
  He ....
  It ....

6 They think he has escaped from prison.
  He ....
  It ....
7 They expect he'll pass his exams.
  He ....
  It ....
8 They say she lied to the police.
  She ....
  It ....
9 They say they miss too many lessons.
  They ....
  It ....
10 They know she was always late for work.
  She ....
  It ....

139 *Complete the sentences using the words in bold. Use two to five words.*

1 The teacher scolded Jim for not paying attention.
  was Jim ...*was scolded by the teacher*... for not paying attention.
2 Her parents named her after her grandmother.
  was She .... her grandmother.
3 Most people think that broken homes cause a lot of social problems.
  thought It .... cause a lot of social problems.
4 An editor will check the article.
  be The article .... an editor.
5 The traffic warden will give you a ticket if you park there.
  be You .... if you park there.
6 A lot of men enjoy football.
  is Football .... a lot of men.
7 The builder will have finished the extension by July.
  been The .... by July.
8 The teacher has given the students their homework.
  have The .... their homework.

6 Passive Voice / Causative Form

9 They are blaming Martin for the accident.
is Martin .... for the accident.

10 They are going to preview the film tomorrow evening.
is The film .... tomorrow evening.

11 They will have settled the matter by this afternoon.
been The matter .... by this afternoon.

140 Look at the notes, then write a report using the passive.

Yet again we experienced an earthquake last night.

A remote area in northern Spain/shake/by an earthquake last night. Several villages/totally destroy/and many people/leave/homeless. The total extent of the damage/still not known/but luckily few casualties/ report as people/warn/of the danger earlier and many villages/evacuate. Victims of the earthquake now/ offer/shelter in local churches/where food and drink/provide.

141 Rewrite the following text in the passive.

After 20 years of civil war, the Lebanese government is rebuilding Beirut. They will construct new offices and hotels. The authorities must also expand Beirut airport. Luckily, bombing did not destroy archaeological sites. By the year 2000, building companies will have completed most of the work. Lebanon's new look will attract many tourists in the future. A few groups have already visited this Middle Eastern paradise.

142 Rewrite the following text in the passive.

The critics have greeted with enthusiasm "Turning Point", Marvin Morton's new play. They regard it as his most mature work. Morton wrote it after he had studied people's behaviour for a considerable time. On the opening night the audience called Morton onto the stage and applauded him loudly. They are staging the play at the Apollo Theatre where they expect thousands of people to see it. Film companies have asked Morton to write a script for a film based on the play. We do not know yet whether Morton will seriously consider the proposal.

Oral Development 9

Look at the picture and the prompts and make sentences using the passive. You can also use your own ideas.

Cues: sea/pollute - waste/dump / for years - companies/fine/last year - action/take - new laws/ introduced/soon - protest marches/organised/recently - people/ask not swim/at present - fishermen/advise/ fish elsewhere - hope/problem solve/two years - volunteers/ask/help/clean up

eg. **The sea has been polluted. etc**

Causative Form

● We use **have + object + past participle** to say that we arrange for someone to do something for us. *He asked the mechanic to repair his car. He* **had his car repaired.** *(He didn't do it himself - the mechanic did it.)*

Present Simple	She **looks after** her children.	She **has** her children looked after.
Present Cont.	She **is looking after** her children.	She **is having** her children looked after.
Past Simple	She **looked after** her children.	She **had** her children looked after.
Past Continuous	She **was looking after** her children.	She **was having** her children looked after.
Future Simple	She **will look after** her children.	She **will have** her children looked after.
Future Cont.	She **will be looking after** her children.	She **will be having** her children looked after.
Present Perfect	She **has looked after** her children.	She **has had** her children looked after.
Present Perf. Cont.	She **has been looking after** her children.	She **has been having** her children looked after.
Past Perfect	She **had looked after** her children.	She **had had** her children looked after.
Past Perfect Cont.	She **had been looking after** her children.	She **had been having** her children looked after.
Infinitive	She can **look after** her children.	She can **have** her children looked after.
-ing form	She likes **looking after** her children.	She likes **having** her children looked after.

● The verb **to have,** when used in the causative, forms its **negations** and **questions** with **do/does** (Present S.) and **did** (Past S.). *She **doesn't have** the flowers arranged. **Did** you **have** the clothes ironed?*

● **Get** can be used instead of **have** in the causative. *Did you **have/get** your hair cut?*

● The **causative** can be used instead of the passive to express **accidents** or **misfortunes**. *He **had** his cheek bruised in a fight. (= His cheek was bruised in a fight.)*

143 *Read the situations, then write sentences using the causative form.*

1 The optician is testing her eyes. What is she doing?
   ...*She's having her eyes tested*....
2 If he doesn't drive more carefully, the police will take away his licence. What will happen to him? ....
3 This time tomorrow an artist will be painting her son's portrait. What will she be doing? ....
4 Someone is cutting down the tree in our garden at the moment. What are we doing? ....
5 They can vaccinate your children against smallpox. What can you do? ....
6 She will hire someone to build a shed for her. What will she do?
   ....
7 The dentist is polishing Tom's teeth. What is Tom doing?
   ....
8 The police are towing away his car. What is happening to him?
   ....
9 Someone dry-cleans his suits every month. What does he do?
   ....
10 He has been paying a therapist to massage his back. What has he been doing? ....
11 Sally gets a hairdresser to dye her hair every month. What does she do?
   ....

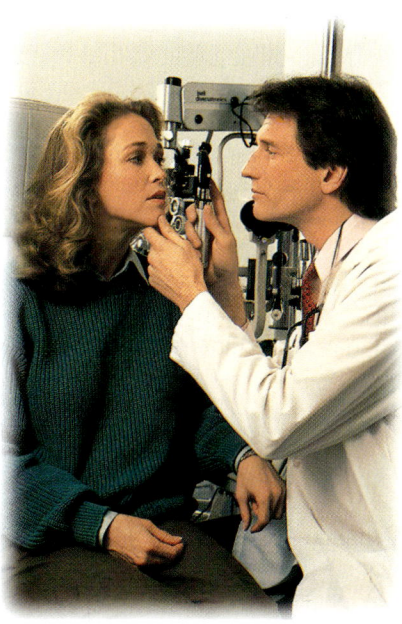

6 Passive Voice / Causative Form

144 Write sentences in the causative form as in the example:

1 Do you ask someone to type your essays? ...*Do you have your essays typed?*....
2 Her photographs haven't been developed yet. ....
3 She doesn't like asking people to do her shopping. ....
4 Have you asked them to install a burglar alarm for you? ....
5 I didn't use to employ someone to do the housework for me. ....
6 The doctor examined her wound. ....
7 He isn't going to take his glasses to be adjusted today. ....
8 Did the detective order the constable to follow the suspect? ....
9 You should ask someone to collect your mail while you are away. ....
10 Did the doctor set Gary's broken leg? ....
11 Will she get someone to check her washing machine for her? ....
12 We're going to ask them to send us a copy of the contract. ....
13 Has the chauffeur been driving Mary's kids to school for years? ....
14 Was his arm broken in a car crash? ....
15 How many times has the plumber fixed John's tap this year? ....

- **Make/have + object + bare infinitive** are used to express that someone causes someone else to do something, but their meaning is slightly different.
  He **made Liz send** a fax. *(He insisted that Liz should send a fax.)*
  He **had Liz send** a fax. *(He asked Liz to send a fax.)*
- **Get + object + to -inf** is used to show that someone **persuades** someone else to do something.
  She **got her husband to cut** the grass. *(She persuaded her husband to cut the grass.)*

145 Rephrase the following using have, make or get as in the example:

1 He insisted that Peter left immediately. ...*He made Peter leave immediately.*....
2 Janet persuaded Diane to drive her to the airport. ....
3 My car radio is being fitted by Gary today. ....
4 She asked her sister to translate the article. ....
5 I finally persuaded the landlord to change the locks. ....
6 My mother insisted that I should wear a dress to the wedding. ....
7 I'll ask John to pick me up at the station. ....
8 Sue persuaded her colleagues to change their minds. ....
9 She is going to ask them to rewrite the assignment. ....
10 I can't believe he asked me to return the cheque. ....
11 He insisted that they should stay at home. ....
12 I'll try to persuade him to give you the money he owes you. ....
13 The receptionist asked her to wait outside his office. ....
14 The doctor insisted that she should go to hospital. ....
15 He asked the porter to carry his luggage. ....

146 Complete the sentences using the words in bold. Use two to five words.

1 They arranged for medical supplies to be flown into the region.
   had   They ...*had medical supplies flown*... into the region.
2 A shark bit Tony's leg off.
   got   Tony .... by a shark.
3 A lawyer will have to sign this document for you.
   have   You .... this document signed by a lawyer.
4 Why did you insist that I buy this horrible cheese?
   make   Why .... this horrible cheese?

5 She pays someone to clean the windows every month.

cleaned   She .... every month.

6 The labourers were forced to work seven days a week.

made   They .... seven days a week.

7 Someone will probably mug you if you walk through that part of town.

get   You .... if you walk through that part of town.

8 They will take away your licence if they catch you driving that way.

have   You .... away if they catch you driving that way.

9 She arranged for her neighbour to walk her dog while she was away.

had   She .... by her neighbour while she was away.

10 Please don't insist that I cook dinner tonight.

make   Please .... dinner tonight.

11 Someone stole their car while they were asleep.

had   They .... while they were asleep.

12 Her nose was broken in the accident.

got   She .... in the accident.

13 Did you insist they should rewrite the composition?

make   Did .... the composition?

14 She hired someone to make new curtains for her house.

had   She .... for her house.

15 He got someone at the garage to adjust the brakes.

adjusted   He .... at the garage.

Oral Development 10

Architects are looking at plans for a luxurious hotel for Smithson International. In pairs comment on the jobs that have already been done, are being done, will be done, or will have been done, then make sentences using the causative. You can use your own ideas.

10 June

Things done : decorate VIP suites, build staff accommodation block, paint reception area

Things being done: build swimming pool, decorate dining room, furnish lounge, paint bedrooms

Things to be done: landscape gardens, build car park

Things that will have been done by the end of next month: install phones, fit bathrooms, equip sports centre

eg. They have had the VIP suites decorated.

6 Passive Voice / Causative Form

147 Complete the sentences using the words in bold. Use two to five words.

1 Fire has completely destroyed the left wing of the house.
  been   The left wing of the house ...*has been completely destroyed by*... fire.

2 Under no circumstances must you remove books from the library.
  removed   Under no circumstances .... from the library.

3 It's still possible to find copies of their album at selected music stores.
  found   Copies of their album .... at selected music stores.

4 Don't you object to people asking you for favours all the time?
  being   Don't you object to .... all the time?

5 The teacher insisted that all latecomers remain behind at the end of the class.
  made   The teacher .... at the end of the class.

6 I don't appreciate people not paying me on time.
  being   I don't appreciate .... on time.

7 You have to wear safety helmets at all times.
  worn   Safety helmets .... at all times.

8 These remains are believed to date back to the Bronze Age.
  that   It .... back to the Bronze Age.

9 Why did they make the decision without consulting me?
  made   Why .... without their consulting me?

10 Anne persuaded her brother to lend her the money.
  got   Anne .... her the money.

11 John has invited me to his birthday party.
  have   I .... John's birthday party.

12 I'd better get a mechanic to look over the car before we set off for Spain.
  looked   I'd better .... before we set off for Spain.

13 We have not yet finalised details for the wedding.
  been   Details .... for the wedding.

14 Aren't you going to ask someone to repair the roof before winter sets in?
  have   Aren't you .... the roof before winter sets in?

15 The office now handles all transactions on computer.
  handled   All transactions .... on computer.

148 Find the word which should not be in the sentence.

1 He has been being offered an interesting job.	**1** *being*
2 Were you be shown how to fix it?	**2**
3 He likes to having his photograph taken.	**3**
4 The criminal is believed to have been left the country.	**4**
5 This painting it is believed to be his masterpiece.	**5**
6 He was seen to leaving the farm at dawn.	**6**
7 All the silverware was disappeared without trace.	**7**
8 The film star is expected that to give a press conference this afternoon.	**8**
9 She was had a new cooker delivered yesterday.	**9**
10 Have you been had the report typed yet?	**10**
11 We should to have a new garage built.	**11**
12 He insists on having his office is cleaned twice weekly.	**12**
13 Did you have had the reception organised by an agency?	**13**
14 We had the locksmith to open the door.	**14**
15 Did you get an application form be mailed to you?	**15**
16 They had been had a burglar alarm installed.	**16**

Consolidation 6

▶ Phrasal Verbs

go about with: keep company with
go ahead: go in front
go back on: break a promise, agreement, etc
go down with: become ill
go for: 1) attack, 2) apply for
go in for: enter a competition
go off: 1) explode, 2) (of food) go bad
go out: 1) be extinguished, 2) mix socially
go over: 1) examine details, 2) repeat
go round: be enough for everyone to have a share

• • • • • • • • • • • • •

hold back: 1) hesitate, 2) control, 3) keep a secret
hold on: wait
hold out: 1) endure, 2) last
hold up: 1) delay, 2) rob (sb or sth)

149 *Fill in the correct particle(s).*

1 Go ...*over*... the rules of the game once more.
2 You go ....and we'll follow close behind.
3 I've decided to go ....the teaching job.
4 The bomb will go ....in two minutes.
5 She is so beautiful she is going .... a beauty contest.
6 He stayed in bed after going ....the flu.
7 My father disapproves of the people I go ....
8 Bring some wood; the fire is going ....
9 You should never go ....a promise.
10 There weren't enough sandwiches to go ....
11 She went .... him with a knife.
12 The bank has been held ....twice this year.
13 Hold ....a minute while I get my jacket.
14 Will the car hold ....until we get to a garage?
15 The road works held ....the traffic.
16 Don't hold ...., tell me everything.
17 I was upset and unable to hold ....my tears.

150 *Look at Appendix 1, then fill in the correct preposition.*

1 He has absolutely no taste ...*in*... clothes.
2 He succeeded .... upsetting all his friends.
3 I think I was a bit mean .... Paula yesterday.
4 Are you having trouble .... your car?
5 Not many people have such a talent .... acting.
6 Cathy is very sensitive .... the needs of others.
7 This ticket is valid .... two days only.
8 I took pity .... the beggar and gave him £1.
9 She is completely unaware .... the trouble she has caused.
10 Children should be warned .... the dangers of drugs.
11 The government feels uneasy .... the current political situation.
12 There is no solution .... your problem.
13 Don't you have any pity .... the poor man?
14 Don't interfere .... their papers.
15 I've been longing ...... some peace and quiet.
16 The detective went .... search .... the stolen painting.
17 The flat smells .... paint.
18 This ice-cream tastes .... almonds.
19 It's important to make good use .... your dictionary.
20 She's not used .... being spoken to like that.
21 This voucher is valid .... all Smiths stores.
22 Don't worry .... Garfield. He'll be OK.
23 I'm not worthy .... such an honour.
24 The children were throwing stones .... the window.

151 *Complete the sentences using the words in bold. Use two to five words.*

1 He had no right to treat me so rudely.
   have   He ...*shouldn't have treated me*... so rudely.
2 The conference took place in a large hotel.
   held   The conference .... hotel.
3 He has a good relationship with his parents.
   gets   He .... his parents.
4 He missed the end of the film because he fell asleep.
   due   He missed the end of the film .... asleep.
5 I'm sure the suspect is telling lies.
   be   The .... lies.
6 People believe she lives in New York.
   believed   She .... in New York.

Consolidation **6**

152 *For questions 1 - 15, read the text below and decide which word A, B, C or D best fits each space. Mark your answers in the answer boxes provided.*

Developing countries

There are **(0)** ... 140 countries which **(1)** ... to the Third World and which are **(2)** ... as developing, less developed and poor countries. Although there are great **(3)** ... between them, they do have a number of **(4)** ... in common. For **(5)** ..., much of the Third World is in poverty. A few exceptions to this rule are Saudi Arabia, Kuwait and Libya. However, because the economies of these three countries **(6)** ... largely on one export, oil, they are still vulnerable in the world market. Most of the developing countries **(7)** ... have very little industry. Farming is often the only**(8)** .... in which the country can make money. **(9)** ... worse, many of the countries only produce enough food to **(10)** ... their own populations alive. India is a classic example of this, as **(11)** ... less than 70 percent of its 870 million people work the land **(12)** ... a living. Another feature which links less developed countries is life expectancy. People die younger in the Third World because of the poverty in **(13)** ... they live. The poor have much less healthy diets **(14)** ... in developed countries, and health care is also more **(15)** ... to be inadequate.

0 A mostly	**B** roughly	**C** partly	**D** evenly
1 A include	**B** attach	**C** connect	**D** belong
2 A said	**B** known	**C** told	**D** taken
3 A changes	**B** disagreements	**C** differences	**D** varieties
4 A features	**B** sides	**C** faces	**D** signs
5 A case	**B** instance	**C** reason	**D** fact
6 A decide	**B** insist	**C** lean	**D** depend
7 A then	**B** although	**C** while	**D** still
8 A way	**B** type	**C** model	**D** method
9 A Most	**B** More	**C** Quite	**D** Even
10 A have	**B** keep	**C** hold	**D** make
11 A a	**B** the	**C** no	**D** too
12 A as	**B** for	**C** of	**D** to
13 A which	**B** where	**C** that	**D** whose
14 A as	**B** than	**C** like	**D** or
15 A likely	**B** probable	**C** possible	**D** definite

	A	B	C	D
0		■		
1				
2				
3				
4				
5				
6				
7				
8				
9				
10				
11				
12				
13				
14				
15				

153 *Read the text carefully. Some of the lines are correct and some have a word which should not be there. If a line is correct, put a tick (✔) in the space provided. If a line has a word which should not be there, write it in the space provided.*

Football Cup

0	The most important match of the English football season	✔	0
00	was on in last weekend. Manchester United, the favourites,	in	00
1	were playing Everton, an another team from the North		1
2	of England. My father has been an Everton fan since that		2
3	he was a young boy, but unfortunately I wasn't there		3
4	to watch the match with him as I am studying at abroad.		4
5	A group of about fifteen English students met in the French		5
6	College bar to cheer our teams. None one of us could		6
7	believe it when the presenter appeared and apologised		7
8	for not being able to get a picture. Instead of we were		8
9	being shown a long stretch of adverts. Every so often		9
10	the presenter would appear again for to apologise		10
11	for the lack of picture. At half-time I phoned home		11
12	and asked what the score was it. My dad was full		12
13	of joy. Apparently Everton had got to a goal		13
14	in the thirtieth minute. Fortunately we could see to the		14
15	second half, so that we watched Everton win the Cup.		15

154 *For questions 1 - 10, read the text below. Use the word given in capitals at the end of each line to form a word that fits in the space in the same line. Write your word in the answer boxes provided.*

Learning for the future

One of the biggest problems facing secondary (0) .... **EDUCATE**
today is providing some form of (1) .... or **TRAIN**
(2) .... for those young people who don't want **QUALIFY**
to apply for (3) .... to university and who aren't **ADMIT**
interested in taking traditional (4) .... . **EXAMINE**
Many students leave school and face (5) .... **EMPLOYMENT**
because they are completely (6) .... . Modern **SKILLED**
secondary education should include more (7) .... **PRACTICE**
subjects and be flexible enough for students to
get credit for their (8) .... even if they don't **ACHIEVE**
pass written tests. Industry is generally (9) .... **ENTHUSIASM**
about introducing job-related education, hoping that
it will lead to a more (10) .... and efficient workforce. **PROFESSION**

0	education
1	
2	
3	
4	
5	
6	
7	
8	
9	
10	

Practice test ◆ 3

For questions 1 - 15, read the text below and decide which word A, B, C or D best fits each space. Mark your answers in the answer boxes provided.

Does the moon affect your behaviour?

For thousands of years the moon has caught our **(0)** .... Although it can be seen during the day, it is associated **(1)** .... things that come out after **(2)** .... like werewolves and witches. For thousands of years the moon has been considered to have magical **(3)** .... and it is still a symbol of the supernatural. Despite moon-landings in the **(4)** .... half of this century, the idea that the moon **(5)** .... our minds and bodies remains **(6)** .... American studies have reported more murders at full moon, more bleeding during surgery, a greater number of accidents and suicides, and more disturbed **(7)** .... in psychiatric hospitals. This **(8)** .... lunar influence has been called the "Transylvania effect". In **(9)** .... there are at least two theories put **(10)** .... by scientists claiming to explain this effect. **(11)** ...., Ivan Kelly of the University of Saskatchewan and James Rotton of Florida International University found that the "Transylvania effect" did not **(12)** .... exist at all. Furthermore, they **(13)** .... the "Transylvania effect" theories, saying they were scientifically incorrect. Kelly claims "moon moods" are probably **(14)** .... by psychological factors. "If you believe the moon affects you, you alter your behaviour accordingly. There is no magic **(15)** .... at all."

0	**A** breath	**B** thoughts	**C** imagination	**D** minds
1	**A** for	**B** at	**C** to	**D** with
2	**A** night	**B** dark	**C** day	**D** light
3	**A** talents	**B** gifts	**C** powers	**D** strengths
4	**A** other	**B** second	**C** present	**D** nearer
5	**A** affects	**B** reacts	**C** adopts	**D** moves
6	**A** contemporary	**B** popular	**C** famous	**D** modern
7	**A** manners	**B** taste	**C** actions	**D** behaviour
8	**A** appearing	**B** plain	**C** open	**D** apparent
9	**A** time	**B** places	**C** fact	**D** order
10	**A** on	**B** away	**C** forward	**D** up
11	**A** However	**B** Moreover	**C** Otherwise	**D** Probably
12	**A** frequently	**B** hardly	**C** eventually	**D** actually
13	**A** sacked	**B** rejected	**C** dropped	**D** refused
14	**A** caused	**B** made	**C** invented	**D** thought
15	**A** involved	**B** concerned	**C** mixed	**D** included

	A	B	C	D
0			■	
1				
2				
3				
4				
5				
6				
7				
8				
9				
10				
11				
12				
13				
14				
15				

Part 2

For questions 16 - 30, read the text below and think of the word which best fits each space.
Use only one word in each space. Write your answers in the answer boxes provided.

The Isle of Wight

The Isle of Wight is a small island just **(0)** .... the south coast of England near the towns of Portsmouth and Southampton.

Queen Victoria loved the island **(16)** .... much that she had Osborne House built, which has not changed at **(17)** .... since the days when she used to visit with her huge family. **(18)** .... tourist attractions include Butterfly World, where, **(19)** .... the name suggests, visitors can see a large range **(20)** .... butterflies, and two zoos. In summer it is usually warm and sunny **(21)** .... for holidaymakers to enjoy the miles of clean beaches.

Alternatively, for those **(22)** .... want to be out of doors but don't like sunbathing, the Isle of Wight is an excellent place for cyclists. There are numerous little paths which lead **(23)** .... picturesque villages all **(24)** .... the island. Newport, the island's capital, is also **(25)** .... a visit. It is a busy little town with **(26)** .... of small specialist shops.

(27) .... the beginning of August, there is the most famous yachting week **(28)** .... the world, which takes **(29)** .... at Cowes. During that week Cowes is full **(30)** .... carnival atmosphere and every bar and restaurant is packed.

0	off	0 ▬
16		16
17		17
18		18
19		19
20		20
21		21
22		22
23		23
24		24
25		25
26		26
27		27
28		28
29		29
30		30

Part 3

For questions 31 - 40, complete the second sentence so that it has a similar meaning to the first sentence. Use the word given and other words to complete each sentence. You must use between two and five words. Do not change the word given. Write your answers in the answer boxes provided.

0 I'm sure they worked hard on the project.
   have
   They .... on the project.

| 0 | *must have worked hard* | ▢ **0** ▮ |

31 It's possible that he didn't understand you.
   may
   He .... you.

| 31 | | 31 ▢ ▢ |

32 The programme was difficult to install because the manual was badly written.
   made
   The badly written manual .... the programme.

| 32 | | 32 ▢ ▢ |

33 She locked the gate so that the dog wouldn't escape.
   prevent
   To .... , she locked the gate.

| 33 | | 33 ▢ ▢ |

34 My offer of help was rejected.
   turned
   They .... of help.

| 34 | | 34 ▢ ▢ |

35 I do not run as fast as I did when I was younger.
   used
   I .... I do now.

| 35 | | 35 ▢ ▢ |

36 I don't really want to get up so early in the morning.
   prefer
   I .... up so early in the morning.

| 36 | | 36 ▢ ▢ |

37 We can find a temporary replacement for you.
   stand
   We can find someone .... you.

| 37 | | 37 ▢ ▢ |

38 Although it was raining, we still went swimming.
   of
   In ...., we still went swimming.

| 38 | | 38 ▢ ▢ |

39 Coaches are usually cheaper than trains.
   expensive
   Coaches are not usually .... trains.

| 39 | | 39 ▢ ▢ |

40 She will probably get the job.
   likely
   She .... the job.

| 40 | | 40 ▢ ▢ |

Part 4

For questions 41 - 55, read the text below and look carefully at each line. Some of the lines are correct and some have a word which should not be there. If a line is correct, put a tick (✔) by the number in the answer boxes provided. If a line has a word which should not be there, write the word in the answer boxes provided.

Big Ben

0	Big Ben is in fact the bell which it tolls on the hour in the	
00	clock tower of the Houses of Parliament and not, as is	
41	commonly supposed, the tower and clock by itself. It is	
42	thought about to have been named after Sir Benjamin Hall.	
43	The bell was been completed on April 10th, 1858.	
44	With a weight of more than over 13 tons, it was the heaviest	
45	bell in Britain at that time. It began to striking the time	
46	in July, 1859, but cracked later that year and was	
47	consequently silent for the next three years. The crack is	
48	plainly being visible even today. An electric motor is	
49	now used to wind the clock mechanism, and checks with	
50	Greenwich Observatory they have rarely shown an error	
51	of more than one second. On some occasions the clock has	
52	stopped accidentally, but almost seldom due to mechanical	
53	problems. Radio made Big Ben as a symbol, and on New	
54	Year's Eve in 1923 Big Ben has made its first broadcast.	
55	It has been heard of nightly ever since.	

0	*it*
00	✓
41	
42	
43	
44	
45	
46	
47	
48	
49	
50	
51	
52	
53	
54	
55	

Part 5

For questions 56 - 65, read the text below. Use the word given in capitals at the end of each line to form a word that fits in the space in the same line. Write your word in the answer boxes provided.

Hypochondriacs

There are people who spend years suffering from
an **(0)** .... which doctors are not usually
(56) .... towards. Hypochondria is a
(57) .... term which describes a highly
(58) .... level of worry about your health.
Sufferers regularly visit their doctors with
(59) .... of serious symptoms
which doctors cannot explain. Hypochondriacs are
always **(60)** .... about their health and often imagine
that they are suffering from **(61)** .... or
(62) .... diseases. They waste the
(63) .... time of doctors when really they are perfectly
(64) .... . Sufferers can be taught to control their
(65) .... through relaxation techniques.

ILL	0	*illness*
SYMPATHY	56	
MEDICINE	57	
NORMAL	58	
COMPLAIN	59	
	60	
PESSIMISM	61	
DANGER	62	
CURABLE	63	
VALUE	64	
HEALTH		
ANXIOUS	65	

7 Reported Speech

Direct Speech gives the exact words someone said. We use inverted commas in Direct Speech. *"It's quite warm,"* she said.	**Reported Speech** gives the exact meaning of what someone said but not the exact words. We do not use inverted commas in Reported Speech. *She said **it was quite warm**.*

Say - Tell - Ask

We use **say** in Direct Speech. We also use **say** in Reported Speech when **say** is not followed by the person the words were spoken to.	*"I can't help you,"* he **said**. ➡ He **said (that)** he couldn't help me.
We use **tell** in Reported Speech when it is followed by the person the words were spoken to	*"I can't help you,"* he said to me. ➡ He **told me** he couldn't help me.
We use **say + to-infinitive** but never ~~say about~~. We use **tell sb, speak/talk about**, instead.	*Mum **said to be** home by 10 o'clock.* *She **spoke/talked about/told us about** her adventures.*
We use **ask** in reported questions and commands, or in direct questions.	*He said to me, "Help me!"* ➡ He **asked me** to help him. *He **asked**, "Are you OK?"* ➡ He **asked me if** I was OK.

Expressions with say, tell and ask

Expressions with **say**	say good morning/evening etc, say something, say one's prayers, say a few words, say so, say no more, say for certain/sure etc
Expressions with **tell**	tell the truth, tell a lie, tell (sb) the time, tell sb one's name, tell a story, tell sb a secret, tell sb the way, tell one from another, tell sb's fortune, tell sb so, tell the difference etc
Expressions with **ask**	ask a favour, ask the time, ask a question, ask the price etc

155 *Fill in say, tell or ask in the correct form.*

1 My parrot can ...*say*... a few words in English.
2 Please .... me what you think of my new dress.
3 He .... that he couldn't reply to any more questions.
4 My mother used to .... me a story before I went to bed.
5 He promised to .... no more about the matter.
6 She stopped to .... the time because she thought she was late.
7 The little girl .... her prayers and then went to sleep.
8 Sally couldn't .... for certain whether or not she would be staying.
9 He had taken an oath so he had to .... the truth in court.
10 With identical twins you can rarely .... the difference between them.
11 The old man always .... good morning to his neighbours.
12 "I'd love to go," she .... to me.
13 When I was younger I used to .... my sister all my secrets.
14 "Could you help me with these bags?" she .... me.
15 Rachel keeps .... me that she's going to change jobs, but she never does.

There are three types of Reported Speech: statements, questions and commands/requests/suggestions.

Statements

● Reported statements are introduced with say or tell. Inverted commas are omitted in Reported Speech. That is optional in the reported sentence.
"She is sleeping," Tom said. ➡ Tom **said (that)** she was sleeping.

● Tenses change as follows:

	Direct Speech	Reported Speech
Present Simple	*"He **plays** well," she said.*	➡ *She said (that) he **played** well.*
Present Cont.	*"He **is playing** well," she said.*	➡ *She said (that) he **was playing** well.*
Past Simple	*"He **played** well," she said.*	➡ *She said (that) he **had played** well.*
Past Cont.	*"He **was playing** well," she said.*	➡ *She said (that) he **had been playing** well.*
Future Simple	*"He **will play** well," she said.*	➡ *She said (that) he **would play** well.*
Future Cont.	*"He **will be playing** well," she said.*	➡ *She said (that) he **would be playing** well.*
Present Perfect	*"He **has played** well," she said.*	➡ *She said (that) he **had played** well.*
Present Perf. Cont.	*"He **has been playing** well," she said.*	➡ *She said (that) he **had been playing** well.*

● Note that Past Perfect and Past Perfect Continuous remain the same in Reported Speech.

● Tenses do not change in Reported Speech when

the reporting verb (said, told etc) is in the Present, Future or Present Perfect.	*"The weather is hot," she **says**.* ➡ *She **says** (that) the weather **is** hot.*
the speaker expresses general truths, permanent states or conditions.	*"Water freezes at 0˚C," he said.* ➡ *He said (that) water **freezes** at 0˚C.*
the speaker is reporting something immediately after it was said (up to date).	*"The hotel **is** awful," he said.* ➡ *He said (that) the hotel **is** awful. (up to date)*
the reported sentence deals with unreal past, conditionals type 2/type 3 or wishes.	*"I wish I **were** rich," she said.* ➡ *She said she wished she **were** rich.*

● If the speaker expresses something which is believed to be true, the tenses may change or remain unchanged. *"I love the place," she said.* ➡ *She said she **loves/loved** the place.*

● However, if the speaker expresses something which is believed to be untrue, the tenses change. *"China is a small country," he said.* ➡ *He said (that) China **was** a small country.*

● The Past Simple changes to the Past Perfect or remains the same. When the reported sentence contains a time clause, the tenses remain unchanged. *"The car broke down **while I was driving** to work," he said.* ➡ *He said the car had broken down **while he was driving** to work.*
Note: If the reported sentence is out of date, the tenses change, but if it is up to date, the tenses can remain the same. *"He **moved out** a month ago," he said.* ➡ *He said that he **had moved out** a month before. (speech reported after he had moved out - out of date)* *"I **am going** to the cinema tonight," she said.* ➡ *She said she **is going** to the cinema tonight. (speech reported before she goes to the cinema - up to date)*

● Personal pronouns and possessive adjectives change according to context. *"No, I won't lend **you my** new car!" he said.* ➡ *He said he wouldn't lend **me his** new car.*

● Certain words change as follows depending on the context.
Direct Speech:	this/these	here	come	*"Will you **come** to my house for dinner?" she said.*
Reported Speech:	that/those	there	go	*She asked him to **go** to her house for dinner.*

7 Reported Speech

● **Time words** can change or remain the same depending on the time reference.

Direct Speech		Reported Speech
tonight, today, this week/month/year	➡	that night, that day, that week/month/year
now	➡	then, at that time, at once, immediately
now that	➡	since
yesterday, last night/week/month year	➡	the day before, the previous night/week/month/year
tomorrow, next week/month/year	➡	the following day/the day after, the following/next week/month/year
two days/months/years etc ago	➡	two days/months/years etc before

*"I'm sitting an exam **tomorrow**," he said.* ➡ *He said he was sitting an exam **the next/following day**. (out-of-date reporting) "I'm sitting an exam **tomorrow**," he said.* ➡ *He said he **is sitting** an exam **tomorrow**. (up-to-date reporting)*

156 *Turn the following sentences into Reported Speech.*

1 "I'm visiting Greece," says Angela. (up-to-date reporting)
   ...*Angela says she's visiting Greece*....
2 "I've never been to Paris before," said John. (out-of-date reporting) ....
3 "I'm taking my driving test next week," she said. (up-to-date reporting) ....
4 "I don't speak Spanish," said Sarah. ....
5 "My house is not far from the town centre," he says. ....
6 "Water boils at 100°C," he said. ....
7 "Australia is a very big country," he said. ....
8 "If I see him, I'll invite him to the party," said Mary. (out-of-date reporting) ....
9 "I was locking the car when a traffic warden turned up," she said. ....
10 "I'm not going on holiday next week," he said. (up-to-date reporting) ....
11 "I've written five letters this morning," said Eddy. (up-to-date reporting) ....
12 "I saw a really bad car accident last night," he said to me. ....
13 "I met David while I was working in Manchester," she said. ....
14 "I'll see you later tonight," she said to him. (out-of-date reporting) ....
15 "It's time you got a job," his mother said to him. ....
16 "If you had studied harder, you would have passed your exam," the teacher said to Tom. ....
17 "If I were rich, I would buy a mansion in Beverly Hills," she said. ....
18 "He doesn't really like his new job," said Theresa. ....
19 "I won't be home late," she said to her husband. (out-of-date reporting) ....
20 "I've been living here for five years," she said. (out-of-date reporting) ....

Reported Questions - Indirect Questions

● **Reported questions** are used to report someone else's questions, suggestions, offers or requests. In reported questions we use affirmative word order and the question mark becomes a full stop. Inverted commas are omitted. To report a question we use: a) **ask + question word** (who, which, where, how etc) when the direct question begins with a question word; b) **ask + if/whether** when the direct question begins with an auxiliary verb (do, have, can etc). Tenses, personal pronouns, possessive adjectives, time words etc change as in statements.

Direct questions	Reported questions
He asked her, "What is your name?"	He asked her **what her name was**.
He asked her, "Do you like tea?"	He asked her **if/whether she liked** tea.

157 Turn the following sentences into Reported Speech.

1 "Will you be going to San Francisco next summer?"
his boss asked. *His boss asked him if he would*
be going to San Francisco the following summer.
2 "Why were you in a hurry?" she asked me. ....
3 "Do you want a lift to work tomorrow?" he asked her. ....
4 "What time have you arranged to meet Clare?" he asked her. ....
5 "How long has Jane been working here?" she asked me. ....
6 "Who left the door open?" she asked them. ....
7 "Did you actually see the man fall?" the reporter asked the bystander. ....
8 "Will you give me a hand lifting the piano?" the workman asked his helper. ....
9 "Can you check the brakes please?" she asked the mechanic. ....
10 "Have they finished renovating their house?" he asked me. ....
11 "Is Mary still having a party next Saturday?" she asked me. ....
12 "Where does your father work?" the teacher asked him. ....
13 "Will they be hiring new staff for the summer?" she asked. ....
14 "Which of their songs do you like best?" he asked me. ....
15 "Where will you be going this weekend?" Jean asked her. ....

● **Indirect questions** are used to ask for information/advice. They are introduced with: **Could you tell me...?, Do you know...?, I wonder..., I want to know..., I doubt ...,** etc and the verb is in the affirmative. If the indirect question starts with **I wonder..., I want to know ...** or **I doubt ...,** the question mark is omitted. Question words (**what, who, where** etc) or **whether** can be followed by an infinitive in the indirect question if the subject of the question is the same as the speaker.

Direct questions	Indirect questions
He asked me, "How old is Thomas?"	*Do you know **how old Thomas is**?*
He asked me, "Is it correct?"	*He wondered **if/whether it is/was** correct.*
He asked me, "Where can I leave it?"	*He wanted to know **where he could leave** it/**where to leave** it.*

158 Turn the following sentences into Indirect Questions. Omit question marks where necessary.

1 Where did I leave my glasses? (I wonder ...) ...*I wonder where I left my glasses....*
2 Is John planning to call a meeting? (Did you know ...) ....
3 Have they ever had a hit single before? (Do you know ...) ....
4 When are you leaving? (I want to know ...) ....
5 Did he tell the truth? (I doubt ...) ....
6 Where is the nearest swimming pool? (Could you tell me ...) ....
7 Who left that message on our answerphone? (She wondered ...) ....
8 What time are they due to arrive? (He wanted to know ...) ....

Reported Commands/Requests/Suggestions

● To report **commands, requests, suggestions** we use an introductory verb (**advise, ask, beg, offer, suggest** etc) (see pages 111,112) followed by a **to-infinitive,** an **-ing form** or a **that-clause** depending on the introductory verb.

"Be careful," he said to me.	➡ *He told me to **be careful**. (command)*
"Please don't talk," he said to me.	➡ *He asked me **not to talk**. (request)*
"Let's watch TV," he said.	➡ *He **suggested watching** TV. (suggestion)*
"You'd better go to the dentist," he said.	➡ *He **suggested that I (should)** go to the dentist. (suggestion)*

7 Reported Speech

159 **Turn the following sentences from Direct to Reported Speech.**

1 "Don't run down the corridors, please," he said to us. ...*He asked us not to run down the corridors*....
2 "May I leave the room, please?" said the student. ....
3 "Let's turn on the television," said Paul. ....
4 "Soldiers! Stand to attention!" said the Major. ....
5 "Can you open the window?" she said to me. ....
6 "Shall we go ice-skating on Saturday?" said Miles. ....
7 "Don't touch the statue!" he said to us. ....
8 "Shall we go camping this summer?" said my brother. ....
9 "Let's have a picnic tomorrow," said John. ....
10 "You'd better go to bed now," he said to the children. ....

Modal Verbs in Reported Speech

● Some modal verbs change in Reported Speech when the reported sentence is out of date, as follows: will/shall ➡ **would**, can ➡ **could** (present reference)/**would be able to** (future reference), may ➡ **might/could**, shall ➡ **should** (asking for advice) / **would** (asking for information) / **offer** (expressing offers), must ➡ **must/had to** (obligation) (* "must" remains the same when it expresses possibility or deduction), needn't ➡ **didn't need to / didn't have to** (present reference) / **wouldn't have to** (future reference).

Direct Speech	Reported Speech
He said, "I'll phone you this evening."	➡ He said that he **would** phone me that evening.
He said, "I **can** speak French."	➡ He said (that) he **could** speak French.
He said, "I **can** join you next weekend."	➡ He said (that) he **would be able** to join us the next weekend.
He said, "I **may** be late home."	➡ He said (that) he **might** be late home.
He said, "How **shall** I get there?"	➡ He asked how he **should** get there. (advice)
He said, "Where **shall** we go?"	➡ He asked where they **should** go. (information)
He said, "**Shall** I take you home?"	➡ He **offered** to take me home. (offer)
He said, "You **must** try harder."	➡ He said (that) I **had to** try harder. (obligation)
He said, "You **must** be joking."	➡ He said (that) I **must** be joking. (deduction)
He said, "You **should** take a holiday."	➡ He said (that) I **should** take a holiday.
He said, "She **had better** tidy her room."	➡ He said (that) she **had better** tidy her room.
He said, "She **needn't** know who he was."	➡ He said (that) she **didn't need to/have to** know who he was.
He said, "You **needn't** meet me tomorrow."	➡ He said (that) I **wouldn't have to** meet him the next day.

160 **Turn the following sentences into Reported Speech.**

1 He said, "Shall I carry your bags?" ...*He offered to carry my bags.*
2 He said, "She needn't see the report." ....
3 He said, "I'll pick you up at 4 o'clock." ....
4 He said, "You should get away for a while." ....
5 He said, "Kevin may need your help later." ....
6 He said, "You must control your feelings.". ....
7 He said, "You need to let me know tomorrow." ....
8 He said, "She had better not say that again." ....
9 He said, "We must be cousins." ....
10 He said, "I can run faster than you." ....
11 He said, "I can meet you next week." ....
12 He said, "Who shall I go to for help?" ....
13 He said, "Where shall we go to eat tonight?" ....
14 He said, "Shall I lend you the money?" ....

Special Introductory Verbs

Introductory verb	Direct Speech	Reported Speech
agree + to-inf **demand** **offer** **promise** **refuse** **threaten** **claim**	*"Yes, I'll be happy to help you."* *"Tell the truth!"* *"Would you like me to open the door?"* *"I'll definitely be here early."* *"No, I won't lend you any money."* *"Hand over your money or I'll shoot you."* *"I saw him steal the car."*	➡ He **agreed to help** me. ➡ He **demanded to be told** the truth. ➡ He **offered to open** the door. ➡ He **promised to be** there early. ➡ He **refused to lend** me any money. ➡ He **threatened to shoot** me if I didn't hand over my money. ➡ He **claimed to have seen** him steal the car.
advise + sb + to-inf **allow** **ask** **beg** **command** **encourage** **forbid** **instruct** **invite sb** **order** **permit** **remind** **urge** **warn** **want**	*"You should see a doctor."* *"You can borrow my car."* *"Please, turn the light off."* *"Please, please stop shouting so loudly."* *"Leave the room!"* *"Go ahead, drive the car."* *"You must not arrive late tonight."* *"Lift the receiver and wait for the dialling tone."* *"Would you like to come out to dinner with me?"* *"Close the door immediately."* *"You may leave now."* *"Don't forget to water the plants."* *"Try to be punctual."* *"Don't go near the edge of the cliff."* *"I'd like you to study harder."*	➡ He **advised me to see** a doctor. ➡ He **allowed me to borrow** his car. ➡ He **asked me to turn** the light off. ➡ He **begged me to stop** shouting so loudly. ➡ He **commanded us to leave** the room. ➡ He **encouraged me to drive** the car. ➡ He **forbade me to arrive** late that night. ➡ He **instructed me to lift** the receiver and wait for the dialling tone. ➡ He **invited me to go** out to dinner with him. ➡ He **ordered me to close** the door immediately. ➡ He **permitted/allowed me to leave** then. ➡ He **reminded me to water** the plants. ➡ He **urged me to try** to be punctual. ➡ He **warned me not to go** near the edge of the cliff. ➡ He **wanted me to study** harder.
accuse sb of + -ing form **apologise for** **admit (to)** **boast about** **complain to sb about** **deny** **insist on** **suggest**	*"You stole my handbag!"* *"I'm sorry I was rude to you."* *"Yes, I broke the window."* *"I'm more intelligent than you."* *"You always leave the door open."* *"No, I didn't break the window."* *"You must take all the medicine."* *"Let's go out for a walk."*	➡ She **accused me of stealing** her handbag. ➡ He **apologised for being** rude to me. ➡ He **admitted (to) breaking/having broken** the window. ➡ He **boasted about being** more intelligent than me. ➡ He **complained to me about my** always **leaving** the door open. ➡ He **denied breaking/having broken** the window. ➡ He **insisted on me/my taking** all the medicine. ➡ He **suggested going** out for a walk.
agree + that-clause **boast** **claim** **complain** **deny** **exclaim** **explain** **inform sb** **promise** **suggest**	*"Yes, it's a great idea."* *"I'm the best player of all."* *"I know who stole your car."* *"You never help me."* *"I never touched the vase!"* *"It's a success!"* *"It's a difficult theory to follow."* *"Your application is under review."* *"I won't forget again."* *"You ought to help her out."*	➡ He **agreed that** it was a great idea. ➡ He **boasted that** he was the best player of all. ➡ He **claimed that** he knew who had stolen my car. ➡ She **complained that** he never helped her. ➡ He **denied that** he had ever touched the vase. ➡ He **exclaimed that** it was a success. ➡ He **explained that** it was a difficult theory to follow. ➡ He **informed me that** my application was under review. ➡ He **promised that** he wouldn't forget again. ➡ He **suggested that** I help her out.
explain to sb + how	*"That's how I crashed the car."*	➡ He **explained to me how** he had crashed the car.

7 Reported Speech

Introductory verb	Direct Speech	Reported Speech
wonder where/what why/how + clause (when the subject of the introductory verb is **not the same** as the subject in the reported question)	He asked himself, "How can she do that?" ➡ He asked himself, "Where have they gone?" ➡ He asked himself, "Why is Tom so rude?" ➡ He asked himself, "What will they do?" ➡	He **wondered how** she could do that. He **wondered where** they had gone. He **wondered why** Tom was so rude. He **wondered what** they would do.
wonder + whether + to-inf or clause **wonder where/what/ how + to-inf** (when the subject of the infinitive is the **same** as the subject of the verb)	He asked himself, "Shall I take the job?" He asked himself, "Where did I leave my glasses?" He asked himself, "What shall I do next?" He asked himself, "How can I break the news?"	➡ He **wondered whether** to take the job. ➡ He **wondered whether** he should take the job. ➡ He **wondered where** he had left his glasses. ➡ He **wondered what** to do next. ➡ He **wondered how** to break the news.

161 First write an appropriate introductory verb, then report the following sentences.

1 "You took my bag, didn't you?" ...accuse... *She accused me of taking her bag.*
2 "I'll bring my homework tomorrow." ....
3 "Get out of the room now!" ....
4 "The train leaves at 6 o'clock." ....
5 "Don't forget to make a dental appointment." ....
6 "Please, please help me!" ....
7 "You must give us a call when you get back!" ....
8 "I won't help you." ....
9 "Would you like to go out with us?" ....
10 "If you do that again, I'll punish you." ....
11 "I didn't break the vase!" ....
12 "Will the rain ever stop?" ....
13 "First turn this knob, then flick the switch." ....
14 "Yes, you're right." ....
15 "What about going for a walk?" ....
16 "You should go on a diet." ....
17 "You mustn't touch the camera." ....
18 "Don't cross the road without looking both ways." ....
19 "Would you like me to water your plants?" ....
20 "Yes, it was me who broke the teapot." ....
21 "It is a difficult situation, you see." ....
22 "I met the Queen once, you know." ....
23 "You always leave the bathroom in a mess!" ....
24 "You may use the fax machine whenever you want." ....
25 "You must stay until 5 o'clock every day!" ....
26 "Give me the money!" ....
27 "I crossed the Atlantic single-handed." ....
28 "You may call me by my first name." ....
29 "Please, empty all the ashtrays before you leave the room." ....
30 "Cease fire!" ....
31 "Go on, tell us what's on your mind." ....
32 "I'd like you to cook dinner tonight." ....
33 "I'm sorry I spoilt the surprise party." ....
34 "Sure, I'd be glad to lend a hand." ....
35 "I'll never let you down again." ....

Reporting a dialogue or a conversation

● In conversations or dialogues we use a mixture of statements, commands and questions. When we report dialogues or conversations, we use: and, as, adding that, and he/she added that, explaining that, because, but, since, so, and then he/she went on to say, while, then etc or the introductory verb in the present participle form. Exclamations such as: Oh!, Oh dear!, Well! etc are omitted in Reported Speech.

Direct Speech

"I was sorry to hear you haven't been well. I hope you're feeling better now," she said.

"What a brilliant idea!" she exclaimed. "Why didn't I think of that?"

"Can you make dinner tonight, Tom?" she said. "I'm working late."

Reported Speech

➡ *She said she was sorry to hear I hadn't been well* **and added that** *she hoped I was feeling better.*

➡ *She exclaimed that it was a brilliant idea* **and** *wondered why she hadn't thought of it.*

➡ *She asked Tom if he could make dinner that night,* **explaining that** *she was working late.*

Exclamations - Yes/No short answers - Question tags

● **Exclamations** are replaced in Reported Speech with **exclaim, thank, wish, say, cry out in pain** etc, **give an exclamation of surprise/horror/disgust/delight** etc. The exclamation mark becomes a full stop. Exclamatory words such as **Oh!, Eek!, Wow!** etc are omitted in the reported sentence.
"Wow!" she said when she saw the huge cake. ➡ *She* **cried out in surprise** *when she saw the huge cake.*

● **Yes/No short answers** are expressed in Reported Speech with a **subject + appropriate auxiliary verb** or **subject + appropriate introductory verb**. *"Can you help me?" she said. "No," he said.* ➡ *She asked him if he could help her but he said he* **couldn't**. *or She asked him if he could help her but he* **refused**.

● **Question tags** are omitted in Reported Speech. We can use an appropriate introductory verb to retain their effect. *"They haven't made up their minds yet, have they?" she said.* ➡ *She* **wondered** *if they had already made up their minds.*

162 *Rewrite the following conversations in Reported Speech.*

A "Hello John. Have a seat, won't you?" Mr Williams said.
"Thank you, sir," John replied. "I'm sorry I'm a bit late but the traffic was dreadful."
"Don't worry John, it's not important," Mr Williams said. "You see, I finally made up my mind last night to give you Alan Tomkin's job, since he's retiring."
"That's excellent news Mr Williams, and I give you my word I'll do my best to do a good job," John replied.
"Why don't you take your new contract home tonight and study it, John?" Mr Williams said.

...Mr Williams greeted John, and invited him to sit down...
....
....
....

B "I've got a job interview today. Can you give me some advice?" said Graham. "Well," said Tracy, "You should dress smartly. You needn't wear a suit, but you had better wear a tie. You must arrive on time. And you ought to prepare some questions about the company." "Thanks," said Graham. "I'll let you know how I get on." "Yes, phone me tonight," Tracy replied.

....
....
....
....

7 Reported Speech

Punctuation in Direct Speech

- We capitalise the first word of the quoted sentence. The full stop, the question mark, the exclamation mark and the comma come inside the inverted commas. The comma comes outside the inverted commas only when "he said/asked" precedes the quoted sentence. *"She is working,"* he said. He said, *"She is working." "She,"* he said, *"is working."* **We do not use a comma after the question mark.** *"Can I leave now?"* I asked but: I asked, *"Can I leave now?"*
- When the subject is a pronoun, it comes before the reporting verb (said, asked etc) but when the subject is a noun, it often comes after "said", "asked" etc at the end or in the middle of the quoted sentence. *"He crashed his car,"* she said. *"He crashed his car,"* said Anna. *"He,"* said Anna, *"crashed his car."* but: She/Anna said, *"He crashed his car."* (not: ~~Said Anna,~~ *"He crashed his car."*)
- Each time the speaker changes, we normally start a new paragraph.

163 *Turn the following into a conversation. Mind the punctuation.*

The ballerina claimed that she couldn't perform that evening. The theatre manager demanded to know the reason but the ballerina refused to discuss it. The manager insisted that she should perform and reminded her that she had signed a contract. Then he threatened not to pay her if she didn't dance. The ballerina exclaimed that this was a disgraceful way to treat a star and she reminded him how famous she was. Then she warned him that she might never dance for the company again. The manager apologised for losing his temper, suggested that they should be reasonable about the matter and begged her not to let the public down. Then he politely asked her why she couldn't perform and she explained that she had twisted her ankle.

........*"I can't perform this evening," said the ballerina*... ....
....
....
....

Subjunctive

- The bare infinitive form of the subjunctive is used after certain verbs and expressions to give emphasis. These are: **advise, ask, demand, insist, propose, recommend, request, suggest, it is essential, it is imperative, it is important, it is necessary, it is vital** followed by **(that) + subject**. In British English we normally use should + simple form instead of the bare infinitive form of the subjunctive. *It is essential (that) you* **finish** *this work today. (less usual) It is essential* **that you should finish** *this work today. (more usual)*

164 *Give the correct form of the verbs in brackets. Some of the verbs are passive.*

1 It is imperative that we ..*should follow*... (follow) his orders to the last letter.
2 He insisted that he .... (pay) for the meal.
3 He proposed that women .... (admit) into the club.
4 It is important that you .... (take) these pills three times a day.
5 He demanded that no one else .... (allow) to see the contract.
6 She recommended that we .... (stay) at the other hotel.

165 *Turn the following sentences into Direct Speech.*

1 He denied spending the rent money. ...*"No, I didn't spend the rent money," he said*....
2 She exclaimed that it was a brilliant idea. ....
3 He explained to me how he had become a millionaire. ....
4 I offered to help her with her composition. ....
5 They permitted us to swim in their pool. ....

6 She insisted on his wearing a tuxedo at the wedding. ....

7 He wondered where to send his application. ....

8 She complained to me about my leaving the car unlocked. ....

9 They encouraged their son to take piano lessons. ....

10 He instructed me to unplug it first and then use a screwdriver. ....

166 *Turn the following dialogue into Reported Speech.*

John: "I feel really awful today, Mum."

Mum: "Why, what's the matter?"

John: "I've got a dreadful headache and I feel a bit dizzy."

Mum: "Oh dear, that sounds quite serious."

John: "I know. I wonder what's wrong with me. I've been feeling like this for a few days."

Mum: "Maybe you should go and see a doctor."

John: "Yes, I think so."

Mum: "I'll make you an appointment. And perhaps you should take the day off school."

John: "But Mum, I can't take the day off school just for a headache. I've got a test today."

...*John said he felt really awful that day.* ...

167 *Turn the following into a conversation, taking care to use the correct punctuation.*

A policewoman was questioning a possible witness about a bank robbery in North London yesterday. She wanted to know if the man had any information which would help the police. The witness claimed to have seen three men run out of the bank and get into a red van which was parked nearby. He insisted that one of the men had been carrying a large suitcase. The policewoman then asked the witness to describe the three men, but he admitted that he had not been able to get a good look at them. The policewoman suggested that he come to the police station to look at some photographs of possible suspects. The man agreed and promised that he would do whatever he could to help.

...*A policewoman was questioning a possible witness about a bank robbery in North London yesterday. "Do you have any information...*

168 *Turn the following into Direct Speech.*

Mr Granger said good morning to everyone and thanked them all for coming. He said that he expected that they were all wondering why he had called the meeting, and promised that he wouldn't keep them in suspense much longer. He explained that a large multinational company had offered to buy the factory for £10 million and he went on to invite people to give their views on whether or not they should sell. He warned them that it was a very important decision they had to make and urged them to think about the matter very carefully as everyone's future could depend on it.

169 *Rewrite the following sentences in Reported Speech.*

1 "Don't come home late," she said to me. "You've got to get up early tomorrow morning."

...*She advised me not to come home late as I had to get up early the next morning.*...

2 "Can I borrow a cup of sugar?" she asked. "I've run out." ....

3 "Why are you always making fun of Jane?" she asked him. "She gets really upset." ....

4 "Would you like to come over for lunch on Sunday?" she asked. "We are having a barbecue."

....

5 "Are you staying in tonight?" Jim asked her, "Or aren't you?" ....

6 "No, I didn't take your ticket," he said, "but I know who did." ....

7 "Betty can't come shopping with us," she said. "She's got a driving lesson." ....

8 "Okay, so I made a mistake," he said. "I'm sorry." ....

9 "Can you come home early?" she said to me. "I've got a surprise for you." ....

10 "Let's go for a picnic," he said. "It's such a lovely day." ....

11 "Why are you leaving now?" she asked. "The party's just beginning." ....

12 "I'm going to study hard," he said. "I want to pass this test." ....

13 "I really like the pink dress," she said to the sales assistant. "How much is it?" ....

14 "I saw Victoria in the supermarket," he said. "She didn't look very well." ....

15 "This is delicious," she said to him. "You should cook professionally."

....

16 "O.K. I'll go to the cinema with you," she said, "but let's have dinner first." ....

17 "Tell me where you've been," he said, "and don't stay out late again." ....

18 "Come to dinner on Saturday," she said. "Don't forget, I live at 34 Green Street." ....

19 "You really should go to college," he said. "A secretarial course is always useful." ....

20 "Hurry up," she said, "the performance is starting in half an hour." ....

21 "If you don't cooperate, we'll fall behind schedule," he said. ....

22 "Do you want me to take you home after school?" he asked. "It's too far for you to walk."

....

23 "You can go in and see her now," he said. "She's just woken up." ....

24 "Where have I put my keys?" he asked himself. "Did I leave them at my mother's?"

....

25 "Don't forget to lock the door twice," she said, "to make sure no one can get in." ....

26 "Do you think you could help me?" she said. "I seem to have lost my way."

....

27 "I won't wear my hat," the child said. "It looks silly." ....

28 "There's been an accident," the policeman said, "and I'm afraid your son was involved."

....

29 "I don't believe what you've done," Jeremy said to his sister. "We're supposed to be saving this for the party." ....

30 "You'd better not hurt her," he told the man, "or I'll report you to the police."

....

170 *Complete the sentences using the words in bold. Use two to five words.*

1 "I got better marks in the test than you did," she said.
   about   She ...*boasted about getting better marks*... in the test than I had.

2 "How about going to the Caribbean for our honeymoon?" she asked.
   suggested She .... to the Caribbean for their honeymoon.

3 "You must do your homework now," he said.
   on   He .... my homework immediately.

4 "First you turn right and then left to get to the shop," he said.
   how   He .... to get to the shop.

5 "No, I won't lie for you any more," she said to him.
   to   She .... any more.

6 "Get this dog out of the house now!" he shouted at me.
   demanded   He .... the dog out of the house immediately.

7 "You'd better not do that again or I'll lose my temper," he said to me.
   warned   He .... that again or he'd lose his temper.

8 "Don't forget to move everything out of the hall," she said to us.
   reminded   She .... everything out of the hall.

9 "You're right, he is a bit strange," she said.
   agreed   She .... a bit strange.

10 "Shall I go tonight?" he asked himself.
   to   He .... go that night.

11 "I think you should stay in bed and get plenty of rest," the doctor told her.
   she   The doctor .... in bed and get plenty of rest.

12 "Will I see him again soon?" she asked herself.
   would   She .... see him again soon.

13 "What a wonderful new outfit you're wearing!" she said.

exclaimed   She .... a wonderful new outfit.

14 "You mustn't forget to buy a Father's Day card this year," she told me.

reminded   She .... a Father's Day card that year.

15 "Nobody must find out where I'm hidden," he said.

found   He said that it was vital .... where he was hidden.

16 "I'm the greatest footballer of all time," he said.

boasted   He .... the greatest footballer of all time.

17 "I'll never forget the way we met," he said.

would   He .... the way they had met.

18 "Tidy your room before you go out," she said to me.

on   She .... my room before I went out.

19 "Let's go for a walk," she said to them.

go   She .... for a walk.

20 "Do your shoelaces up or you'll fall over," she said.

me   She .... my shoelaces, otherwise I'd fall over.

21 "I don't like this settlement," he said.

complained   He .... like that settlement.

22 "Where's Sally going on holiday?" asked Jane.

was   Jane .... on holiday.

23 "Don't touch that saucepan because it's hot," she said to me.

not   She .... the saucepan because it was hot.

24 "I'm sorry I missed the appointment," he said.

apologised   He .... the appointment.

25 "You need to leave now," he said to me.

necessary   He told me that it was .... at once.

26 "Please, please don't go Suzie," she cried.

begged   She .... go.

27 "You broke that window Tom," said Mr Smith.

of   Mr Smith .... window.

28 "Oh, you look so beautiful," he said to her.

remarked   He .... very beautiful.

29 "You needn't come tomorrow," said Grandma to me.

have   Grandma said .... to go the next day.

30 "You shouldn't stay in the sun for longer than fifteen minutes," the doctor told us.

advised   The doctor .... in the sun for longer than fifteen minutes.

31 "You must not enter the room without permission," he said to us.

to   He .... the room without permission.

32 "Do try and practise a bit more," she said to us.

urged   She .... a bit more.

33 "I would like you to be there by 6 o'clock," she said to them.

wanted   She .... there by 6 o'clock.

34 "OK, I'll wait a little longer," she said.

to   She .... a little longer.

35 "Of course I didn't take your wallet," she said.

denied   She .... his wallet.

36 "Yes, I think it is the best option," she said.

that   She .... best option.

37 "Leave this building immediately!" he said to us.

ordered   He .... the building immediately.

38 "You mustn't get out of the car," my mother said to us.

forbade   My mother .... of the car.

39 "Will I ever see them again?" he asked himself.

whether   He .... ever see them again.

40 "You might book a room before you go," she said to us.

suggested   She .... a room before we went

7 Reported Speech

171 Find the word which should not be in the sentence.

1	*about*
2	
3	
4	
5	
6	
7	
8	
9	
10	
11	
12	
13	
14	
15	
16	
17	
18	
19	
20	

1 The boss said about we were going to be given a few days off.
2 Sophie told to me she was looking for a better job.
3 He wanted to know if I did went to that party last night.
4 The reporter he asked the Prime Minister to comment on the election results.
5 Tony asked me if I was wanted to play golf with him that afternoon.
6 They wanted to know if that they were allowed to keep pets in the flat.
7 Celia asked Jim what time he was being leaving for the airport.
8 The student asked the teacher for to repeat what he had said.
9 The shop assistant told us do not to touch any of the items on display.
10 My mother said that I had better to leave early.
11 She told me she was leaving and explaining that she was too tired.
12 He asked me if I could do the ironing and I said I could so.
13 Nicki promised that to pay me back as soon as possible.
14 She denied that she had been taken any money from them.
15 Fiona suggested that he would talk to the manager in person.
16 He wondered what had to do to set the situation right.
17 They threatened to will dismiss him if he didn't change his attitude.
18 He asked me that what I intended to do when the term was over.
19 It is important that he should be told them the truth.
20 The doctor recommended that he should to stay at home for a few days.

Oral Development 11

In pairs, students look at the first picture and make up a short dialogue according to the situation given. Next, a pair of students act out the dialogue while the rest of the class takes notes. Then students report the conversation. Do the same with the other picture.

Yesterday Nicki and Rob, who are colleagues, spent their lunch hour together for the first time. What could they have been talking about?

Last week Pamela ran into an old school friend, Louise, while shopping. They had coffee together. What could they have been saying?

Consolidation 7

▶ *Phrasal Verbs*

keep at sth: continue working on sth
keep away (from): stay away
keep back: 1) stay back, 2) conceal
keep behind: make sb remain after others have left
keep sb/sth down: control
keep (oneself) from: 1) prevent from, 2) avoid
keep in with: remain friendly with
keep sb/sth off: (cause) to stay at a distance
keep on: continue
keep up with: stay level with (sb/sth)

● ● ● ● ● ● ● ● ● ● ● ● ●

let sth down: lengthen a garment
let sb down: disappoint
let sb off: not to punish
let on: reveal a secret
let out: make (a garment) looser, larger etc
let up: lessen, stop gradually

172 *Fill in the correct particle(s).*

1 She hired an assistant because she couldn't keep ...*up with*... the work.
2 The firefighter told us to keep .... from the burning building.
3 It's a good idea to keep .... John as he might be helpful to you later.
4 He's going to keep .... taking his driving test until he passes.
5 He put up a "No Trespassing" sign to keep walkers .... his land.
6 Tell me the whole story; don't keep anything ..... .
7 The judge let the boys .... with a warning.
8 When she put on weight she had to let ...... all her clothes.
9 It was raining hard earlier but it's letting ...... now.
10 John didn't let .... that Jim had broken the window.
11 This skirt is rather short. You'd better let it ....
12 I thought I could trust Sam, but he let me ....

173 *Look at Appendix 1, then fill in the correct preposition.*

1 There was a long queue ...*at*... the bus stop.
2 We have to win this election .... all costs.
3 His gambling habit left him seriously .... debt.
4 She left the oven on all day .... accident.
5 Many Asian countries, India .... instance, use English as a second language.
6 My pen pal and I have a lot .... common.
7 The officer was .... charge of 20 men.
8 .... all accounts, he's a very capable diplomat.
9 .... the beginning of the play the hero sees the heroine for the first time.
10 I thought he was honest .... the beginning, but I was wrong.
11 I don't like being taken .... granted!
12 By the end of the film the viewers were .... tears.
13 Dr Milton discovered the vaccine .... chance.
14 Please don't change all your plans just .... my sake.
15 Read the text .... detail, then answer the questions.
16 The scandal has been .... the news for weeks now.
17 We can offer you a 10% discount if you pay .... cash.
18 Payment can be made .... cheque or with a credit card.
19 Martha was .... a loss to explain why she'd been sacked.
20 There's a beautiful cottage .... sale in our village.
21 You're .... a good mood today! Have you had some good news?
22 Your order will be sent ...... post within 3 days.
23 There's a restaurant .... the top of the Eiffel Tower.
24 The books were piled one .... top of the other.
25 We regret that the lift is not .... use today.
26 I'm sorry. I took your jacket .... mistake this morning.
27 The judges announced their decision .... the end of the competition.
28 We were worried at first but .... the end everything went well.
29 Let's go out to dinner .... a change.
30 The offices are .... 77 Oxford St.
31 He lives .... the suburbs and commutes to the city every day.
32 The mirror lay .... pieces on the floor.

174 *Complete the sentences using the words in bold. Use two to five words.*

1 How long will it take you to build the shelves?
building   When ...*will you finish building*... the shelves?
2 Perhaps she got caught in traffic.
have   She .... in traffic.

3 The management won't let passengers smoke on the train.

are Passengers .... on the train.

4 "Why is he so secretive?" she asked herself.

was She .... so secretive.

5 People say he is very clever.

be He .... very clever.

6 She is proud of her beautiful house.

pride She .... beautiful house.

7 We couldn't sleep at night as the air conditioning was faulty.

difficult The faulty air conditioning .... to sleep at night.

8 "You've caused a lot of pain to my family," she said to him.

causing She .... a lot of pain to her family.

9 She is scared to be alone in the house at night.

afraid She .... in the house at night.

10 She won't tolerate his rudeness any longer.

put She won't .... any longer.

11 It's likely that they will go to the party.

are They .... the party.

12 You will be collected from your hotel at 8.00 by taxi.

call A taxi .... at your hotel at 8.00.

175 *For questions 1 - 15, read the text below and think of the word which best fits each space. There's an example at the beginning (0).*

World Population

By 1993, **(0)** ...*the*... world's human population had reached 5.5 thousand million and, **(1)** .... the growth has slowed **(2)** .... in recent years, it will be many decades **(3)** .... it stops. The reason **(4)** .... this growth is causing so **(5)** .... concern is that we cannot keep up

(6) .... the corresponding increase **(7)** .... demand for food, water, healthcare, jobs, education and housing. It also increases the likelihood of damage **(8)** .... the environment. Much of the growth has been in the poorer countries of the world, but overpopulation is also a problem for some rich countries, including Britain. **(9)** .... a population of approximately 58 million, Britain has 233 inhabitants **(10)** .... square kilometre. Furthermore, it is estimated that the **(11)** .... of people in the country will have increased to 62 million by 2031, at **(12)** .... time it will start to decline again. Populations not **(13)** .... increase because of higher birth rates, but also because of people moving from poor to rich countries, and from the countryside to the towns. In **(14)** ...., the latter cause is greater **(15)** .... general population growth and is creating many problems in the towns and cities, especially in poorer parts of the world.

176 *Fill in the following collocation grid .*

	a bank	a purse	time	a house	a person	an office	a car	a shop
rob	✔							
burgle								
steal								

177 *Read the text carefully. Some of the lines are correct and some have a word which should not be there. If a line is correct, put a tick (✔) in the space provided. If a line has a word which should not be there, write it in the space provided.*

Letter of apology

0	Thank you for your letter of 25th March informing	**0** ✔
00	us of the faulty equipment we were sent you.	**00** were
1	We would like to express about our deep regret	**1**
2	for the error, together with an explanation of it what	**2**
3	happened. There was a mix-up with the orders at the	**3**
4	manufacturing plant and they sent us the wrong	**4**
5	equipment already packaged and sealed. Our clerk he failed	**5**
6	to check the equipment inside and much carelessly	**6**
7	sent on the box to you. We assure you of the actual	**7**
8	equipment is not faulty but so simply the wrong	**8**
9	model. We would like for you to accept our	**9**
10	sincere apologies for the incident and we promise that	**10**
11	this will not to happen again. Please find	**11**
12	enclosed a cheque for all the shipping and	**12**
13	transportation costs as well as and a cheque	**13**
14	for £200 for an inconvenience caused. We hope	**14**
15	you will continue to do the business with us in the future.	**15**

178 *For questions 1 - 10, read the text below. Use the word given in capitals at the end of each line to form a word that fits in the space in the same line. Write your word in the answer boxes provided.*

Hawaii

The Hawaiian islands **(0)** .... are a tropical paradise. — **REAL** — **0** really

Palm trees, **(1)** .... views and breathtaking sunsets — **SCENE** — **1**

add up to many people's ideal holiday. At the — **2**

(2) .... resort of Waikiki you'll find a wide — **FAME** — **3**

(3) .... of restaurants, bars and nightclubs, with — **VARY**

prices ranging from **(4)** .... reasonable — **FAIR** — **4**

to very **(5)** .... . By day the beaches are buzzing — **EXPENSE** — **5**

with **(6)** .... and, as the sun sets, nightlife of every — **ACTIVE** — **6**

(7) .... can be experienced. If you're not keen on — **DESCRIBE** — **7**

busy beaches, then there's the **(8)** .... of taking — **POSSIBLE** — **8**

one of the many excursions around the islands or — **9**

even snorkelling in the **(9)** .... bays. The final — **FASCINATE**

(10) .... on how you spend your time is yours, — **DECIDE** — **10**

but few people ever regret going there.

Conditionals/Wishes/Unreal Past

	If-clause (hypothesis)	Main clause (result clause)	Use
Type 1 real present	**If + any present form (Present S., Present Cont. or Present Perfect)**	**Future/Imperative can/may/might/must/should + bare inf/Present Simple**	**true or likely to happen in the present or future**
	*If the weather **is** nice, we **will go** on an excursion.* *If you **have done** your homework, you **can watch** TV.* *If you **have** a headache, **take** an aspirin.*		
Type 2 unreal present	**If + Past Simple or Past Continuous**	**would/could/might + bare infinitive**	**untrue in the present; also used to give advice**
	*If I **were** you, I **wouldn't speak** to him again. (advice)* *If he **didn't eat** so many sweets, he **wouldn't have** a problem with his teeth.* *(but he eats a lot of sweets - untrue in the present)*		
Type 3 unreal past	**If + Past Perfect or Past Perfect Continuous**	**would/could/might + have + past participle**	**imaginary situation contrary to facts in the past; also used to express regrets or criticism**
	*If she **had known** how to use the mixer, she **wouldn't have broken** it.*		

Conditionals

- **When the if-clause precedes the result clause, we separate the two clauses with a comma.** *If he had been more careful, he wouldn't have caused the accident. but: He wouldn't have caused the accident if he had been more careful. (no comma)*
- **Conditionals are usually introduced by** if. **Other expressions are:** unless **(=if not),** providing, provided (that), as long as, in case, on condition (that), but for + -ing form/noun, otherwise, or else, what if, supposing, even if, only if. *Unless you work more efficiently, you'll be fired. I will do it only if you promise not to tell anyone.*
- **After "if" we normally use** were **instead of** was **for all persons in conditionals type 2 in formal English.** *If I were/was you, I would tell her everything.*
- **We do not normally use** will, would **or** should **in if-clauses.** *If you want this, you can have it. (not: if you will want.)* **However,** will, would **or** should **can be used in if-clauses to make a** request **or express** annoyance, doubt/uncertainty **or** insistence. *If he should come, show him in. (doubt/uncertainty - I doubt that he will come ...) If you will/would be more patient, I'll be with you in a minute. (request - Will you please be more patient?)*

179 Put the verbs in brackets into the correct tense, then identify the types of conditionals.

1 If you ...*don't put up*... (not/put up) this shelf, you won't have anywhere to put your books. *(1st type)*
2 If he .... (change) jobs, he would be a lot happier.
3 If I were you, I .... (tell) her how you feel.
4 If you continue to shout so loudly, you .... (wake up) the baby.
5 Even if he .... (ask) them, they wouldn't have agreed to come.
6 Unless you .... (feel) any better, you can take the rest of the day off.
7 If she .... (not/threaten) him, he wouldn't have left.
8 I .... (not/trust) him if I were you.
9 If you're patient for a few minutes, I .... (be able) to finish this.
10 He .... (not/go) with her if he had known she would behave so irresponsibly.

11 I wouldn't have been able to do it unless she .... (help) me.
12 Sometimes if you .... (take) a chance, it pays off.
13 If he .... (wake up) earlier, he wouldn't have been late for work.
14 If they will go on making so much noise, I .... (have to) punish them.
15 If we .... (intend) to spend the day in London, we would have bought a day pass.
16 Keep your voice down in case he .... (overhear) us.
17 If she .... (be) more experienced, she would be more likely to get the job.
18 If the food .... (not/be) so bad, we wouldn't have complained.
19 Sales will increase provided that the advertising campaign .... (be) successful.
20 If you .... (spend) less on clothes, you would be able to save some money.

180 Rewrite the following as conditional sentences.

1 You need to go to Egypt to see the Sphinx.
   If ...*you go to Egypt, you can see the Sphinx.* ...
2 John didn't leave early so he didn't get there on time.
   If ....
3 She used factor 12 suntan lotion as she gets sunburnt easily. If ....
4 The fax machine is broken so I'll have to send it by post. If ....
5 Calling her might make her feel better.
   If ....
6 There'll be an election if the president resigns.
   Providing ....
7 More tickets need to be sold, otherwise the concert will be cancelled.
   If ....
8 You'll have trouble selling your house if you're not prepared to accept a lower offer.
   Unless ....
9 He cancelled his trip because he had run out of money.
   If ....
10 Tom didn't wear a coat and caught a cold.
   If ....
11 You need to study to pass this exam.
   Unless ....
12 You really ought to go somewhere sunnier to get a suntan.
   Unless ....

181 Complete the text by putting the verbs in brackets into the correct tense.

If I were world leader, I 1) ...*would try*... (try) to stop the destruction of the earth and I 2) .... (make) the world a better place for all people. If the world's problems had been tackled sooner, the quality of life 3) .... (improve) long ago. First of all, I would try to bring about peace in the world. As long as there is fighting between nations, millions of people 4) .... (continue) to suffer and die. If wars continue, children 5) .... (be left) without parents and 6) .... (grow up) in a world of misery and fear. But as long as people disagree over land and possessions, the fighting 7) .... (go on). Therefore, I would ensure that all people were treated as equals and given the same opportunities in life. It would also help if all countries 8) .... (stop) producing arms so there would no longer be the weapons with which to fight. In addition, I would introduce laws to reduce pollution. If pollution levels had been controlled earlier, life 9) .... (not/become) so unbearable. If I 10) .... (have) the power, I would ban all cars from city centres and increase public transport. If there were more trees, the air we breathe 11) .... (be) cleaner. Unless measures are taken soon, it 12) .... (be) too late both for ourselves and our children.

8 Conditionals / Wishes / Unreal Past

182 *Rephrase the following in as many ways as possible using the words from the list below.*

**only if, otherwise, as long as, unless, providing,
on condition that, if**

1 Should you go to Rome, you must see the
   Colosseum.
2 You can swim but there must be an adult with you.
3 Drive carefully so that you won't have an accident.
4 He will get a bonus if productivity increases.
5 I'll lend you the money, but you must pay me back
   soon.

Omission of "if"

If can be omitted in if-clauses. In this case **should**, **were** and **had** (Past Perfect) come before the
subject. ***If he should*** win the race, he'll be very happy. ➡ ***Should he win*** the race, he'll be very happy.
If I were you, I wouldn't tell him. ➡ ***Were I*** you, I wouldn't tell him.
If I had known the truth, I'd have called the police. ➡ ***Had I known*** the truth, I'd have called the police.

---

183 *Rewrite the following sentences omitting "if".*

1 If I were you, I would think twice before accepting his offer.
   ...*Were I you, I would think twice before accepting his offer.*
2 If you had brought more money with you, we could have gone on holiday.
   ....
3 If I were you, I'd leave an hour earlier to be sure of getting there on time.
   ....
4 If you get through to the theatre, could you reserve four tickets for tonight's performance?
   ....
5 If you had paid the telephone bill on time, your phone wouldn't have been cut off.
   ....

Mixed Conditionals

All types of conditionals can be mixed. Any tense combination is possible if the context permits it.

	If-clause	Main clause	
Type 2	If they **were working** all day, (They were working all day	they **will be** tired now. so they are tired now.)	**Type 1**
Type 2	If I **were** you, (You are not me) If he **were** a better driver, (He is not a good driver	I **would have accepted** the job. so you didn't accept the job.) he **wouldn't have crashed** the car. so he crashed the car.)	**Type 3**
Type 3	If she **had finished** earlier, (She didn't finish earlier	she **would be going** to the party tonight. so she isn't going to the party.)	**Type 2**

---

184 *Rewrite the following as mixed conditional sentences as in the example:*

1 He is not an honest person so he didn't tell the truth.
   ...*If he were an honest person, he would have told the truth.*
2 They were awake all night so they are tired now.
   ....

3 You didn't tell me earlier so we are not going to the cinema tonight.

....

4 She didn't cancel the milk so the milkman keeps delivering it.

....

5 The ship left Plymouth yesterday so it will be in Spain now.

....

6 They were painting the house all day so they are covered in paint now.

....

7 She didn't do her homework so she's in trouble with her teacher.

....

8 She is so disorganised that she missed the deadline.

....

9 The children were playing in the garden all day so they are very dirty now.

....

10 He doesn't take his job seriously so he wasn't promoted.

....

185 *Complete the following sentences with an appropriate conditional clause.*

1 Should you go to London, you ...*must visit the Houses of Parliament.* ...
2 If he doesn't practise more, he ....
3 Unless you get permission, ...
4 Only if we ban the hunting of whales ....
5 If I could afford it, ...
6 If you had booked a table in the restaurant, ...
7 Should you meet George, ...
8 Were she in my shoes, ...
9 The fire wouldn't have started if ....
10 But for his money, she ....
11 Had you followed my advice, ...
12 Only if we stop cutting down trees ....
13 Were she more sincere, ...
14 If you had watered the plants, ...

186 *Complete the sentences using the words in bold. Use two to five words.*

1 I would have lent you my car but I didn't know you needed to borrow it.
   had   If ...*I had known you*.. needed to borrow my car, I would have lent it to you.
2 As long as you are very careful, you can use my CD player.
   provided   You can use my CD player .... very careful.
3 If there isn't an interpreter at the conference, she won't be able to understand the speakers.
   unless   She won't be able to understand the speakers .... at the conference.

4 He didn't get the job because he was late for the interview.
   would   If he hadn't been late for the interview, he .... job.

5 I only learnt to drive because you taught me.
   never   I .... drive if you hadn't taught me.

6 You'd better see a doctor.
   were   If .... see a doctor.

7 Tim will be able to operate the machine but somebody must show him how.
   only   Tim will be able to operate the machine .... how.

8 She didn't take an umbrella so she got completely soaked.
   have   If she had taken an umbrella, she .... soaked.

9 I will buy a new car but I must save enough money first.
   save   Provided .... first, I will buy a new car.

10 She broke her leg so she couldn't go skiing.
   broken   If .... leg, she could have gone skiing.

11 Kay can't be at home, otherwise she would have answered the phone.
   would   If Kay .... have answered the phone.

12 I would be grateful to receive any information you may have.
   could   I would be grateful .... any information you may have.

13 Karen can make the pie but she must have the recipe.
   long   Karen can make the pie .... the recipe.

14 If you see Miles, can you ask him to contact me immediately?
   see   Should .... ask him to contact me immediately?

15 Chris wants to phone his boss but he hasn't got the number.
   would   If Chris .... phone his boss.

Wishes

	Form	Use
I wish (if only) **(wish/regret about the present)**	**+ Past tense**	**wish/regret about a present situation we want to be different**
*I wish we **were** in Paris now. (It's a pity we aren't.)*		
I wish (if only) **(wish/regret about the present)**	**+ could + bare infinitive**	**wish/regret in the present concerning lack of ability**
*I wish I **could** swim. (but I can't)*		
I wish (if only) **(regret about the past)**	**+ Past Perfect**	**regret that something happened or didn't happen in the past**
*I wish you **had told** me earlier. (but you didn't)*		
I wish (if only) **(impossible wish for a future change)**	**+ subject + would + bare inf** (a. "wish" and "would" should have a different subject. We never say: ~~I wish I would, He wishes he would~~ etc b. wish + inanimate subject + would is used to express the speaker's lack of hope or disappointment	**wish for a future change unlikely to happen or wish to express dissatisfaction; polite request implying dissatisfaction or lack of hope**

*I wish he **would stop** smoking. (But I don't think he will - wish for a future change unlikely to happen.)*
*I wish students **would pay** more attention. (dissatisfaction)*
*I wish the wind **would stop** blowing. (But I'm afraid it won't stop blowing - wish implying disappointment)*
*I wish you **would be** more careful. (Please, be more careful - request implying lack of hope)*

● After **I wish** we can use **were** instead of **was** in all persons. *I wish she **were**/**was** more patient.*

187 **Put the verbs in brackets into the correct tense.**

Dear Mum,

I feel really unhappy! I wish I 1) ...*hadn't taken*... (not/take) this job. If only I 2) .... (give) it more thought before I made the decision to come here. I wish the people here 3) .... (be) more friendly - that would make it much better. If only I 4) .... (have) longer breaks. Looking at a computer screen all day is tiring and sometimes I find myself wishing it 5) .... (explode)! I wish my boss 6) .... (give) me something different to do. I wish there 7) .... (be) someone here I could talk to but I haven't made any friends. If only I 8) .... (make) some, but it's very difficult. I wish you 9) .... (live) nearer to me! Please write. I miss you!

Love,
Jenny

188 *Write sentences as in the example:*

1   You felt sick and you missed your friend's birthday party.
    .*I wish I hadn't felt sick. If I hadn't felt sick, I wouldn't have missed my friend's birthday party.*
2   You got up late and you missed the train.
    ....
3   You weren't offered the job because you weren't qualified.
    ....
4   You're not a senior staff member so you can't use the car park.
    ....
5   You didn't go to the meeting so you didn't hear about the safety inspection.
    ....
6   You want to go away for the weekend but you've got lots of homework.
    ....
7   You want a pet but you're allergic to animals.
    ....
8   You damaged the video because you didn't know how to connect it.
    ....
9   You like chocolate but you're on a diet.
    ....
10 You enjoy playing tennis but you have twisted your ankle.
    ....

189 *Complete the sentences using the words in bold. Use two to five words.*

1   It's a pity I can't go to the beach today, but I have to stay at home and study.
    could   I wish ...*I could go to the beach* ... today, but I have to stay at home and study.
2   If it weren't raining, we could go on a picnic.
    stop   I wish .... so we could go on a picnic.
3   It's a shame we didn't see the exhibition.
    had   We wish .... the exhibition.
4   George needs a new car but he can't afford to buy one.
    could   George wishes .... a new car.
5   It's a pity Jenny wasn't invited to the party.
    been   Jenny wishes .... to the party.
6   I've been offered a job in Paris but I can't speak French.
    speak   I wish ...., because I've been offered a job in Paris.

7 George never arrives on time when we arrange to go out.
only If .... on time when we arrange to go out.
8 I would really like to be lying on the beach now.
were I .... on the beach now.

190 *Put the verbs in brackets into the appropriate form.*

Mary was telling Julie about her planned trip to a tropical island. It sounded wonderful. "If I were you, I **1)** ...*would be*... (be) so excited," Julie said. "I am," replied Mary," but I wish you **2)** .... (come) with me. We **3)** .... (have) such fun!" "I know. If only I **4)** .... (know) earlier, I **5)** .... (not/spend) all my money on redecorating the kitchen. Anyway, what clothes are you planning to take with you?" "Well, I'm hoping to buy some new ones. If you **6)** .... (finish) work early today, we **7)** .... (go) shopping in town." "If I **8)** .... (be) you, I'd make sure I took light clothes and lots of insect repellent. What **9)** .... (you/do) when you get there?" "Sunbathe, swim and go for long walks on the beach." "Make sure you **10)** .... (send) me a postcard and take lots of pictures." "Don't worry, I will."

191 *Rewrite the letter using wishes or if-clauses as in the example:*

Dear Christine,

I just had to drop you a line and let you know what a terrible day I've had today.
Well, first of all, I thought I would let the canaries out of their cage to fly around for a while. What a mistake! They flew straight out of the open window and I haven't seen them since!
Then I decided to surprise my husband by putting up some new bookshelves in the lounge. Oh dear! I drilled a hole straight into the wiring in the wall and cut off the whole street's electricity supply. What a disaster! The neighbours are furious with me.
On top of that, when my husband came home from work he tripped over the bucket I had left in the middle of the floor. Unfortunately, he hurt his ankle and he was angry with me. I shouldn't have left the bucket there.
Anyway, hopefully tomorrow will be better than today.

With love,
Elise

...I wish I hadn't had such a terrible day yesterday. ...

192 *Complete the following sentences.*

1 If only I had kept my appointment with the dentist yesterday, ...*I wouldn't have toothache now.*...
2 I wish I had paid my electricity bill, ...
3 If I were Prime Minister, I ....
4 If it rains tomorrow, ...
5 Pete wishes he had worked harder at school, ...
6 Sarah will go to the party if ....
7 If only I had more money, ...
8 Liz wishes she had got up earlier, ...
9 If only Jo hadn't locked her keys in the car, ...
10 If John gets a promotion at work, ...
11 If the government bans smoking in public areas, ...
12 If only I hadn't shouted at Julie, ...
13 If Jenny had locked the front door, ...
14 If you are late for a job interview, ...
15 If you have a headache, ...

Unreal Past

The Simple Past can be used to talk about imaginary, unreal or improbable situations in the present and the Past Perfect can be used to talk about imaginary, unreal or improbable situations in the past. This is called Unreal Past. Unreal Past is used as follows:

Past Simple	Past Perfect
● **Conditionals Type 2 (unreal in the present)** *If I were you, I wouldn't do that.*	● **Conditionals Type 3 (unreal in the past)** *If he had warned me, this wouldn't have happened.*
● **wish (present)** *I wish she were more cooperative.*	● **wish (past)** *If only I hadn't lost all my money last night.*
● **I'd rather/sooner sb ... (present)** *I'd rather you paid me today.*	● **I'd rather/sooner sb ... (past)** *I'd rather you had not told everyone.*
● **Suppose/Supposing** *Suppose your father caught you smoking, what would you do?*	● **Suppose/Supposing** *Suppose he had left before the boss came, what would have happened?*
● **as if/as though (untrue situation in the present)** *She behaves as if she were the Queen.*	● **as if/as though (untrue situation in the past)** *Soon after being introduced, they were talking to each other as if they had been friends for years.*
● **it's (about/high) time ...** *It's time you started work.*	

would rather = I'd prefer

● when the subject of **would rather** is also the subject of the following verb	**I'd rather +**	**Present bare infinitive** (present/future reference) **Perfect bare infinitive** (past reference)
	I'd rather play tennis. I'd rather not have gone out with him yesterday.	
● when the subject of **would rather** is different from the subject of the following verb	**I'd rather sb +**	**Past Simple** (present/future reference) **Past Perfect** (past reference)
	I'd rather you stopped smoking. *I'd rather you had mentioned that before.*	

● **prefer + gerund/noun + to + gerund/noun** (general). *I prefer (drinking) tea to (drinking) coffee.*
● **prefer + full infinitive + rather than + bare infinitive** (general preference)
I prefer to drink coffee rather than (drink) tea.
● **would prefer + full infinitive + rather than + bare infinitive** (specific preference)
I'd prefer to live in London rather than (live in) Swansea.
● **would rather + bare infinitive + than + bare infinitive.** *I'd rather fly to Munich than go there by car.*

had better = should

● **I had better + present bare inf (present/future reference)**
He had better consult a lawyer. (= He should consult a lawyer.)
● **It would have been better if + Past Perfect (past reference).** *It would have been better if you hadn't talked to James last night. (= You shouldn't have talked to James last night.)*

8 Conditionals / Wishes / Unreal Past

193 Put the verbs in brackets into the correct form.

1 Suppose they ...*had cancelled*... (cancel) the flight. How would you have got home?
2 We'd rather you .... (take out) separate holiday insurance.
3 I hate it when you speak to me as if I .... (be) a child.
4 She'd rather .... (not/show) him her passport.
5 It's high time he .... (face) up to his responsibilities.
6 If only I .... (not/leave) the window open!
7 If they .... (go) out less, they'd have more money.
8 Chris prefers .... (work) mornings rather than evenings.
9 Suppose Helen .... (invite) your ex-boyfriend, would you still go to the party?
10 I'd rather Sam .... (not/play) his music so loud.
11 Sylvia wishes she .... (have) long hair.
12 She had only lived there three months but she spoke the language as if she .... (live) there longer.
13 Tom's mother made him go to school although he would rather .... (stay) at home.
14 I feel a bit sick now. I wish I .... (eat) so much.
15 He much prefers .... (listen) to CDs to .... (go) to live concerts.
16 I'd prefer .... (ride) my bicycle to the shops rather than .... (take) the bus.
17 I'd rather .... (live) alone than .... (share) a flat with a stranger.
18 I prefer .... (talk) with friends rather than .... (watch) television.
19 If she .... (work) harder, she wouldn't have failed her exams.
20 You'd better .... (go) to bed as we have to be up early tomorrow.

194 Complete the sentences using the words in bold. Use two to five words.

1 Your mother's worried about you. You should phone her.
   better   You ...*had better phone*... your mother as she's worried about you.
2 Will you ever think about finding a flat of your own?
   time   It's .... about finding a flat of your own.
3 Look at how he lives - he thinks he's a millionaire.
   if   He lives .... a millionaire.
4 This summer, I would rather book a holiday in Monaco than Lyons.
   prefer   This summer, I .... a holiday in Monaco rather than Lyons.
5 Why didn't you tell me yourself that you were leaving?
   rather   I'd .... me yourself that you were leaving.
6 She wants to be more like her mother.
   wishes   She .... more like her mother.
7 I should have taken that job in Canada last year.
   only   If .... that job in Canada last year.
8 You should have checked the oil before you set out.
   better   It .... you had checked the oil before you set out.

195 Fill in the gaps with the appropriate auxiliary verb.

1 He hasn't got a yacht but he wishes he ...*had*... .
2 She can't afford a maid but she wishes she ....
3 I didn't pay attention in class but I wish I ....
4 He had his hair cut really short but now he wishes he ....
5 He's going to the dentist this afternoon but he wishes he ....
6 She made a terrible mistake but now she wishes she ....
7 They probably won't change their minds but I wish they ....
8 He always brings his dog to my house but I really wish he ....
9 I forgot to enclose the cheque but I wish I ....
10 He won't let me leave early but I wish he ....

196 *Put the verbs in brackets into the correct form.*

Dear Jenny,

Sorry I didn't answer your last letter. If I 1) ...**had realised**... (realised) how serious the situation was, I would have written to you straightaway. You obviously need my advice. I only wish I 2) .... (be) with you now to help you. I think it's about time you 3) .... (leave) your job and 4) .... (start) to look for a new one. If your boss 5) .... (insist) on treating you so unfairly, then you have very little choice. You say that you'd rather 6) .... (have) a job you hate than no job at all, but is that really true? If you 7) .... (be) worried about money, don't be. You can come home and live with your father and me for a while. I'd rather you 8) .... (live) nearer home anyway. Your old boss at the library, Mr Green, says you could have your old job back if you 9) .... (want) it. You could have been Head Librarian by now if you 10) .... (not/leave)! Anyway, I'll let you know if I 11) .... (hear) about any other suitable jobs. Take care and let me know if you 12) .... (make) any decisions.

Love,
Mum

197 *Complete the sentences using the words in bold. Use two to five words.*

1 I didn't pass my exams and now I can't go to university.
   wish   I ...*wish I had passed*.. my exams; then I could go to university.
2 I was about to buy the painting, when I realised it was a fake.
   if   I would have bought the painting .... it was a fake.
3 I didn't see the TV programme because I didn't know it was on.
   known   If .... the TV programme was on, I would have seen it.
4 I think you should go on holiday.
   were   If ...., I would go on holiday.
5 You shouldn't have told Sally my secret.
   told   I'd .... Sally my secret.
6 You'd think he was a politician.
   though   He behaves .... a politician.
7 You should be in bed now. It's late.
   went   It's .... to bed.
8 It would have been better if you had passed on the message.
   only   If .... the message.
9 If the teacher asked you to answer that question, what would you say?
   asked   Suppose .... to answer that question, what would you say?
10 It's a pity it's raining.
   stop   I .... raining.
11 She couldn't tell you because she didn't know.
   would   Had .... told you.
12 Why did I listen to John? He always tells lies.
   listened If .... to John. He always tells lies.
13 We should have left by now if we don't want to miss the bus.
   time   It's .... if we don't want to miss the bus.
14 I would have liked you to have informed my parents about my change of plan.
   rather   I .... my parents about my change of plan.
15 It would have been better if they had got the earlier train.
   only   If .... the earlier train.
16 You ought to have set a wedding date by now.
   time   It's .... a wedding date.

198 *Find the word which should not be in the sentence.*

1 Unless you not know the details, you can't reach a decision.
2 If they will finish this assignment on time, they'll be rewarded.
3 Even if he offered to make up for the damage, otherwise I wouldn't accept.
4 If were I had accepted the job, I would be earning a lot of money now.
5 If she were be me, she would have done exactly the same.
6 You won't be allowed to attend the reception unless you will receive an invitation.
7 I wish if they would stop criticising our efforts to change things.
8 I'll give them my new address in case they will want to forward my post.
9 If only he had been taken our advice.
10 As long as you will promise to behave yourself, you can stay overnight at your friend's.
11 I wish for Sarah would give up her dream of becoming an opera singer.
12 He looked as if that he hadn't slept for days.
13 It's time they had decided what they want to do.
14 She'd better to take a course in French before she moves to France.
15 I'd rather they had stayed at a hotel the next time they're in town.
16 John would rather to buy a new car than a second-hand one.
17 She would prefer to have invest the money rather than spend it.
18 Unless we will have the car repaired, we won't be able to make our journey.
19 Don't you wish you were being someone famous?
20 Had if I waited longer, I would have seen the parade.

1	*not*
2	
3	
4	
5	
6	
7	
8	
9	
10	
11	
12	
13	
14	
15	
16	
17	
18	
19	
20	

Oral Development 12

Students look at the pictures below then, in turns, make sentences using conditionals or wishes to say what the man is thinking.

S1: *I wish the wind would change direction.*
S2: *If the wind changes direction, we'll avoid the rocks.   etc*

Consolidation 8

Phrasal Verbs

look after: take care of
look down on: despise (opp. **look up to**)
look for: search for
look forward to: anticipate
look into: investigate
look on: 1) be a spectator, 2) regard; consider
look out (for): watch out
look over: inspect carefully
look through: study carefully (sth written)
look up: 1) look for an address, name, etc in the relevant book or list, 2) visit sb after a lapse of time (specially sb living at some distance)

● ● ● ● ● ● ● ● ● ● ● ● ●

make for: move quickly towards
make up: 1) invent (story, poem etc), 2) make an amount complete, 3) compose, 4) reconcile, 5) prepare (by mixing)
make oneself up: put cosmetics on
make up for: compensate for
make out: 1) complete; fill in, 2) distinguish, 3) understand

199 *Fill in the correct particle(s).*

1 I've been looking ...*for*... my diamond ring everywhere.
2 The hotel manager will look .... your complaint.
3 I must look .... this essay before I hand it in tomorrow.
4 Now that he's rich, he looks .... all his friends who still work at the factory.
5 He looks .... his father who he considers to be a hero.
6 Look .... for sharks when you go swimming.
7 Look .... her phone number in the directory if you can't remember it.
8 John looks .... the children while Mary goes to work.
9 I'm sure he made the whole story ....
10 I'll make .... forgetting our anniversary.
11 We decided to make .... the nearest beach.
12 He made .... the cheque to me personally.
13 Your writing is so bad, I can't make .... what you've written.
14 She spends hours making herself .... every morning.

200 *Complete the sentences using the words in bold. Use two to five words.*

1 Although his mother warned him, the boy continued to play in the road.
   despite The boy continued to play in the road ...*despite being/having been warned by*.. his mother.
2 Their garden is much bigger than ours.
   nearly Our garden is .... theirs.
3 He could read before he was three years old.
   able He .... before he was three years old.
4 She hired a professional gardener to prune the trees.
   had She .... a professional gardener.
5 I won't go with you unless you let me pay my own way.
   if I won't go with you .... me pay my own way.
6 I regret ever telling her about my plans.
   wish I .... her about my plans.
7 He can't tolerate his neighbours' behaviour much longer.
   put He .... his neighbours' behaviour much longer.
8 She started to ride when she was ten years old.
   been She .... she was ten years old.
9 "You really shouldn't have said that to her," he said to me.
   criticised He .... that to her.
10 They hired him because of his excellent qualifications.
   due They hired him .... had excellent qualifications.
11 He was late every day so he lost his job.
   result He was late every day .... lost his job.
12 In general, I'd much rather walk than ride a bike.
   walking In general, I .... a bike.
13 He hasn't signed the contract yet.
   still The contract .... signed.

Consolidation 8

201

Look at Appendix 1, then fill in the missing preposition(s).

1 The contents of the parcel were broken ...*on*... arrival.
2 The situation is getting .... control; we must take action immediately.
3 The policeman took his family to the theatre as he was .... duty.
4 We heard about the plane crash .... the news.
5 He hasn't played tennis for a while so he's .... practice.
6 The new safety measures are still .... discussion.
7 You're supposed to avoid eating sweets as you're .... a diet.
8 The balloon landed .... a farm quite unexpectedly.
9 The parachutist landed .... a field.
10 You are .... arrest; you have the right to call your lawyer.
11 All medicines must be kept .... reach of children.
12 The factory is .... fire; vacate the area!
13 My favourite china teapot smashed .... pieces on the floor.
14 Someone planted a bomb .... a platform in Victoria Station.
15 Typewriters are going .... use as they're being replaced by computers.
16 The politician would only agree to speak to me .... the record.
17 Let's go .... a cruise around the Mediterranean.
18 Drinking alcohol is .... the law in many countries.
19 I'm sure the bus will arrive .... long.
20 This must be posted .... delay!
21 I was .... the impression he was abroad.
22 He doesn't like to carry cash, so he buys everything .... credit.
23 This newspaper is two weeks .... date!
24 I'm writing .... regard to your recent application.
25 .... our surprise, he won the competition.
26 They could recite the entire play .... memory.
27 Hurry up please. We're a bit .... schedule.
28 .... second thoughts, I'd rather not go out tonight.

202

Put the verbs in brackets into the correct tense.

If you 1) ...*want*... (want) to see the highest waterfall in the world, you have to go to Venezuela. There, you 2) .... (find) the Angel Falls - a spectacular sight. We 3) .... (go) there last year and we were very impressed. We 4) .... (walk) in the countryside for about an hour when suddenly we 5) .... (hear) the sound of water. As we 6) .... (approach) the waterfall, we 7) .... (cannot) believe how loud the water was. It was the first time we 8) .... (ever/see) a waterfall and if we had known how amazing it was, we 9) .... (take) a video camera with us. We hope we 10) .... (return) one day to see this wonder of nature again.

203

Fill in the correct form of the infinitive or the -ing form.

In the past decade academics have been involved in 1) ...*investigating*... (investigate) differences between men and women. Researchers have been especially interested in 2) .... (discover) what women can 3) .... (do) better than men. As far as language is concerned, studies show that girls begin 4) .... (talk) before boys and are capable of 5) .... (produce) more varied and sophisticated sentences. In addition to 6) .... (have) a better command of the language, women also appear 7) .... (have) better social skills and are more likely 8) .... (be) complimentary than men. Another area that has been investigated is how men and women lead. Women try 9) .... (share) power and make their employees 10) .... (feel) more worthwhile. Men, on the other hand, like 11) .... (demonstrate) their authority more formally and seem 12) .... (care) more about hierarchy. However, it is worth 13) .... (remember) that study results reflect averages, and there will always be exceptions.

204 *For questions 1 - 15, read the text below and decide which word A, B, C or D best fits each space. Mark your answers in the answer boxes provided.*

"Diamonds are Forever"

It has been **(0)** .... practice in recent years for a man to buy his fiancée a diamond to **(1)** .... their engagement. Diamond rings have been bought by the aristocracy since the **(2)** .... of the century, but until the 1950's they were considered an expensive and **(3)** .... accessory for a working-class wedding. **(4)** ...., it was around this time that De Beers, the biggest producers of diamonds in the world, decided that they needed to **(5)** .... their market. As a **(6)** .... they launched an advertising campaign which was **(7)** .... at couples with a slightly smaller budget. It was one of the most successful campaigns in the company's **(8)** .... For this campaign, the advertisers wanted to sell the idea that, **(9)** .... diamonds are an expensive luxury, they are also the **(10)** .... of everlasting love. Thus a diamond engagement ring was supposed to signify the husband's life-long **(11)** .... to his wife. The idea was expressed in the **(12)** .... which was first conceived by De Beers' advertisers: "Diamonds are Forever". This **(13)** .... to be highly profitable because the public bought the idea and **(14)** .... bought diamond rings by the thousands. De Beers, who now have almost total **(15)** .... over diamond production worldwide, have never looked back.

	A	B	C	D
0	usual	common	average	regular
1	prove	notice	show	mark
2	beginning	first	origin	front
3	unwanted	unnecessary	invaluable	needless
4	Although	However	While	When
5	stretch	grow	continue	extend
6	fact	result	conclusion	reaction
7	aimed	pointed	guided	led
8	history	past	story	tale
9	even	but	although	nevertheless
10	post	signal	fact	symbol
11	devotion	trust	relationship	faith
12	word	phrase	part	remark
13	turned	proved	ended	confirmed
14	after	though	consequently	following
15	force	check	control	strength

Answer 0: B

Consolidation 8

205

Read the text carefully. Some of the lines are correct and some have a word which should not be there. If a line is correct, put a tick (✔) in the space provided. If a line has a word which should not be there, write it in the space provided.

In-Flight Video Magic

0	British Airways calls itself the world's favourite	**0**	✔
00	airline. Whether this is true or if not, they are	**00**	*if*
1	planning a new entertainment, information and	**1**	
2	communication services for the near future.	**2**	
3	On long flights they will intend to give people	**3**	
4	control over to personal video screens. Travellers will be	**4**	
5	able to select the videos of which their choice	**5**	
6	from a list of several dozen. As well as to being able	**6**	
7	to plug into a wide variety of music, passengers	**7**	
8	will have a large number of multilingual games	**8**	
9	at their hand, from the latest teenage crazes to	**9**	
10	intellectual favourites, like as chess. In addition,	**10**	
11	travellers will be able to get information on flight	**11**	
12	connections, the weather and their of current flight's	**12**	
13	progress. They will also be able to make up phone	**13**	
14	calls anywhere in all the world and arrange	**14**	
15	themselves business or social appointments.	**15**	

206

For questions 1 - 10, read the text below. Use the word given in capitals at the end of each line to form a word that fits in the space in the same line. Write your word in the answer boxes provided.

Letters

A really **(0)** .... thing when you're alone abroad and surrounded by **(1)** .... is to receive a letter from a friend or **(2)** .... from home. It's always **(3)** .... to know what people are up to. But in responding, the hardest thing is to **(4)** .... a whole new way of life and **(5)** .... of ideas, not to mention new friends and unfamiliar **(6)** .... . Those receiving your letters can never have a full **(7)** .... of your new job and your **(8)** .... routine; but you can make the picture clearer by providing a **(9)** .... of these, adding a **(10)** .... of unexpected details.

COMFORT	**0**	*comforting*
STRANGE	**1**	
RELATE	**2**	
INTEREST	**3**	
SUMMARY	**4**	
COLLECT	**5**	
SURROUND	**6**	
UNDERSTAND	**7**	
DAY	**8**	
DESCRIBE	**9**	
VARY	**10**	

Practice test  4

Part 1

For questions 1 - 15, read the text below and decide which word A, B, C or D best fits each space. Mark your answers in the answer boxes provided.

Diaries

A diary is a daily **(0)** ..... of events, thoughts and feelings **(1)** ..... either for the writer's own personal satisfaction or for **(2)** ..... use. Most diarists **(3)** ..... expect nor necessarily want anyone else to read what they have written, so, on the **(4)** ..... only they and perhaps their relatives and **(5)** ..... friends ever see their writings. On the other hand, some people do write with the **(6)** ..... of informing and entertaining the public, although often diaries are only **(7)** ..... and published after the author's death.
One example of a diarist who never expected his diary to be **(8)** ..... by the public was Samuel Pepys, who lived in the 17th century. His diary is the most impressive **(9)** ..... the English language, recording some of the greatest **(10)** ..... in English history, yet it is also the story of a **(11)** .... lovable man's life. Another example is that of Anne Frank, a young Jewish girl who was in **(12)** .... from the Nazis in Amsterdam **(13)** ..... the Second World War. It is a unique and moving **(14)** ..... of her unbearable life and the courage she needed to **(15)** ..... it.

0	**A** memorandum	**B** record	**C** narration	**D** shorthand
1	**A** possessed	**B** held	**C** kept	**D** stocked
2	**A** later	**B** latter	**C** late	**D** then
3	**A** not	**B** either	**C** none	**D** neither
4	**A** all	**B** general	**C** whole	**D** everything
5	**A** narrow	**B** close	**C** near	**D** tight
6	**A** reason	**B** fact	**C** intention	**D** function
7	**A** explored	**B** excavated	**C** discovered	**D** invented
8	**A** seen	**B** revealed	**C** shown	**D** exhibited
9	**A** to	**B** for	**C** of	**D** in
10	**A** stories	**B** facts	**C** events	**D** happenings
11	**A** most	**B** much	**C** many	**D** more
12	**A** save	**B** hiding	**C** search	**D** rescue
13	**A** through	**B** during	**C** over	**D** for
14	**A** file	**B** report	**C** account	**D** collection
15	**A** pass	**B** outlive	**C** suffer	**D** tolerate

Answer boxes:

	A	B	C	D
0		■		
1				
2				
3				
4				
5				
6				
7				
8				
9				
10				
11				
12				
13				
14				
15				

Part 2

For questions 16 - 30, read the text below and think of the word which best fits each space.
Use only one word in each space. Write your answers in the answer boxes provided.

BUYING A NEW BIKE

Until recently, few people went cycling, but **(0)** .... the last few years more bikes have **(16)** ....
.... sold in Britain **(17)** .... cars. Now approximately two million are bought each year, the majority of **(18)** .... are mountain bikes.

There are over 500 different models to choose **(19)** .... and the prices vary enormously. The
cheapest can be bought for under £200, **(20)** .... you will need over £4,000 for a bike at the top
end of the range. The reason **(21)** .... this difference is the quality of the frame. Bikes costing less
than £350 are not recommended **(22)** .... they are very heavy and therefore not much fun to ride.
Furthermore, they often break because they are not very **(23)** .... made. The more expensive
models are **(24)** .... lighter because they are made **(25)** .... metals like aluminium.

When buying a new bike it is best to go to a specialist bike shop **(26)** .... than a toy shop or
garage. One reason for this is that a specialist will make **(27)** .... that the bike fits you properly,
as a bike which is the wrong size can be **(28)** .... uncomfortable and dangerous.

To reduce the risks of injury, cyclists are advised to wear a helmet. **(29)** .... bikes travel at
slower speeds than motorbikes, you can still suffer serious injuries to the head **(30)** .... you fall off.

0	*during*	0
16		16
17		17
18		18
19		19
20		20
21		21
22		22
23		23
24		24
25		25
26		26
27		27
28		28
29		29
30		30

Part 3

For questions 31 - 40, complete the second sentence so that it has a similar meaning to the first sentence. Use the word given and other words to complete each sentence. You must use between two and five words. Do not change the word given. Write your answers in the answer boxes provided.

0 I'm sure they worked hard on the project.
have
They .... on the project.

| 0 | *must have worked hard* | 0 ▭ ▬ |

31 The new musical failed to impress the critics.
succeed
The new musical .... the critics.

| 31 | | 31 ▭ ▭ |

32 It's a good idea to keep your savings in the bank.
should
Your savings .... in the bank.

| 32 | | 32 ▭ ▭ |

33 The doctor told me to reduce the amount of fat I ate.
down
I was told .... the amount of fat I ate.

| 33 | | 33 ▭ ▭ |

34 Although she is rich, she doesn't spend much money on clothes.
being
She doesn't spend much money on clothes .... rich.

| 34 | | 34 ▭ ▭ |

35 Our house really needs to be redecorated.
had
It's about .... redecorated.

| 35 | | 35 ▭ ▭ |

36 After he lost his job, he couldn't pay the rent on time.
fell
After he lost his job, he .... rent.

| 36 | | 36 ▭ ▭ |

37 "Why don't you paint the doors blue?" said Martin.
painting
Martin .... blue.

| 37 | | 37 ▭ ▭ |

38 People say a strange creature lives in Loch Ness.
said
A strange creature .... in Loch Ness.

| 38 | | 38 ▭ ▭ |

39 I don't think we should go to a club tonight.
rather
I'd .... to a club tonight.

| 39 | | 39 ▭ ▭ |

40 He went to drama school in order to become an actor.
aim
He went to drama school .... an actor.

| 40 | | 40 ▭ ▭ |

For questions 41 - 55, read the text below and look carefully at each line. Some of the lines are correct and some have a word which should not be there. If a line is correct, put a tick (✔) by the number in the answer boxes provided. If a line has a word which should not be there, write the word in the answer boxes provided.

Women Drivers

0	For the years women drivers have traditionally	0	*the*
00	been seen as bad drivers. However, a survey	00	✔
41	carried out for the British television network, the	41	
42	BBC, seems to be tell a different story. Over	42	
43	three times like as many men as women confess to	43	
44	bad driving habits. According to of the survey, men	44	
45	are more likely to drive too close up to the car in	45	
46	front or read a map while they are being driving! More	46	
47	men they appear to drive when they are tired and in	47	
48	danger of falling asleep. Women stop at more red	48	
49	traffic lights and have fewer of serious accidents.	49	
50	Is this due to being traditional female characteristics	50	
51	such as gentleness compared with typical male characteristics	51	
52	such as aggression or a difference in the intelligence?	52	
53	According to the Royal Automobile Club,	53	
54	things change as men get more older. After the	54	
55	age of 30, so they tend to become safer!	55	

Part 5

For questions 56 - 65, read the text below. Use the word given in capitals at the end of each line to form a word that fits in the space in the same line. Write your word in the answer boxes provided.

Dolphins

Humans are destroying dolphins at an (0) .... rate. Long fishing nets called "Walls of Death" are mainly to blame. Since their (56) .... in the 1960's millions of dolphins, whales and seals have been (57) .... caught up in them and killed. Most caring people feel that this situation is (58) .... . It is known that dolphins are (59) .... creatures and killing them is both (60) .... and a foolish waste.
Now, the (61) .... of some charities to raise money for the (62) .... of dolphins means that this (63) .... may soon be stopped. One large charity (64) .... sells products such as T-shirts and jewellery and uses the profits to pay for their (65) .... .

ALARM	0	*alarming*
	56	
INTRODUCE	57	
ACCIDENT	58	
ACCEPTABLE	59	
INTELLIGENCE	60	
HUMANE	61	
EXIST	62	
CONSERVE	63	
DESTROY	64	
ORGANISE	65	
ACTIVE		

Pre - test 2

Choose the correct item.

1 I'll have James .... these figures.
  A to checking   **B** to check
  C check   **D** checking

2 She threatened .... the meeting.
  A to leave   **B** leave
  C to leaving   **D** leaving

3 He was made .... a fine.
  A pay   **B** paying
  C to pay   **D** to paying

4 We'd rather go camping than .... in a hotel.
  A staying   **B** stay
  C to stay   **D** to staying

5 If you had looked harder, you .... him at the station.
  A will see   **B** would see
  C see   **D** would have seen

6 It's time I .... my summer holiday.
  A will organise   **B** organise
  C have organised **D** organised

7 Unless she .... in the next ten minutes, we will have to go without her.
  A phones   **B** phoned
  C will have phoned **D** will phone

8 .... I look after the children for you?
  A Will   **B** Ought
  C Would   **D** Shall

9 I don't know when we ...... house.
  A will move   **B** had moved
  C move   **D** have moved

10 .... I've read the book three times, I still don't understand it.
  A Nevertheless   **B** Despite
  C However   **D** Although

11 I wish he .... give up his idea of becoming a rock star.
  A will   **B** would
  C had   **D** can

12 I prefer classical music .... popular music.
  A rather   **B** than
  C to   **D** from

13 Peter denied .... anything to do with the missing money.
  A having   **B** have
  C to have   **D** to have had

14 My luggage is twice as .... as yours.
  A heaviest   **B** heavier
  C more heavy   **D** heavy

15 I .... her to phone the office for me.
  A had   **B** made
  C got   **D** insisted

16 They .... him of lying in court.
  A denied   **B** accused
  C charged   **D** insisted

17 She gave me a .... belt for my birthday.
  A wonderful blue leather
  B leather blue wonderful
  C blue leather wonderful
  D leather wonderful blue

18 If I were a magician, I .... a peaceful world.
  A would have created **B** will create
  C create   **D** would create

19 I wish I .... better in last week's test.
  A had done   **B** would do
  C did   **D** will do

20 He .... a scholarship last month.
  A was offered   **B** is offered
  C has been offered **D** will be offered

21 Can't you do this .... quicker?
  A even   **B** any
  C much   **D** very

22 The teacher .... us to stand up.
  A spoke   **B** said
  C talked   **D** asked

23 She insisted on .... for everything.
  A to pay   **B** paying
  C to paying   **D** pay

24 She .... the silverware polished yesterday.
  A will have   **B** had
  C is having   **D** has

B *Fill in the gaps with the correct form of the verb in brackets.*

Many people wish they **1)** .... (have) a job that paid as well as Harold's, so if they heard him complain about it they way he does, they probably **2)** .... (not/have) much sympathy for him. "If only I **3)** .... (run) my own business," he says, "I **4)** .... (be) much happier. I wish the bank **5)** .... (give) me a loan when I asked for one last year. If they had done, I **6)** .... (be able to) start up my own company there and then." But, as everyone knows, if you **7)** .... (work) for yourself, you **8)** .... (have to) work very hard indeed, and there is no guarantee of success.

C *Put the verbs in brackets into the correct form.*

I wish I **1)** .... (can) play a musical instrument. If I **2)** .... (have) the choice, I **3)** .... (be) a pianist, and play in a jazz band. If only my parents **4)** .... (make) me take lessons when I was a child! When I asked my mother about this, she said: "We **5)** .... (buy) you a piano if you **6)** .... (ask) us, but you never mentioned it." How I wish I **7)** .... (say) something! Still, I suppose if I start saving up now, I **8)** .... (be able to) buy myself one in a couple of years.

D *Complete the sentences using the words in bold. Use two to five words.*

1 The steak was so tough that we couldn't eat it.
such It .... that we couldn't eat it.
2 You'd better not be late again.
were If I .... be late again.
3 "OK, I'll prepare lunch now," he said.
to He .... at once.
4 Emily and Kim have the same number of pencils.
as Emily .... Kim.
5 Julie is not as artistic as her mother.
less Julie .... her mother.
6 You must fasten your seatbelts securely before takeoff.
fastened Seatbelts .... before takeoff.
7 "Don't touch the iron; it's hot," he said.
warned He .... the iron because it was hot.
8 I haven't had a chocolate bar for two months.
time The .... a chocolate bar was two months ago.
9 The builders will have finished the repairs by Thursday.
been The repairs .... by Thursday.
10 As people get older, they become more forgetful.
the The .... forgetful they become.
11 I ate more than was necessary last night.
need I .... so much last night.
12 As long as you impress the interviewer, you may be offered the job.
provided You may be offered the job .... the interviewer.
13 That's the field we play football in.
where That's .... football.
14 Someone stole my bike last night.
had I .... last night.
15 Matthew is less friendly than Thomas.
so Matthew isn't .... Thomas.
16 You should have called them last night.
better It .... you had called them last night.
17 This is Sarah and she works for the BBC.
who This is Sarah .... the BBC.

18 Why did you insist that we should appoint Mr Vermont chairman?
make   Why .... Mr Vermont chairman?
19 She doesn't know much about sport but she acts like an expert.
though   She acts .... an expert on sport.
20 "Don't forget to reserve the tickets," she said to him.
reminded She .... the tickets.

E *Fill in the blanks with the correct particle(s).*

1 The manager will look .... your complaint.
2 She is a good friend; she never lets me ....
3 I can't make .... his handwriting.
4 My boss and I get .... really well.

5 She made .... a story to tell her children.
6 You shouldn't look .... poor people.
7 It took him three weeks to get .... the flu.
8 I was held .... for two hours by heavy traffic.

F *Fill in the blanks with the correct preposition(s).*

1 He paid for his shopping .... cash.
2 His lack of punctuality resulted .... his dismissal from work.
3 He was unaware .... the consequences.
4 Chris is very determined to succeed .... his profession.

5 Which one of the twins are you referring .....?
6 The relationship .... my father and me isn't good.
7 I found this silver brooch .... chance.
8 Keep the food .... reach of the dog or he'll eat it.

G *Correct the following sentences by taking out the inappropriate word.*

1 It took me twenty minutes to start over the car this morning.
2 The city turned out to be a very hot in the summer.
3 Frank seems that to be a very clever person.
4 Despite of being nervous, I managed to pass the interview.
5 He has a lots of good friends.
6 One of the most best things about summer is the weather.
7 Sarah is a famous and too highly respected songwriter.
8 My mother she works in a bank.
9 The new teacher seems like very kind and patient.
10 Unless he is not here by ten, we will leave without him.
11 He was not neither happy nor excited the day he won the lottery.
12 The people in general go on holiday once a year.

1	
2	
3	
4	
5	
6	
7	
8	
9	
10	
11	
12	

H *Fill in the correct word derived from the words in bold.*

1 I'm grateful for your .... help.
2 This organisation deals with the .... of wildlife.
3 Tamsin has a special .... of animals.
4 A lot of .... research is being done into the greenhouse effect.
5 Mr Scotts is a .... film producer.
6 Winning a gold medal in the Olympics was his greatest ....
7 Everyone has been so .... since I lost my job.
8 Single mothers get little .... from society for their hard work.
9 This magazine has a .... of articles on topical issues.
10 There's a .... that you'll get the job.
11 The teacher asked the students to write a .... of the text.
12 The shop had an .... window display.

VALUE
PROTECT
UNDERSTAND
SCIENCE
FAME
ACHIEVE
SYMPATHY
RECOGNISE
VARY
POSSIBLE
SUMMARISE
IMPRESS

9 Nouns / Articles

Nouns

- **Nouns are: abstract** (*invasion, visit etc*), **concrete** (*invader, visitor etc*), **proper** (*David, Madrid, Japan etc*), **collective** (*audience, family, government etc*) **and common** (*book, sofa etc*).

The Plural of Nouns

Nouns are made plural by adding:

- **-s** to the noun. (*book - books etc*)

- **-es** to nouns ending in **-s, -ss, -x, -ch, -sh.** (*bus - buses, class - classes, fox - foxes, church - churches, rash - rashes etc*)

- **-ies** to nouns ending in **consonant + y.** (*body - bodies, party - parties etc*)

- **-s** to nouns ending in **vowel + y.** (*boy - boys, play - plays etc*)

- **-es** to nouns ending in **-o** (*potato - potatoes*)

- **-s** to nouns ending in: **vowel + o** (*video - videos*), **double o** (*taboo - taboos*), **abbreviations** (*photograph/ photo - photos*), **musical instruments** (*cello - cellos*) **and proper nouns** (*Navajo - Navajos*). **Some nouns ending in -o can take either -es or -s. These are: buffaloes/buffalos, mosquitoes/ mosquitos, volcanoes/volcanos, zeroes/zeros, tornadoes/tornados etc**

- **-ves** to some nouns ending in **-f/-fe.** (*scarf - scarves*) **(but: chiefs, roofs, cliffs, safes etc)**

- Some nouns of Greek or Latin origin form their plural by adding Greek or Latin suffixes. (*basis - **bases**, crisis - **crises**, terminus - **termini**, criterion - **criteria**, medium - **media** etc*)

Compound nouns form their plural by adding -s/-es:

- to the second noun if the compound consists of two nouns. (*corkscrew - corkscrews*)

- to the noun if the compound consists of an adjective and a noun. (*steering wheel - steering wheels*)

- to the first noun if the compound consists of two nouns connected with a preposition or to the noun if the compound has only one noun. (*doctor of philosophy - doctors of philosophy, hanger-on - hangers-on*)

- at the end of the compound if this is not made up of any nouns. (*runaway - runaways*)

Irregular Plurals: man - **men**, woman - **women**, foot - **feet**, tooth - **teeth**, louse - **lice**, mouse - **mice**, child - **children**, goose - **geese**, sheep - **sheep**, deer - **deer**, fish - **fish**, trout - **trout**, ox - **oxen**, salmon - **salmon**, spacecraft - **spacecraft**, aircraft - **aircraft**, means - **means**, species - **species**, hovercraft - **hovercraft**

207 *Write the plural of the following words:*

1	potato	*...potatoes...*	11	zoo	....
2	house	....	12	fishing rod	....
3	photo	....	13	fox	....
4	dessert spoon	....	14	child	....
5	fish	....	15	trout	....
6	video	....	16	louse	....
7	lorry	....	17	teacher	....
8	toy	....	18	baby	....
9	calf	....	19	workman	....
10	wolf	....	20	ship	....

21	boyfriend	....
22	mother-in-law	....
23	stepmother	....
24	type	....
25	stereo	....
26	mosquito	....
27	superstar	....
28	story	....
29	flyover	....
30	bunch	....

Countable - Uncountable Nouns

Nouns can be **countable** (those that can be counted) *1 egg, 2 eggs etc* or **uncountable** (those that can't be counted) *bread, wood etc.* Uncountable nouns take a singular verb and are not used with **a/an**. **Some, any, no, much** etc can be used with them. *Luggage is obtained from the Luggage Reclaim Area. Can I have* **some bread***, please?* but: **a relief, a pity, a shame, a wonder, a knowledge (of sth), a help.** *What* **a relief!** *What* **a pity!** *What* **a shame!**

Uncountable nouns are:

- **Mass nouns** (fluids, solids, gases, particles): *beer, blood, bread, butter, air, oxygen, corn, flour etc.*
- **Subjects of study**: *history, literature, maths, physics, accountancy, chemistry, economics etc*
- **Languages**: *Spanish, French, Japanese, Portuguese, Italian, Chinese etc*
- **Games**: *baseball, billiards, football, golf, darts, rugby, cricket, cycling etc*
- **Diseases**: *flu, pneumonia, measles, mumps, chickenpox, tuberculosis etc*
- **Natural phenomena**: *darkness, fog, gravity, hail, snow, sunlight, shade etc*
- **Some nouns**: *accommodation, advice, anger, applause, assistance, behaviour, business, chaos, countryside, courage, dirt, education, evidence, homework, housework, information, intelligence, knowledge, luck, music, news, peace, progress, seaside, shopping, traffic, trouble, truth, wealth, work etc*
- **Collective nouns**: *baggage, crockery, cutlery, furniture, jewellery, luggage, machinery, money, rubbish, stationery etc*
  Note: With expressions of duration, distance or money meaning "a whole amount" we use a singular verb. *Two months* **was** *too long to spend in hospital.*

Many uncountable nouns can be made countable.

a **piece** of paper/cake/information/advice/furniture; a **glass**/**bottle** of water/beer/wine; a **jar** of jam; a **rasher** of bacon; a **pint** of beer; a **box**/**sheet** of paper; a **packet** of tea; a **slice**/**loaf** of bread; a **pot** of yoghurt; a **pot**/**cup** of tea; a **kilo**/**pound** of meat; a **tube** of toothpaste; a **bar** of chocolate/soap; a **bit**/**piece** of chalk; an ice **cube**; a **lump** of sugar; a **bag** of flour; a **pair** of trousers; a **game** of soccer; a(n) **item**/**piece** of news; a **drop**/**can** of oil; a **can** of Coke; a **carton** of milk; a **block** of wood; a **flash**/**bolt** of lightning; a **clap**/**peal** of thunder etc

Plural Nouns

- **objects consisting of two parts**: **garments** *(trousers, pyjamas etc)*, **instruments** *(binoculars, compasses etc)*, **tools** *(scissors, pliers etc)*
- **arms, ashes, barracks, clothes, congratulations, earnings, (good) looks, outskirts, people, police, premises, riches, stairs, surroundings, wages etc.** *The police* **are looking** *for the bank robbers.*
  Group nouns (army, audience, class, club, committee, company, council, crew, crowd, headquarters, family, jury, government, press, public, staff, team etc) can take either a singular or a plural verb depending on whether we see the group as a whole or as individuals. *The* **staff** *of the company* **works** *really hard to increase production.* (the staff as a group) *The* **staff were given** *a bonus at Christmas.* (each member of the staff separately as individuals)

Note how certain nouns can be used in the singular and plural with a different meaning.

Singular	Plural
Give me a **glass** of water, please.	I've been wearing **glasses** since I was 8 years old.
Has she always had short **hair**?	There are so many **hairs** in the sink!
How would you rate this on a **scale** of 1 to 10?	Can you put that fish on the **scales** for me please?
In Japan it is not a **custom** to kiss your friends.	Our bags were thoroughly searched at **customs**.
Have you got any lined **paper** I could use?	He showed his **papers** to the customs officer.
She's wearing a ring made of **wood**.	John loves his Sunday afternoon walk in the **woods**.
I can't talk now; I have a lot of **work** to do.	A lot of Dali's **works** are on display in this museum.
We had at least 200 **people** at our wedding.	The **peoples** of Europe are hoping for change.
The **rain** is falling really heavily now.	The villagers are hoping for the **rains** to come soon.
You need **experience** for this job.	I had a lot of interesting **experiences** visiting Asia.
We used a **compass** to find our direction.	Use your **compasses** to draw some circles.

9 Nouns / Articles

208 Underline the correct verb form.

1. Mathematics is/are my favourite subject.
2. Wood come/comes from trees.
3. The news was/were interesting this evening.
4. Her advice was/were useful.
5. Your furniture is/are so tasteful.
6. Tennis is/are a game played by 2 or 4 people.
7. Butter contain/contains a lot of fat.
8. The scissors cut/cuts really well.
9. Your hair is/are so shiny.
10. Japanese is/are difficult to learn.
11. Most people is/are worried about the future.
12. Children usually like/likes sweet things.
13. This company has/have six branches.
14. That jewellery really suit/suits you.
15. Water is/are necessary for survival.
16. My luggage was/were lost by the airline.
17. Measles is/are infectious.
18. This machinery is/are very noisy.
19. £300 is/are too much to spend on that dress.
20. Your scales is/are not very accurate.

209 Write the correct form of the verbs in brackets.

1. The people of Africa ...*believe*... (believe) in various religions.
2. 20 years .... (be) a long time to spend in prison for theft.
3. The staircase .... (be) too steep for my grandmother to climb.
4. Cathay Pacific .... (be) an Asian airline.
5. Happiness .... (be) the key to success.
6. Flu .... (make) you feel miserable.
7. A loaf of bread .... (cost) more now than it did ten years ago.
8. I think olive oil .... (add) a lot of flavour to cooking.
9. The committee .... (meet) every Wednesday in the boardroom.
10. It is said that lightning never .... (strike) in the same place twice.
11. My favourite pyjamas ..... (be) the ones with red and white stripes.
12. All the members of staff .... (get) together in the staff room.
13. Some people think French .... (sound) so romantic.
14. There .... (be) too much sugar in my tea.
15. Physics .... (involve) a lot of theoretical study.
16. Gravity .... (pull) things towards the centre of the Earth.
17. Good looks .... (be) all you need to be a model.
18. A crew of over five people .... (work) in most commercial aeroplanes.
19. Decorating a house .... (be) a lot of trouble.
20. Your trousers .... (go) nicely with this blue top.

210 Finish the sentences without changing the meaning of the first sentence.

1. She has got scruffy hair. Her hair ...*is scruffy*....
2. You need some teaching experience before we employ you. Some ....
3. He was given some very useful information. Some ....
4. He bought a new suit for the wedding. A new suit ....
5. An alarm protects this shop from burglaries. This shop ....
6. People use sand to make glass. Sand ....
7. I like playing darts more than any other game. Darts ....
8. Nowadays men and women wear trousers. Trousers ....
9. You are not allowed to park here. Parking ....
10. You need binoculars to see that far. Binoculars ....
11. Models always wear smart clothes. Smart clothes ....
12. This greengrocer's always has fresh vegetables. The vegetables ....
13. The government is passing new laws. New laws ....
14. I found physics very difficult at school. Physics ....
15. The man found the advice very useful. The advice ....

Word Formation

- To describe people we add **-ar, -er, -or, -ee** to the end of verbs, or **-ist, -ian** to the end of nouns or verbs making any necessary spelling changes. *employ - employee, lie - liar, drive - driver, act - actor, art - artist , music - musician*

Nouns can be formed from verbs

-age *(drain - drainage)*, **-al** *(propose - proposal)*, **-ance** *(hinder - hindrance)*, **- ation** *(investigate - investigation)*, **-ence** *(refer - reference)*, **-ion** *(protect - protection)*, **-ment** *(employ - employment)*, **-sion** *(decide - decision)*, **-sis** *(analyse - analysis)*, **-tion** *(repeat - repetition)*, **-y** *(injure - injury)*

Nouns can be formed from adjectives

-ance *(arrogant - arrogance)*, **-cy** *(fluent - fluency)*, **-ence** *(patient - patience)*, **- ion** *(desperate - desperation)*, **-iness** *(lonely - loneliness)*, **-ity** *(familiar - familiarity)*, **-ment** *(content - contentment)*, **-ty** *(anxious - anxiety)*, **-y** *(honest - honesty)*

211

For questions 1 - 10, read the text below. Use the word given in capitals at the end of each line to form a word that fits in the space in the same line. Write your word in the answer boxes provided.

Choosing the right career to suit your **(0)** .... and one that lives up to your **(1)** .... can be rather difficult. We usually take certain factors into **(2)** .... when making such a **(3)** .... . First of all, what are the **(4)** .... of the job? You need to find out what **(5)** .... are necessary before you hand in your **(6)** .... form. Then, think of your career prospects and consider whether there is ample **(7)** .... for **(8)** .... . Finally, you need to decide on the level of **(9)** .... you would be happy with and whether you will achieve a sense of job **(10)** .... equal to the work you put in.

PERSONAL	0	*personality*
EXPECT	1	
CONSIDER	2	
DECIDE	3	
REQUIRE	4	
QUALIFY	5	
APPLY	6	
OPPORTUNE	7	
PROMOTE	8	
RESPONSIBLE	9	
SATISFY	10	

212

For questions 1 - 10, read the text below. Use the word given in capitals at the end of each line to form a word that fits in the space in the same line. Write your word in the answer boxes provided.

Most people's political **(0)** .... is limited to voting in an **(1)** .... every few years. Other, more committed, people regularly attend **(2)** .... about particular political issues. Then, there are those who enter into **(3)** .... with the **(4)** .... who represents them. They may write with **(5)** .... to some national law which concerns them, with a **(6)** .... for a change in party policy, or something concerned purely with local **(7)** .... - anything, in fact, which they feel deserves the **(8)** .... of their Member of Parliament. However, waiting for a reply requires a lot of **(9)** ...., and few would expect a profound and lengthy **(10)** .... of their original letter.

ACTIVE	0	*activity*
ELECT	1	
DEMONSTRATE	2	
CORRESPOND	3	
POLITICS	4	
REFER	5	
PROPOSE	6	
GOVERN	7	
ATTEND	8	
PATIENT	9	
ANALYSE	10	

9 Nouns / Articles

213 For questions 1 - 10, read the text below. Use the word given in capitals at the end of each line to form a word that fits in the space in the same line. Write your word in the answer boxes provided.

Great composers offer us a unique **(0)** .... of the world around us. Achieving this takes both **(1)** .... and a degree of **(2)** .... that few of us possess. Shut away in the **(3)** .... of their studios, free from the **(4)** ....of day-to-day concerns, they strive for the perfect **(5)** .... of what they know and feel. **(6)** .... usually comes slowly, and being over-sensitive to **(7)** .... may lead to **(8)** .... . On the other hand, enthusiastic praise from critics and the public can relieve the composer's **(9)** .... and bring him or her a degree of **(10)** .... that few but creative artists ever experience.

	INTERPRET
	INSPIRE
	COMMIT
	PRIVATE
	DISTRACT
	EXPRESS
	RECOGNISE
	CRITICISE
	DISCOURAGE
	ISOLATE
	SATISFY

0	*interpretation*	0 ▬
1		1 ▭ ▭
2		2 ▭ ▭
3		3 ▭ ▭
4		4 ▭ ▭
5		5 ▭ ▭
6		6 ▭ ▭
7		7 ▭ ▭
8		8 ▭ ▭
9		9 ▭ ▭
10		10 ▭ ▭

Indefinite article (A/An) / Definite article (The)

- **A/An** is used with singular countable nouns to talk about indefinite things. *There's **a** man standing at the door. (indefinite)* We can use **some** in the affirmative with plural countable nouns or uncountable nouns and **any** in questions and negations. *There are **some people** at the bus stop. Give me **some milk** please. **Are there any cups** in the cupboard? There **isn't any sugar** left.*
- **A/An** can also be used meaning "per" *(He goes to the gym twice **a/per** week)* or with money *(**a/one** pound)*, fractions *(**a/one** quarter)*, weight/measures *(**a/one** metre)*, whole numbers *(**a/one** thousand)*, price/weight *(£2 **a** kilo)*, frequency/time *(three times **a** week)*, distance/fuel *(60 miles **a** gallon)*, distance/speed *(60 km **an** hour)*, and illnesses *(**a** fever, **a** cold, **(a)** toothache, **(a)** backache)*.
- **The** is used with singular and plural nouns, countable and uncountable ones, to talk about something specific or when the noun is mentioned for a second time. *Can I try on **the** blue dress, please? (Which dress? The blue one; specific) There was a rat in the kitchen. I killed **the** rat with my boot.*
- **A/An** or **the** is used before singular countable nouns to refer to a group of people, animals or things. ***A/The** dolphin lives in the sea. (We mean all dolphins).* **A/An** or **the** is never used before a noun in the plural when it represents a group. *Dolphins are intelligent animals. (not: ~~The dolphins~~ are intelligent animals)*

214 Fill in a, an, the, any or some where necessary.

1. I need ...*a*... car and I know .... kind of car I want. It must do 100 miles .... hour and also do 40 miles .... gallon.
2. "Have you got .... money? I had .... this morning but I did .... shopping, and .... fruit was so expensive! 50p .... kg for .... apples! It's .... disgrace!"
3. .... everyone knows .... lion is .... king of .... jungle but is .... shark .... king of .... sea? I can't think of .... fish which will eat .... shark!
4. .... man came to .... door this morning and asked to see the water meter. I asked him if .... price of .... water was going up and he said it would increase by 10p .... cubic metre.
5. "How much is .... dress material in .... window?" "£5 .... metre, madam." "Do you have any in .... blue?" "Yes, there's .... blue material in .... stockroom."
6. Let me give you .... advice. If you need .... help with .... work I've given you, go to .... person who runs your department.

The is used before	The is omitted before

The is used before

- **nouns which are unique.** *the Earth, the Colosseum*

- **names of cinemas** *(The Plaza),* **hotels** *(The Savoy),* **theatres** *(The Palladium),* **museums** *(The Prado),* **newspapers/magazines** *(The Independent)* **but:** *(Time),* **ships***(The Cutty Sark),* **institutions** *(The British Council),* **galleries** *(The Tate Gallery)*

- **names of rivers** *(the Nile),* **seas** *(the Black Sea,)* **groups of islands/states** *(the Shetland Isles, the USA)* **mountain ranges** *(the Himalayas),* **deserts** *(the Sahara desert),* **oceans** *(the Atlantic),* **canals** *(the Manchester Canal)* **and names or nouns with "of".** *(the Valley of the Kings, the Garden of Gethsemane)* **Note:** *the equator, the Arctic/Antarctica, the South of France, the South/West/North/East*

- **musical instruments, dances.** *the piano, the samba*

- **names of families** *(the Hunters),* **nationalities ending in -sh, -ch or -ese** *(the English, the Dutch, the Japanese etc).* **Other plural nationalities are used with or without the.** *(the North Americans, the Austrians etc)*

- **titles** *(the Patriarch, the Duchess of Windsor, the King).* but: **"The" is omitted before titles with proper names.** *King Carlos*

- **adjectives used as plural nouns** *(the young, the unemployed, the homeless, the blind etc)* **and the superlative degree of adjectives/ adverbs.** *He's **the most** friendly boy in the group.*

- **Note:** **"most"** used as a determiner followed by a noun, does not take "the". ***Most people*** *like swimming.* **but:** *Of all European countries, Greece has **the most ancient** monuments.*

- **the words: beach, cinema, city, coast, country(side), earth, ground, jungle, radio, pub, sea(side), sky, station, shop, theatre, village, weather, world etc but not before "man".** *eg. She went to the **library** to return some books.* **Note:** "the" is optional with seasons. *(the) summer*

- **morning, afternoon, evening, night.** *I'll be home late in **the** evening.* **but:** *at night, at noon, at midnight, by day/night, at 4 o'clock etc*

- **historical references/events.** *the Russian Revolution, the Renaissance, the Cold War* **(but:** *World War II)*

- **only, last, first (used as adjectives).** *He was **the first** person to arrive.*

The is omitted before

- **proper nouns.** *I'll see **Ann** tomorrow.*

- **names of sports, games, activities, days, months, holidays, colours, drinks, meals and languages (not followed by the word "language").** *He plays football well. He likes red. We speak German.* **but:** ***The ancient Greek language*** *is hardly used now.*

- **names of countries** *(England),* **but:** *the Argentine, the Netherlands, (the) Sudan, the Hague, the Vatican City,* **cities** *(London),* **streets** *(Carnaby Street),* **but:** *the High Street, the Strand, the Mall, the A11, the M4 motorway,* **squares** *(Trafalgar Square),* **bridges** *(Tower Bridge* **but:** *the Bridge of Sighs, the Forth Bridge, the Severn Bridge, the Golden Gate Bridge),* **parks** *(Central Park),* **stations** *(Euston Station),* **individual mountains** *(Kilimanjaro),* **islands** *(Sicily),* **lakes** *(Lake Victoria),* **continents** *(Africa)*

- **possessive adjectives.** *That isn't your pen.*

- **two-word names whose first word is the name of a person or place.** *John F. Kennedy Airport, Windsor Castle* **but:** *The White House, (because the first word "White" is not the name of a person or place)*

- **pubs, restaurants, shops, banks and hotels which have the name of their founder and end in -s or -'s.** *Woolworth's, Lloyds Bank, Tom's Bar* **but:** *the Red Lion (pub) (because "Red Lion" is not the name of a person or place)*

- **bed, church, college, court, hospital, prison, school, university, when we refer to the purpose for which they exist.** *John went to hospital. (He is a patient.)* **but:** *His mother went to **the** hospital to see him last week. (She went to the hospital as a visitor.)* **Work (= place of work) never takes "the".** *She is at **work**.*

- **the words home, Father/Mother when we talk about our own home/parents.** ***Father*** *is at **home**.*

- **means of transport: by bus/by car/by train/by plane etc but:** *in the car, on the bus/train etc.* *She travelled by **bus**.* **but:** *She caught **the** 5 o'clock bus.*

- **We say: flu/the flu, measles/the measles, mumps/the mumps but:** *He's got malaria.*

9 Nouns / Articles

215 Fill in "the" where necessary.

1 Shall we have ..–.. lunch at .... home or go to .... Royal Oak and Castle?

2 .... Prince Philip visited .... Royal Albert Hall today.

3 .... Pete's Bar is situated in .... Terminal 1 at .... Heathrow Airport.

4 .... Browns were .... first to leave .... party at .... midnight.

5 We landed at .... Charles de Gaulle airport in .... Paris and were met by .... ambassador in person.

6 Tim's gone to .... hospital to pick up .... results of .... tests .... Mum had .... last week.

7 .... most world maps are out of date now, due to .... political events which have taken place recently.

8 .... Chicago Bulls, from .... USA are one of .... best-known basketball teams.

9 When .... Berlin Wall was pulled down it was a great moment in .... history.

10 Lots of people go for .... exotic holidays in .... Asia, but you must take care not to catch .... malaria.

11 We decided to go to .... island of Sicily last summer and we've decided to go to an island again this year; either to .... Rhodes or .... Canaries.

12 In .... Jerusalem we visited .... Dome of the Rock, ... Church of the Holy Sepulchre and saw the site of .... Solomon's Temple.

13 Lots of people are without jobs in .... city, so .... government has decided to give .... unemployed special benefits.

14 Tarzan, ... Lord of .... Jungle, had a friend called .... Cheetah.

15 Many people go trekking in .... mountains like .... Alps or .... Himalayas.

16 .... English spend their holidays in hot countries because they enjoy going to .... beach.

17 .... royal yacht sailed across .... Indian Ocean.

18 You'll find my house if you walk along .... Green Street and turn right into .... High Street.

19 Many of .... England's young men died in .... First World War.

20 .... Vatican City is one of .... most beautiful places in .... Rome.

21 .... people from .... Brazil dance .... samba really well.

22 We went to .... pub rather than .... cinema because .... Father wanted to.

216 Fill in "the" where necessary.

Dear George

I've just returned from 1) ..–.. America after spending 2) .... summer working with children at a camp for 3) .... blind. I travelled to 4) .... States by 5) .... aeroplane and while I was on 6) .... plane I met some other people going to work at the camp. There were 7) .... Germans and Italians and also some people from 8) .... Netherlands. However, it was 9) .... French who were 10) .... most noticeable nationality as there were so many of them. Once I arrived, 11) .... most of my time was spent arranging activities such as 12) .... music, sports and crafts. The children learned to play 13) .... guitar, to practise 14) .... swimming and even to speak 15) .... French. After the camp was over, I spent some time travelling. My favourite sights were 16) .... Grand Canyon and 17) .... Lake Michigan. I also visited 18) .... Empire State Building and I loved 19) .... Disneyland. I had a great time, and I hope to be able to do 20) .... same thing next summer after I've finished 21) .... university.

Best wishes,
Alex

217 *Fill in a/an or the where necessary.*

1 ...*The*... Tower of London is on .... north side of .... Thames.
2 He has visited a number of places including .... USA, ... Middle East and .... Asia.
3 .... University of Cambridge is one of .... most famous in .... United Kingdom if not in .... Europe.
4 He took .... job with .... government because he's interested in .... politics.
5 New Year celebrations are held in .... Trafalgar Square in .... London and in .... Times Square in .... New York.
6 .... month I spent in .... France was one of .... best times in my life.
7 After six months in .... hospital my grandmother is coming .... home.
8 .... Sunset Boulevard is .... most famous street in .... Hollywood.
9 .... millionaire purchased .... mansion as .... gift for his wife's birthday.
10 .... Nile flows from near .... Lake Victoria to .... Mediterranean.
11 She goes to .... church every Sunday, and also goes to .... church every Friday to help with the cleaning.
12 My perfect day in London would include shopping at .... Harrods, eating at .... Pierrot's and going to .... opera at .... Covent Garden.
13 .... Mount Everest is in .... Himalayas.
14 .... Falklands are islands in .... South of .... Atlantic Ocean.
15 He came into .... antique gold watch when his grandfather passed away.
16 When I visit .... Netherlands I always stay at .... Park Hotel in .... Amsterdam.
17 Tom teaches at .... university near his home.
18 .... van crashed into .... back of my car in .... Green Street yesterday.
19 Of .... Seven Wonders of the World, I've only visited .... Pyramids.
20 After .... Prime Minister visited .... prison, he promised to improve conditions in .... prisons.
21 We heard .... lovely sermon at .... church in .... Lord Street .... last night.
22 She caught .... cold because she didn't come in from .... rain.

> **A couple of, several, a few, many, a (large/great/good) number of, both** are followed by a countable noun. **(Too) much, a little, a great/good deal of, a large/small amount/quantity of** are followed by an uncountable noun. **A lot of, lots of, hardly any, some, no, plenty of** are followed by a countable or uncountable noun.

218 *Underline the expressions which can be used with nouns as in the example:*

1 The teacher gave us several, <u>a lot of</u>, many, <u>too much</u>, a few homework to do.
2 You've got some, a lot of, both, plenty of, many beautiful furniture.
3 Can you lend me a few, some, a lot of, a couple of, a little money?
4 Jane likes both, a couple of, too much, a little, some your paintings.
5 Have you had a lot of, plenty of, both, a little, too much letters from Suzie?
6 Everyone can do with some, a little, both, a good deal of, several peace and quiet at times.
7 There are a little, a number of, several, a small amount of, no Asian people living in our street.
8 There are much, no, a small amount of, hardly any, lots of people in the shop.
9 He spent a couple of, much, lots of, a good deal of, a few time reorganising his files.
10 The children ate a good deal of, too much, a few, a good number of, a little food at the party.

9 Nouns / Articles

219 Find the word which should not be in the sentence.

1 Very few people can speak the Chinese.
2 Vera is not used to a cold weather.
3 Mark is very good at the painting landscapes.
4 What shall we have for a dinner tonight?
5 He likes all the kinds of modern music.
6 The tennis is one of the oldest sports.
7 They travelled to Nice by a car.
8 The nanny took a great care of the child that had been placed in her charge.
9 The most people are concerned about global warming and its effects.
10 What's on a TV tonight?
11 He had a serious accident so he's been in the hospital for two months.
12 He gave me a valuable advice on how to invest my money.
13 The Christmas is a time to be merry.
14 It gives me a great pleasure to welcome you to our hotel.
15 Our daughter was nervous on her first day at the school.
16 We've got a plenty of time to spare before the show begins.
17 The Sir Lawrence Olivier was born in Britain in 1907.
18 We decided to meet at the Victoria Station.
19 I ran into an old friend on my way to the work this morning.
20 Bats come out at the night.

1	*the*
2	
3	
4	
5	
6	
7	
8	
9	
10	
11	
12	
13	
14	
15	
16	
17	
18	
19	
20	

Oral Development 13

Look at the following list and say each item using "the" where necessary.

Pyramids, Tahiti, Parthenon, Eiffel Tower, Mount Rushmore, Bangkok, Taj Mahal, Dome of the Rock, Suez Canal, Charing Cross, Sultan of Brunei, oriental music ,Louvre, Heathrow Airport, Hong Kong, Leaning Tower of Pisa, Mount Vesuvius, Hanging Gardens of Babylon, River Thames, Cosmopolitan, Paris, Netherlands, Jamaica, Oslo, Unicef, Prince of Wales, Lake Constance, Rocky Mountains, United Nations, Crete, Lake Geneva, Fifth Avenue, Spanish language, English Channel, Pacific, Carlton Hotel, Marks and Spencer, Holy Land, Queen Sofia, Argentine, Ionian Islands

S1: The Pyramids S2: Tahiti   etc

Consolidation 9

▶ Phrasal Verbs

put aside: save (usu money)
put away: put in the usual place
put down: 1) suppress by force, 2) write down; make a note, 3) attribute to, 4) criticize
put forward: propose
put off: postpone
put on: 1) switch on, 2) increase (weight), 3) pretend to be/have
put out: 1) extinguish, 2) cause inconvenience
put through: connect by phone
put up: 1) offer hospitality, 2) erect, 3) raise prices
put up with: tolerate

● ● ● ● ● ● ● ● ● ● ● ● ●

run across: meet or find by chance
run after: chase
run away with: steal
run down: 1) (of a battery) lose power, 2) (passive) be exhausted, 3) knock down, 4) speak badly of sb
run into: 1) meet unexpectedly, 2) collide with
run out of: come to an end
run over: read through quickly; review
run up against: face; encounter
run through: examine quickly; rehearse

220 Fill in the correct particle(s).

1 Please put ...*out*... your cigarettes before takeoff.
2 The hotel receptionist put me .... to room 617.
3 We put .... our wedding for another two months.
4 She has some money put .... for her old age.
5 She puts .... all her thoughts in a diary every night.
6 I'll accept a lift if it doesn't put you .... too much.
7 I can't put .... his rude behaviour any more.
8 He always puts his wife .... by insulting her in public.
9 Could you put .... the air conditioning? It's hot in here.
10 They have run .... money for the political campaign.
11 He ran .... his notes before entering the exam room.
12 The plans for the new road ran .... a lot of local opposition.
13 She feels run .... after working so hard recently.
14 The thief ran .... all the money from the bank.
15 He ran .... his ex-wife in the supermarket.
16 Our car was badly damaged when a van ran .... it.

221 Complete the sentences using the words in bold. Use two to five words.

1 I had difficulty in completing the course.
   complete I found ...*it difficult to complete*... the course.
2 We were delayed at the airport for three hours.
   held We .... airport for three hours.
3 I wish I had stayed at home instead of going to Ann's.
   rather I'd .... than gone to Ann's.
4 Doctors say smoking damages people's health.
   said Smoking .... people's health.
5 I'm sorry I missed your party.
   wish I .... your party.
6 They couldn't go on holiday because their car had broken down.
   prevented They .... on holiday because their car had broken down.
7 Have you decided about taking the job?
   mind Have you .... taking the job?
8 Weight is measured on scales.
   used Scales .... weight.
9 My aunt made me my wedding dress.
   had I .... by my aunt.
10 The grandparents took care of the child.
   looked The child .... the grandparents.
11 Lisa types quicker than Michelle.
   type Michelle .... as Lisa.
12 "I didn't steal Mark's wallet," Ted said.
   stolen Ted .... Mark's wallet.

Prepositions of Time

AT	IN	ON
at 9.30	in the morning/evening/afternoon/night	on Thursday
at Christmas/Easter	in the Easter/Christmas holiday(s)	on Easter Sunday etc
at noon/night/midnight	in October (months)	on Christmas Day
at lunch/dinner/breakfast (time)	in (the) winter (seasons)	on Friday night
at that time	in 1995 (years)	on January 18th
at the moment	in the 20th century	on a winter afternoon
at the weekend (on the weekend: Am. English)	in two hours (two hours from now)	on that day

 Look at the table above, then fill in the correct prepositions.

Health & FITNESS Club

You'll arrive at the health farm **1)** ...*on*... Thursday, that's **2)** .... June 15th. You should try to arrive **3)** .... the morning if you can. **4)** .... the first day we won't be doing a lot, just resting, so you can go and lie by the pool if you like. You'll be expected to get up early **5)** .... Friday morning **6)** .... about 7 o'clock. Your day's programme will be given to you **7)** .... breakfast. **8)** .... the summer we have a lot more guests and so **9)** .... that time you'll be assigned to your different groups. Lunch will be served **10)** .... noon, and **11)** .... lunch you'll be given an opportunity to meet the other trainers. There'll be a rest period **12)** .... the afternoon followed by a swim and sauna for those who are interested. We like to have a bit of a dance **13)** .... Friday night, so bring your party clothes! We will be conducting a period of meditation and relaxation **14)** .... the weekend, but all the trainers will be around to keep you busy. Don't forget that we are also running a second session **15)** .... August and another one **16)** .... Christmas for those who are interested.

223 *Think of the word which best fits each space. Write only one word in each space.*

Italy

Italy is a fascinating country, a wonderland of **(0)** ...*both*... man-made and natural beauty. No **(1)** .... where you go in this small but varied country you **(2)** .... find something to interest, intrigue **(3)** .... delight you. The big cities such **(4)** .... Milan, Rome and Naples are filled **(5)** .... ancient monuments, Renaissance palaces and some of the best examples **(6)** .... modern architecture in the world, while smaller cities like Pisa and Siena are well **(7)** .... exploring for sights: the famous Leaning Tower, churches and museums, not to **(8)** .... their parks, gardens and surrounding countryside. Because Italy covers **(9)** .... a large area **(10)** .... north to south, its climate is **(11)** .... varied as its sights. **(12)** .... in the north you can find lakes, forests and mountains, the far south is a paradise of sunshine, warm sea and sandy beaches. And of course everywhere **(13)** .... is the delicious food, which is a good reason for visiting Italy even **(14)** .... you have decided to ignore every **(15)** .... attraction of this wonderful country.

224

Read the text carefully. Some of the lines are correct and some have a word which should not be there. If a line is correct, put a tick (✔) in the space provided. If a line has a word which should not be there, write it in the space provided.

Wake up to milk

0	Delivered in daily to your door, by your milkman,	0	*in*
00	come rain or shine, milk provides a remarkable	00	✔
1	cocktail of protein, vitamins, minerals and	1	
2	energy for your whole of family, from the	2	
3	youngest to the most oldest. Milk is a delicious,	3	
4	nourishing drink for everyone - not only children.	4	
5	And because of our needs change as we grow	5	
6	older, there's a type of milk for every one member	6	
7	of your family. It's a refreshing, healthy drink	7	
8	that the dentist will be approve of. There's	8	
9	nothing to beat milk: drink it like plain, or as	9	
10	a milk shake flavoured with fresh fruit, chocolate	10	
11	or fruit yoghurt. There are also such many ways	11	
12	to drink milk, so it's no any wonder its popularity	12	
13	never dies. Milk in a bottle is the more "greenest"	13	
14	way to buy it because milk they bottles are generally	14	
15	re-used for between twelve and forty times.	15	

225

For questions 1 - 10, read the text below. Use the word given in capitals at the end of each line to form a word that fits in the space in the same line. Write your word in the answer boxes provided.

Snoring

In Britain alone, over 3 million people snore **(0)** .... enough to disrupt their partner's sleep. In some cases, snoring makes **(1)** .... difficult, causing oxygen **(2)** .... to the brain and heart and thus waking the person up suddenly. It is known to ruin the lives of many people **(3)** .... who are **(4)** .... to sleep properly. The causes are **(5)** ...., but the most common are fat collecting around the upper throat, or blockage of the nasal passage. In **(6)** ...., some people decide to have an **(7)** .... . Although this **(8)** .... is extremely **(9)** ...., it has been shown that it can often **(10)** .... solve the snorer's problem.

LOUD	0	*loudly*
BREATHE	1	
STARVE	2	
	3	
GLOBE	4	
ABLE	5	
VARY	6	
DESPERATE	7	
OPERATE	8	
OPT	9	
PLEASANT	10	
SUCCESS		

10 Emphatic Structures / Inversion

Emphatic Structures

We use emphatic structures to emphasise a particular part of a sentence.

- **it is/was (not) + subject/object + that/who(m)** (statements/negations)
  It was Mary that/who called you. It was the manager that/who(m) I wrote to.
  It was the radio that broke down. (only "that" can be used because the subject is not a person)
  It wasn't me that/who called the police. It isn't the TV that needs to be repaired.

- **is/was it + subject/object + that/who(m)** (questions)
  Is it Jim that/whom you are going to meet?
  Was it his bicycle that got stolen last night?

- **that is/was + question word** (statements)
  That's what he did to save the boy.

- **is/was that + question word** or **question word + is/was it + that** (questions)
  Was that why they moved house?
  Why is it that you are always late for work?

- **question word + subject + verb + is/was**
  What he needs is a long holiday.

- To express **admiration, anger, concern** etc we use question words with **ever**.
  Whatever are you talking about?

- **do/does/did + bare infinitive** is used in the Present Simple, Past Simple or Imperative to give emphasis. *I do promise to keep your secret. Do have some more coffee. He did buy the diamond ring.*

226 *Rewrite the sentences as in the example:*

1 **Ann** decorated the pumpkin.
   ...*It was Ann who/that decorated the pumpkin*....
2 The children need **somewhere to play**. ....
3 Did **you** give him that horrible pair of trousers? ....
4 **What** do you mean by talking to me like that? ....
5 You should **concentrate more while you're driving.** ....
6 **I** telephoned our cousins. ....
7 **Where** are you going to be at Easter? ....
8 You need **a nice cup of tea**. ....
9 **When** did you get home? ....
10 **Why** did you borrow money from Al? ....

227 *Complete the sentences using the words in bold. Use two to five words.*

1 You weren't paying attention when the accident happened.
   that   It ...*was you that wasn't*.... paying attention when the accident happened.
2 The doctor promised that I would be out of bed in a couple of days.
   did   The .... would be out of bed in a couple of days.
3 Alexander Fleming discovered penicillin.
   was   It .... discovered penicillin.
4 Did you meet Marlon Brando in Hollywood?
   met   Was .... Marlon Brando in Hollywood?

5 The committee doesn't want to accept any new members to the club.
   is   What the .... to accept any new members to the club.
6 He said he was coming with us.
   say   He .... with us.
7 Did you go to the Rivera Club last night?
   it   Was .... you went to last night?

Inversion

We can invert the subject and the auxiliary verb in the sentence to give emphasis. This happens:

- **after certain expressions placed at the beginning of a sentence.**
  Barely, Hardly (ever) ... when, In no way, In/Under no circumstances, Little, Never (before), Nor/Neither, No sooner ... than, Not even once, Not only ... but also, Not since, Not till/until, Nowhere, Only by, Only in this way, On no account, On no occasion, Only then, Rarely, Scarcely (ever) ... when, Seldom.   *Little did he say* about his accident. *Rarely does he visit* us.
  Note that when only after, only by, only if, only when, not since, not till/until are put at the beginning of a sentence, we use inversion in the main clause.
  Only when you see him *will you realise* how much he has suffered.

- **after so, such, to such a degree (in result clauses) placed at the beginning of a sentence.**
  So hard does he work that he will soon be promoted.

- **in conditionals when should, were, had (Past Perfect) are placed at the beginning of the sentence.** Note that "if" is omitted.
  Should you go out, leave the key under the mat. (If you should go out ... - Type 1)
  Were I you, I would apologise. (If I were you ... - Type 2)
  Had he been invited, he would have come. (If he had been invited ... - Type 3)

- **after so, neither/nor, as to express agreement.**
  "I enjoy romance films." *"So do I."* ("So" is used to agree with an affirmative statement.)
  "Tim didn't come." *"Neither/Nor did Ann."* ("Neither/Nor" are used to agree with a negative statement.)
  Her students loved her, *as did* her colleagues.

In the following structures we invert the subject and the main verb.

- **after adverbs of place.** *There goes the bus!* (but: There it goes!) Here *is your pen!* (but: Here it is!)

- **in Direct Speech when the reporting verb comes after the quote and the subject is a noun.**
  "What a nice dress!" *said Susan.* (but: "What a nice dress!" she said.)

228 *Complete the sentences using the words in bold. Use two to five words.*

1 We can go on with the plan only if you agree.
   can   Only if ...*you agree can we go*... on with the plan.
2 Edna won't leave the house under any circumstances.
   will   Under .... leave the house.
3 If the river rises any higher, the town will be flooded.
   rise   Should ...., the town will be flooded.
4 If you'd paid on time, you wouldn't have been cut off.
   paid   Had ...., you wouldn't have been cut off.
5 He had just recovered from flu when he caught a bad cold.
   sooner   No .... from flu than he caught a bad cold.
6 He took such a long holiday that he forgot how to do his job.
   did   Such a long holiday .... that he forgot how to do his job.
7 They managed to get our attention only by shouting and waving their arms.
   manage   Only by shouting and waving their arms .... to get our attention.

8 He only asks for help when he is really desperate.
ask Only when he is really desperate .... for help.

9 If I see him, I'll give him your message.
should I'll give him your message .... him.

10 Tom never seems worried about his future.
seem Never .... worried about his future.

11 I've never had such fun anywhere else.
else Nowhere .... such fun.

12 Lynn didn't realise that her mother was so worried about her.
realise Little .... that her mother was so worried about her.

13 The army marched forward into battle.
marched Forward .... into battle.

14 Her parents and her friends warned her not to go alone.
as Her parents warned her not to go alone, ... friends.

15 She sang so well that she was offered a record deal.
sing So .... that she was offered a record deal.

16 Unemployment hasn't been at such a high level at any time since the 1930's.
been Not since the 1930's .... at such a high level.

17 I only watch television if I don't have anything else to do.
do Only when I have nothing else to do .... television.

18 She'd barely finished drying her hair when her first guests arrived.
had Barely .... drying her hair when her first guests arrived.

19 He didn't thank me once for feeding his cat.
once Not .... me for feeding his cat.

20 If there had been a phone nearby, he would have called an ambulance.
there Had .... nearby, he would have called an ambulance.

21 The door to the basement isn't to be left open on any account.
account On .... to the basement to be left open.

22 We won't tell anybody the good news until we're certain it's true.
will Not until we're certain it's true .... anybody the good news.

23 He felt so unwell that he had to cancel their date.
did So .... that he had to cancel their date.

24 Bob forgot his mother's birthday and his sister's too.
did Bob didn't remember his mother's birthday; .... his sister's.

25 He was so anxious that he kept biting his nails.
his Such .... he kept biting his nails.

26 Brown bread is healthier and tastier than white bread.
only Not .... than white bread, but it's healthier too!

27 I didn't expect that they would throw a surprise party for my birthday.
expect Little .... they would throw a surprise party for my birthday.

28 It isn't often that temperatures in Spain fall below 0˚C.
fall Seldom .... below 0˚C in Spain.

29 If I were you, I'd accept the offer.
you Were .... accept the offer.

30 This is the only way the Prime Minister can win the election.
this Only .... the Prime Minister win the election.

229 *Rewrite the sentences using so or such at the beginning of the sentence.*

1 As the exams were difficult, many students complained.
So ...*difficult were the exams that many students complained.*...

2 His dream was so strange that his psychiatrist wrote about it in a medical journal.
So ....

3 The explorers took such a long time to find the tomb that they had nearly run out of supplies.
Such ....

4   Many people think she's English because she speaks the language so fluently.
    So ....

5   She is so ignorant that she has never heard of Shakespeare.
    Such ....

6   He was so surprised that he nearly fell off his chair.
    Such ....

7   The dancer moved so gracefully that he appeared to be skating.
    So ....

230   *Fill in so, neither/nor and the appropriate verb.*

1   "I don't feel like going to work today."
    "...*Neither do I*... . Let's go to the beach instead."

2   "I really like our new teacher."
    "................... . She's really patient, isn't she?"

3   "I can't decide what to buy Chris for his birthday."
    "................... . What can you give a man who has everything?"

4   "I should really start doing some kind of exercise."
    "......................... . I've put on a lot of weight."

5   "I'd really love to go out tonight."
    "................... . Let's go to the new Italian place round the corner."

6   "I can't stand this heat any more."
    "......................... . Let's get in the car and go for a drive."

7   "I had the time of my life at the party last night."
    "......................... . I'll never forget you dancing the tango with old
    Mrs Marple."

8   "I've spent lots of money on clothes this month."
    "......................... . There's hardly any space left in my wardrobe."

9   "I won't be surprised if they don't turn up this evening."
    "............... . They've been known to let people down in the past."

10 "We're thinking of going to Ibiza this summer."
    "......................... . We've heard it's a great holiday resort."

231   *Complete the sentences using the words in bold. Use two to five words.*

1   He broke his leg during the summer holidays.
    that   It was during ...*the summer holidays that*... he broke his leg.

2   He didn't realise a surprise party awaited him.
    know   Little .... a surprise party awaited him.

3   Why did you leave work early today?
    that   Why was .... early today?

4   It was impossible for us to have a day off work.
    could   On no account .... a day off work.

5   You had to be lucky to discover gold in those days.
    could   Only if you .... discover gold in those days.

6   Hillary and Tenzing were the first climbers to reach the summit of Mount Everest.
    who   It was .... reached the summit of Mount Everest.

7   The courier met him at the station.
    who   It was .... him at the station.

8   You should never park on double yellow lines.
    circumstances   Under .... on double yellow lines.

9   He seldom tells us what he's really thinking.
    tell   Seldom .... he's really thinking.

10 You won't be given the job if you don't make a good impression.
    will   Only by .... you be given the job.

10 Emphatic Structures / Inversion

 232 **Find the word which should not be in the sentence.**

1	*did*
2	
3	
4	
5	
6	
7	
8	
9	
10	
11	
12	
13	
14	
15	
16	
17	
18	
19	
20	

1 Only when did she finished her report was she paid.
2 It was Clive who he scored the winning goal.
3 Whatever it is she wearing!
4 Not only is that Bill a good musician, but he also dances well.
5 If will you finish, you can leave.
6 Never before once had he caught such a big fish.
7 That was how had he deceived so many people.
8 Where I haven't been there is Paris.
9 So much loud was the music that we had to leave the bar.
10 Rarely ever are those birds seen in the wild.
11 No sooner when had he got home than he was called back to the office.
12 Only by she trying hard can Ann overcome her weaknesses.
13 It was last year that they did got engaged.
14 Why is it this that you always blame me for your problems?
15 Wherever is did you buy this awful orange and purple hat?
16 So much brilliant was his performance that the audience cheered.
17 Do you sit down please.
18 What you need it is someone to help you.
19 I hate Mexican food and so does hates my husband.
20 He did left early in the morning.

Oral Development 14

Look at the pictures below, then talk about them using emphatic structures or inversion.

eg.   **It was Kirkpatrick who started the fight. Not only was he rude to the referee but he also punched him on the nose.   etc**

Consolidation 10

Phrasal Verbs

see about: deal with; make arrangements for (= **see to**)

see sb off: go with sb to their point of departure

see sb out: accompany sb to the door/exit of a house/building

see over: inspect (a house, flat etc)

see through sb/sth: not be deceived by sb/sth

see sb through: support sb until the end of a difficult time

see to: 1) make arrangements, 2) attend to sth

• • • • • • • • • • • • •

set about: 1) begin to do, 2) attack

set aside: save for a special purpose

set back: 1) delay progress of sth, 2) delay an event till a later date, 3) cost (slang)

set out: 1) begin a journey, 2) start a course of action with a clear aim in mind

set in: start and seem likely to continue

set on: (cause to) attack

set up: 1) start a business, 2) build; erect, 3) establish

233 Fill in the correct particle(s).

1 Don't do the washing up now, I'll see ...*to*... it later.
2 Let's make an appointment to see .... the property with the surveyor.
3 He thinks he's clever but I can see .... his tricks.
4 You look after the children and I'll see .... the tickets.
5 We'll all come to the station to see you ....
6 He sets .... a little money every month.
7 As soon as the last guest had gone, he set .... cleaning the flat.
8 When he finished university he set .... his own computer company.
9 He set .... to become a millionaire before he was thirty.
10 We'll need winter coats now that the cold weather has set ....
11 That leather jacket set me .... £300.
12 The sound equipment has been set .... ready for the concert.
13 The storm did a lot of damage and set construction .... by a week.
14 The gang of hooligans set .... him with sticks.
15 She set .... a committee to oppose the plans for the new building.

234 Look at Appendix 1, then fill in the correct preposition.

1 She was expelled ...*from*... school when they caught her taking some test papers.
2 He forgave me .... arriving late for his performance.
3 Don't worry - you'll be safe .... those men here. They won't find you.
4 I replied .... the invitation for the party.
5 It's so typical .... him to be late for an appointment.
6 Mozart was a genius ...... composing operas.
7 The train to Liverpool departs .... platform 7 at 10.30.
8 He was ashamed ...... the way he had treated his friend.
9 In this city you have to beware .... the busy roads as they're very dangerous.
10 This new hairdryer does not comply .... British safety standards.
11 The boy was named .... his grandfather.
12 Joan is frightened .... spiders.
13 The barrister was very happy .... the jury's verdict.
14 All the tax is included .... the price written on the item.
15 If the boat was going to sink, there would be a great need .... lifejackets.
16 If you persist .... calling me such horrible names, I'm going to tell the teacher.
17 Jimmy agreed .... his fiancée .... where they should get married.
18 I was shocked .... the price they charged.
19 Don't forget to thank your grandmother .... your present.
20 The hijackers surrendered .... the police.
21 It's about time you stopped relying .... your parents.

235 Fill in the following collocation grid.

	the bus	one's temper	weight	a film	money	a target	one's mind	the train
lose								
miss	✓							

Consolidation 10

236 — Complete the sentences using the words in bold. Use two to five words.

1 She said she was sorry for ruining my dress.
   ruined   She ...*apologised for having ruined*... my dress.

2 You'd better reconsider his offer.
   were   If .... reconsider his offer.

3 The house she lives in is just round the corner.
   where   The .... just round the corner.

4 "Why don't you try on the blue dress?" she said to me.
   that   She .... the blue dress.

5 I'd prefer him to be back before 11 o'clock.
   rather   I .... before 11 o'clock.

6 Sheila doesn't agree with John's way of thinking.
   approve   Sheila .... way of thinking.

7 He would never have read the book if you hadn't suggested it.
   for   But ...., he would never have read the book.

8 They are building me a new shed.
   having   I .... built.

9 Katie will move to London but she must find a job.
   finds   Only if Katie .... move to London.

10 She left the house early because she was afraid the traffic might be bad.
   case   She left the house early .... bad.

11 He didn't find time to phone her until midnight.
   round   He didn't .... until midnight.

12 I wish I had curly hair like yours.
   rather   I .... like yours.

237 — Fill in the gaps with the correct form of the verb in brackets.

Mrs Pickles **1)** ...*has been living*... (live) in her two-storey house for over five years. She **2)** ....
(do) most of the housework herself but, once a month, she **3)** .... (clean / upstairs windows) by a professional window cleaner called Fred. At the end of each month Fred calls round **4)** ......

.... (collect) his money. One day, Mrs Pickles **5)** .... (ask) Fred an unusual question. **6)** "....................................... (you/use) the bathroom last time you were here?" Fred blushed. He **7)** .... (use) Mrs Pickles' upstairs bathroom because he **8)** .... (not/want) to wait until he got home. "Yes I did, Mrs Pickles ... I'm sorry." "Don't worry," she laughed. "I don't mind you **9)** .... (use) my bathroom. But if you **10)** .... (need) to use it again **11)** .... (you/try) to remember to unlock the bathroom door before you **12)**....................................... (climb) back out of the window?"

238 *For questions 1 - 15, read the text below and decide which word A, B, C or D best fits each space. Mark your answers in the answer boxes provided.*

Stress

Stress is important. We all need a certain **(0)** .... of it in order to **(1)** ... fulfilling lives. However, if we have too much of it, it can have the opposite **(2)** .... . Some people can tolerate greater **(3)** .... of stress than others, but most of us will **(4)** .... at some time in our lives. It is **(5)** .... a good idea to learn a few stress management techniques. Identifying the **(6)** .... of the problem we have, so that we can **(7)** .... it more effectively, is one of the first **(8)** .... towards reducing stress. The second is talking to a person you can trust, who will listen and, if necessary, **(9)** .... you some positive advice. Not only are smoking and drinking **(10)** .... to our health, they actually increase stress **(11)** .... than reduce it. So, next time you want to relax, **(12)** .... of reaching for that glass of wine or a cigarette, have a warm bath or go for a walk. Walking has more than health benefits, it helps you think more **(13)** .... too. Pets have a calming influence on us, unless they make noise which irritates us. In fact, unwanted noises should be **(14)** ....as far as possible. On the other hand, laughter is one of the best ways to **(15)** .... yourself feel considerably better.

0	**A** number	**B** bulk	**C** amount	**D** load		
1	**A** guide	**B** lead	**C** carry	**D** spend		
2	**A** influence	**B** solution	**C** answer	**D** effect		
3	**A** levels	**B** platforms	**C** grades	**D** scales		
4	**A** undergo	**B** suffer	**C** tolerate	**D** torture		
5	**A** therefore	**B** so	**C** however	**D** nevertheless		
6	**A** purpose	**B** occurrence	**C** cause	**D** reason		
7	**A** rather	**B** solve	**C** do	**D** cope		
8	**A** movements	**B** methods	**C** ways	**D** steps		
9	**A** give	**B** provide	**C** supply	**D** hand		
10	**A** negative	**B** destructive	**C** harmful	**D** hurtful		
11	**A** more	**B** rather	**C** as	**D** quite		
12	**A** ahead	**B** other	**C** because	**D** instead		
13	**A** clearly	**B** well	**C** skilfully	**D** cleanly		
14	**A** subtracted	**B** avoided	**C** limited	**D** transported		
15	**A** succeed	**B** have	**C** do	**D** make		

Answer boxes:

	A	B	C	D
0			■	
1				
2				
3				
4				
5				
6				
7				
8				
9				
10				
11				
12				
13				
14				
15				

Consolidation 10

239

Read the text carefully. Some of the lines are correct and some have a word which should not be there. If a line is correct, put a tick (✔) in the space provided. If a line has a word which should not be there, write it in the space provided.

My First Balloon Flight

0	Two weeks ago I have had a great experience; my first ever
00	flight in a hot air balloon. When I got up that morning
1	I felt rather nervous about and in fact I was considering
2	cancelling my trip! However, as I had already paid, I
3	drove shaking to the balloon field. Four of passengers
4	travelled in the basket, them accompanied by an
5	experienced balloonist. The fire was been lit, the ropes
6	were untied and the balloon rose slowly into the air.
7	As we got more higher, the air smelt fresher and cooler. I
8	could see my wife down on the ground. She is afraid
9	of heights so that she refused to come. From the balloon,
10	houses looked as like matchboxes.
11	An hour later, the balloon began to lose height. The
12	balloonist told to us that we would land in a field on a
13	nearby farm. We landed down surrounded by frightened
14	sheep and an angry bull. It was being an experience
15	that I'll remember for the rest of my own life.

0	*have*	0
00	✓	00
1		1
2		2
3		3
4		4
5		5
6		6
7		7
8		8
9		9
10		10
11		11
12		12
13		13
14		14
15		15

240

For questions 1 - 10, read the text below. Use the word given in capitals at the end of each line to form a word that fits in the space in the same line. Write your word in the answer boxes provided.

How strange are they ...?

The idea that **(0)** .... and creativity are linked is an old one. During the past 30 years or so **(1)** .... have been researching this and have concluded that **(2)** .... writers are more likely to be depressed, visual **(3)** .... are three times more likely to have split personalities, and **(4)** .... scientists are up to ten times more likely to suffer from severe **(5)** .... . However, a study of 400 such eccentric individuals has revealed they are self-confident, **(6)** .... and inquisitive, although sometimes prone to becoming obsessed with many different things at once. This **(7)** ...., they claim, is their recipe for **(8)** .... . Their sense of adventure and **(9)** .... protects them from the "real" world, and so is a form of **(10)** .... .

MAD	
PSYCHOLOGY	
CREATE	
ART	
SUCCESS	
DEPRESS	
HEALTH	
CURIOUS	
HAPPY	
IMAGINE	
ESCAPE	

0	*madness*	0
1		1
2		2
3		3
4		4
5		5
6		6
7		7
8		8
9		9
10		10

Practice test 5

For questions 1 - 15, read the text below and decide which word A, B, C or D best fits each space. Mark your answers in the answer boxes provided.

Why are broken mirrors believed to be unlucky?

Breaking a mirror is said to **(0)** .... seven years' bad luck. Although most people may **(1)** .... that they are not superstitious, they would nonetheless be a **(2)** .... uncomfortable if they did break a mirror. This age-old superstition is **(3)** .... to have come from the ancient belief that when a person **(4)** .... at their reflection, they were seeing their own soul. **(5)** .... that reflection was broken, then the soul would be **(6)** .... The seven-year **(7)** .... probably arises from another ancient belief, that the body **(8)** .... itself every seven years. After this time had **(9)** ...., the soul would then be renewed. Superstitions surrounding mirrors don't **(10)** .... there. Break one in Yorkshire, and you'll **(11)** .... your best friend, and in America, it's not bad luck to break one on **(12)** .... If you do it accidentally, simply **(13)** .... out a dollar bill and make the sign of the cross. In many countries it's a **(14)** .... custom to **(15)** .... any mirrors in the house with a cloth when someone has died.

0	A	carry	B	fetch	C	bring	D	take
1	A	tell	B	claim	C	persist	D	support
2	A	lot	B	small	C	little	D	few
3	A	possible	B	likely	C	probable	D	apparently
4	A	looked	B	saw	C	watched	D	observed
5	A	As	B	Should	C	If	D	Unless
6	A	disappeared	B	crushed	C	exploded	D	destroyed
7	A	period	B	time	C	distance	D	date
8	A	charged	B	replaced	C	removed	D	began
9	A	left	B	spent	C	passed	D	been
10	A	end	B	complete	C	go	D	begin
11	A	overlook	B	misplace	C	miss	D	lose
12	A	purpose	B	accident	C	reason	D	chance
13	A	remove	B	have	C	take	D	bring
14	A	common	B	cultural	C	plain	D	familiar
15	A	dress	B	screen	C	shade	D	cover

	A	B	C	D
0	☐	☐	▬	☐
1	☐	☐	☐	☐
2	☐	☐	☐	☐
3	☐	☐	☐	☐
4	☐	☐	☐	☐
5	☐	☐	☐	☐
6	☐	☐	☐	☐
7	☐	☐	☐	☐
8	☐	☐	☐	☐
9	☐	☐	☐	☐
10	☐	☐	☐	☐
11	☐	☐	☐	☐
12	☐	☐	☐	☐
13	☐	☐	☐	☐
14	☐	☐	☐	☐
15	☐	☐	☐	☐

Part 2

For questions 16 - 30, read the text below and think of the word which best fits each space. Use only one word in each space. Write your answers in the answer boxes provided.

The Brain

Contrary to popular belief, it is not true **(0)** .... we use only 10 percent of our brain power; it is **(16)** .... of the myths of modern times. The brain controls all of our bodily functions as **(17)** .... as carrying out the most complicated processes **(18)** .... thought and imagination.

There must **(19)** ...., be some spare capacity built into the system because brain cells - unlike most of the body's other cells - are not **(20)** .... to divide and therefore are incapable **(21)** .... replacing themselves **(22)** .... they die.

It is possible to increase the abilities of our brain. We do **(23)** .... when we learn to read, **(24)** .... example. Current research shows that the learning process creates new connections **(25)** .... brain cells **(26)** .... increases our mental powers.

But scientists are unable to say exactly how **(27)** .... of our brains we don't use. Despite a lot of research, the brain is still the **(28)** .... mysterious organ in the body and it will be many years **(29)** .... enough information can be gathered to explain all **(30)** .... functions.

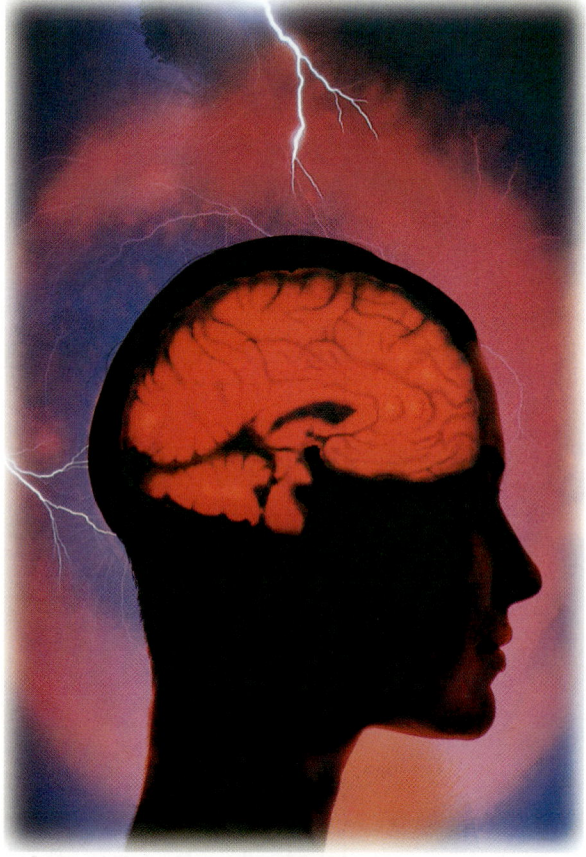

0	that	0 ▭ ▬
16		16 ▭ ▭
17		17 ▭ ▭
18		18 ▭ ▭
19		19 ▭ ▭
20		20 ▭ ▭
21		21 ▭ ▭
22		22 ▭ ▭
23		23 ▭ ▭
24		24 ▭ ▭
25		25 ▭ ▭
26		26 ▭ ▭
27		27 ▭ ▭
28		28 ▭ ▭
29		29 ▭ ▭
30		30 ▭ ▭

Part 3

For questions 31 - 40, complete the second sentence so that it has a similar meaning to the first sentence. Use the word given and other words to complete each sentence. You must use between two and five words. Do not change the word given. Write your answers in the answer boxes provided.

0   I'm sure they worked hard on the project.
   have
   They .... on the project.

| 0 | *must have worked hard* | ▢ 0 ▬ |

31   As well as having a flat, they also have a cottage.
   got
   Not only .... but also a cottage.

| 31 | | ▢ 31 ▢ |

32   Despite meeting lots of people, she feels lonely.
   though
   She feels lonely .... lots of people.

| 32 | | ▢ 32 ▢ |

33   She intends to go back to college in September.
   intention
   It .... back to college in September.

| 33 | | ▢ 33 ▢ |

34   All this exercise has exhausted me.
   worn
   I .... all this exercise.

| 34 | | ▢ 34 ▢ |

35   It would be better if you left your passport at reception.
   rather
   We .... your passport at reception.

| 35 | | ▢ 35 ▢ |

36   We bought more food than we needed.
   have
   We .... much food.

| 36 | | ▢ 36 ▢ |

37   The walk was so long that we were exhausted by the end of it.
   such
   It .... that we were exhausted by the end of it.

| 37 | | ▢ 37 ▢ |

38   The soldier was told to obey all orders.
   carry
   The soldier .... all orders.

| 38 | | ▢ 38 ▢ |

39   He lost the game because he hadn't practised.
   have
   He .... the game if he had practised.

| 39 | | ▢ 39 ▢ |

40   Someone stole Sarah's bag while she was out.
   had
   Sarah .... while she was out.

| 40 | | ▢ 40 ▢ |

Part 4

For questions 41 - 55, read the text below and look carefully at each line. Some of the lines are correct and some have a word which should not be there. If a line is correct, put a tick (✔) by the number in the answer boxes provided. If a line has a word which should not be there, write the word in the answer boxes provided.

Bad Service

0	There's a saying that the customer he is always right.	0	*he*
00	However, they can't have heard it at my local	00	✓
41	supermarket. It's just around about the corner from	41	
42	where I live and work at, but if it wasn't so	42	
43	convenient, I don't think I would to put my foot in	43	
44	the door. The staff there, with a few of exceptions, are	44	
45	very rude. Their manner is being aggressive and not	45	
46	at all helpful. The slightest question comes from	46	
47	you is met with a resentment. At the cash	47	
48	desk, if you haven't got the very correct change,	48	
49	you might as well leave one as they won't help	49	
50	you out. Even if you are quietly minding	50	
51	your own business, looking at the much different	51	
52	kinds of food on offer, you are sure to be in	52	
53	the way of someone other who is trying to rearrange	53	
54	the shelves. Recently, they couldn't find the price of	54	
55	an item so that they wouldn't sell it. Can you believe it?	55	

Part 5

For questions 56 - 65, read the text below. Use the word given in capitals at the end of each line to form a word that fits in the space in the same line. Write your word in the answer boxes provided.

Burglars!

The (0) .... of all burglaries occur when people go on holiday. (56) .... guests often take advantage of an empty house. However, there are many (57) .... measures you can take. It is (58) .... to cancel any doorstep deliveries. Move (59) .... items like TVs away from windows where they can be seen by a potential (60) .... . Put all expensive items of (61) .... in storage; if left, there is every (62) .... they will be found - thieves know all the (63) .... places to look. Finally, for extra (64) .... ask a neighbour to keep a (65) .... eye on your home.

MAJOR	0	*majority*
INVITED	56	
	57	
PREVENT	58	
ADVISE	59	
VALUE		
INTRUDE	60	
JEWEL	61	
LIKELY	62	
TYPE	63	
SECURE	64	
WATCH	65	

11 Determiners / Pronouns

Determiners are: **indefinite article** (a/an), **definite article** (the), **demonstratives** (this - these/that - those), **possessive adjectives** (my, your, his etc), **quantifiers** (some, any, every, no, both, each, either, neither, enough, several, all, most etc) and **numbers** (one, two etc).

Demonstratives (this - these / that - those)

This/These are used

- **for people or things near us.**
  This box is yours.
- **for present/future situations.**
  I'm going out with Ted this week.
- **when the speaker is in or near the place he/she is referring to.** *This house was built in 1856. (The speaker is near or in the house.)*
- **to introduce people or to identify ourselves on the phone.** *"Ann, this is Jane."*

That/Those are used

- **for people or things not near us.**
  That boy over there is my son.
- **for past situations.**
  That day was the worst of his life.
- **to refer back to something mentioned before.**
  "We're moving to York." "That's fantastic!"
- **when speaking on the phone to ask who the other person is.** *"Hello? This is Alan Smith. Who's that, please?"*

Note: This/These - That/Those are not always followed by nouns. *This is all I can do to help you.*

241 *Fill in: this, that, these or those.*

1 "I'll never forget my holiday in Moscow. ...*That*... was the holiday of a lifetime!"
2 "What are you doing .... Thursday?" "Well, I have to go to work as usual."
3 "Didn't you just love .... striped trousers in the shop we just passed?"
4 Mmm! .... is the best soup I've ever tasted!
5 "Do you see .... girl over there? She's my cousin's girlfriend."
6 "Hello, ... is Mrs Cook. Can I speak to Mr Brown please?"
7 "I can't go out in .... dress. It's much too tight."
8 "I've been accepted by my first choice of university." "Congratulations. .... is fantastic!"
9 "................................. were the days when we used to sing and dance every night."
10 Don't you think .... new electronic diaries that we saw in the shop are really clever?
11 " .... belonged to my grandmother," said Tim as he slipped the diamond ring onto Ann's finger.
12 "Don't you think .... trousers suit me?"
13 " .... biscuits are delicious. Did you make them yourself?"
14 "................................. records you threw out were my original hits from the sixties!"
15 Aren't .... boys over there your students?
16 "............................. lamp needs repairing." "............................. is what I was trying to tell you."

242 *Fill in: this, that, these or those.*

"What did you think of 1) ...*that*... dress Priscilla was wearing last night?" "Oh, it was awful, wasn't it? And 2) .... earrings!" "Ugh! Her sense of style is even worse 3) .... days than it was when she was at school." "I wonder what outrageous outfit she'll be wearing to the Windsor's cocktail party 4) .... evening." "5) .... is something that we'll just have to wait and see."

11 Determiners / Pronouns

- **All** refers to more than two people or things. It has a positive meaning and takes a verb in the plural. It is the opposite of **none**. *All the students failed.* ***All of them*** *failed. They* ***all*** *failed.* ***All five of them*** *failed.*
  All + **that-clause** (= the only thing) takes a singular verb. ***All that*** *he said was not to worry.*

- **Both** refers to two people or things. It has a positive meaning and takes a verb in the plural. It is the opposite of **neither/not either**. *Pam and Ann are singers.* ***Both*** *Pam and Ann* ***are*** *singers. They* ***are both*** *singers.* ***Both of them*** *are singers.* ***Both*** *girls* ***are*** *singers.*

- **Whole** (= complete) is used with countable nouns. We always use **a, the, this, my** etc + **whole + countable**. *the whole day = all day*

- **Either** (= any one of two) / **Neither** (= not one and not the other) refer to two people or things and are used before singular countable nouns. ***Neither girl enjoys*** *horror films.* **Neither of/Either of** take a verb either in the singular or plural. ***Neither of them is/are*** *French.*

- **None** refers to more than two people or things. It has a negative meaning and isn't followed by a noun. *"Are there any mistakes?" "No,* ***none.****"* **None of** is used before nouns or object pronouns followed by a verb either in the singular or plural. It is the opposite of **all**. ***None of the three girls/them know(s)*** *how to do it.* **Note:** **no** + **noun**. *There's* ***no room*** *for you.*

- **Every** is used with singular countable nouns. It refers to a group of people or things and means "all", "everyone", "everything" etc. *He goes to the gym* ***every*** *day.*

- **Each** is used with singular countable nouns. It means "one by one", considered individually. ***Each*** *member of the team* ***was*** *given a medal.* Note that **every one** and **each one** have **of** constructions. ***Every one of****/****Each one of*** *the players is to be given a bonus.*

- **One/Ones** are used to avoid repetition of a countable noun. *"Which dress do you like?" "This* ***one****."*

243 Underline the correct item.

1 <u>Both</u> / Neither Mozart and Beethoven were great composers.
2 Neither / Either Sam or David studied physics at school.
3 I finished the all / whole exercise in five minutes.
4 I've kept in touch with all / every my old school friends.
5 Neither / Either of the girls passed the exam. They both failed.
6 Victor goes to the same restaurant every / all day.
7 None / Each of the people he contacted were interested.
8 We have to pay our telephone bill each / every three months.
9 You'll get fat if you eat all / none those biscuits.
10 Either / Both Tom and Lynn had a good time.
11 She spent the whole / all afternoon lying on the beach.
12 Each / All of candidate will be interviewed individually.
13 None of / Every the students believed that the exam results would be released so early.
14 I don't like either / neither of these coats. I'll look for one somewhere else.
15 You'd better read through the all / whole contract before you sign it.
16 You're going to have to look through each / both one of these files separately.
17 There's a leak in both / each the hot water tank and the cold water tank.
18 Neither / Either of the tapes you bought is the one I really wanted.
19 None of / All of the girls were ready for the dance on time. They got there late.
20 "Do you like these boots?" "No, I prefer these one / ones."
21 Each / All one of the candidates was given a questionnaire before the interview.
22 Fiona and I went to the opera. We both / all enjoyed it very much.
23 There's no / none space for a washing machine in my kitchen.
24 All / Every that she wants is another baby. She simply adores big families.
25 I go swimming nearly either / every day.
26 My drama group put on a play but none / all of us were pleased with the performance.

Mozart   **Beethoven**

244 *Fill in: all, both, whole, either, neither, none, every, each or one(s).*

1   ...*None*... of the toxic waste has been cleared up by the company.
2   He's studying .... politics and modern languages at university.
3   "I think these are the .... you like."
4   They spent the .... day packing for their holiday.
5   She spends .... her time studying for her exams.
6   In .... game there is an element of risk.
7   John and Fiona had a lot of work yesterday. .... of them went out.
8   "Do you like this skirt?" "I think that .... is more flattering."
9   The members of the club were .... given copies of the regulations.
10 Both of these dictionaries are excellent - .... one of them will help you in your studies.

- **Both ... and ... + plural verb.** *Both* Ann and Liz *are* vegetarians.
- **Neither ... nor ... / Either ... or ... / Not only ... but also ... + singular** or **plural verb** depending on the subject which follows nor, or, but also. *Neither* Bill **nor** John **is** willing to help. Not only Sue but also **her family are** going to the wedding.

245 *Rewrite the sentences using both...and, neither...nor, either...or, not only... but also.*

1   Kay is a doctor and so is Niall. ...*Both Kay and Niall are doctors.*...
2   Karen will pick you up from the station or else Miles will. ....
3   John hasn't been to Germany and his brother hasn't either. ....
4   Jo and Jim speak French. ....
5   Paul doesn't like going to the cinema. Tim doesn't either. ....
6   James likes going fishing; so does Kate. ....
7   This winter Liz is going skiing; so are her parents. ....
8   Tim will fix your car or else John will. ....
9   Pete and Nicki prepared the dinner. ....
10 Jane is going on a picnic this Sunday and so are her schoolmates. ....

246 *Complete the sentences using the words in bold. Use two to five words.*

1   My aunt lives on a farm and so does my cousin.
    and   Both my ...*aunt and cousin live*... on a farm.
2   Danny can speak Chinese and so can his brother.
    but   Not .... brother can speak Chinese.
3   Gordon is a journalist; his wife is too.
    are   Both .... journalists.
4   The exhibition will be opened by the mayor or the Queen.
    or   Either the .... open the exhibition.
5   Not only Patricia but also her husband want to emigrate.
    and   Both .... to emigrate.
6   She doesn't enjoy sleeping in a tent and nor does her sister.
    nor   Neither .... sleeping in a tent.
7   Bob is about to leave; Helen is about to leave too.
    also   Not only .... about to leave.
8   My father didn't go to university and neither did my mother.
    nor   Neither my .... to university.
9   You can ask John or Tom to help you prune the trees.
    either You can .... to help you prune the trees.

11 Determiners / Pronouns

A lot of - many - much

	countables	uncountables	
Positive	a lot (of)/lots of/ many (formal)	a lot (of)/lots of/ much (formal)	There are **a lot of** animals in the zoo. There is **a lot of** sugar in my coffee.
Interrogative	many	much	Are there **many** books in the library? Did you have **much** time to read any of them?
Negative	many	much	There aren't **many** cakes left. I won't make any more as I don't have **much** flour left.
	a few (= some)/ (very) few (= not many, not enough)	a little (= some)/ (very) little (= not much, not enough)	**A few** students passed the test. **Very few** prisoners escape from prison. **A little** salt gives flavour to food.

- **A lot (of)/Lots of** + countable/uncountable nouns are normally used in positive sentences. **A lot of** people attended the ceremony. She's got **lots of** furniture. **A lot of** can also be used in questions and negations in informal English. Was there **a lot of** disagreement over the proposal?

- **Many + countables / much + uncountables** are normally used in questions or negations. Are there **many** cakes? There isn't **much** Coke. **Many** and **much** are often used in positive sentences after **too, so, how** or in formal English. She didn't realise **how much** money she had spent. You should slow down; you're doing **too much.**

- **A few** (= some, a small number) + **countables** **a little** (= some, a small amount of) + **uncountables** have a positive meaning. I have **a little** money left so I'll buy **a few** sweets.

- **Few** (= not many, almost none) + **countables / Little** (= not much, almost none) + **uncountables** have a negative meaning and are rather formal English. **Very few/very little, only a few/only a little** are more usual. **Few** English people speak a second language. I've had **very little** success with my job applications. He had **only a few** problems in the exam even though he had done **only a little** work for it.

Note: most, all, some, any, many, a few, several, both, one, two, much, (a) little are followed by **of** when a noun follows, preceded by possessives or words such as: this, that, these, those, the or a. How **much of** the money I gave you did you spend? I liked **two of** her books, but I was bored by the others. So **many of** my friends are away that I've got no one to talk to.

247 *Fill in: a lot (of), much or many.*

1 It takes ...*a lot of*... patience to bring up children.
2 There can't be .... people who haven't seen Jurassic Park.
3 She doesn't have .... time to herself these days.
4 Why haven't you washed the dishes? You didn't have .... else to do.
5 He's very popular. He always has .... people at his house.
6 We don't get on very well as we haven't got .... in common.
7 Will there be .... guests at the wedding?
8 You need .... courage to be a firefighter.
9 Have .... new people joined the club this year?
10 There are too .... mistakes in your composition.
11 There's still .... food left over from the party last night.
12 I hope we didn't make .... noise when we came in late last night.
13 She's eaten too .... sweets so she doesn't feel well.
14 There's .... poverty in some African countries.
15 She must have .... money to afford such expensive clothes.

248 *Underline the correct item.*

1 Very <u>few</u> / much / little people can guess what the future will be like.
2 There are very little / too many / much cars on the roads.
3 There's a little / a few / much light coming in through that window.
4 We've had much / very little / a lot of problems with the car.
5 Did you learn many / much / a few English on your summer course?
6 He was late because he had little / few / a lot of work to do.
7 I'm afraid I haven't got much / many / a little information about that matter.
8 Only a few / a lot of / a little people knew it was my birthday.
9 There are a little / much / a few sandwiches left on the table.
10 John's schoolwork leaves lots of / many / few room for improvement.
11 Did you spend many / a few / much money on this blouse?
12 There are only a little / a few / a lot of days left before the holiday.
13 I don't like many / much / little of Woody Allen's films.
14 Sally ate too many / much / little cake and now she feels sick.
15 There are a lot / a little / a few flowers in the garden.
16 I have only a little / a few / a lot of books but I'd like to have more.

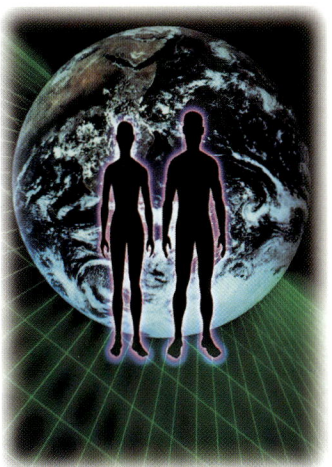

Some - Any - No

	Adjectives	Pronouns	Adverbs	
		people	things	places
Positive	some any	someone/somebody anyone/anybody	something anything	somewhere anywhere
Interrogative	any	anyone/anybody	anything	anywhere
Negative	no/not any	no one/not anyone nobody/not anybody	nothing not anything	nowhere not anywhere
Positive/Negative/ Interrogative	every	everybody (all people) everyone	everything (all things)	everywhere (in all places)

● **Some** is used before countable or uncountable nouns. *I'll buy **some** apples. He gave me **some** money.*
● **Some** and **its compounds** (somebody, something etc) are normally used in positive sentences. **They are also used in questions when we want to make an offer, a request or when we expect a positive answer.** *There's **someone** at the door. (= positive) Would you like **something** to eat? (= offer) Could I have **something** to drink? (= request) Is there **someone** waiting for me? (= I expect there is) but: Is there **anyone** waiting for me? (= I'm asking in general)*
● **Any** is used before countable or uncountable nouns. *Is there **any** sugar?* **Any** and **its compounds** **(anyone, anything etc) are normally used in questions.** *Is there **anyone** here?* **They are also used in positive sentences meaning "It doesn't matter how/what/which/when/who/where".** *You can go **anywhere** you want.* **Any** and **its compounds** **can be used after** if **in a positive sentence.** *If **anything** is broken, I will hold you responsible.*
● **No/not any** **are used before countable and uncountable nouns.** **No/not any** and **their compounds** **(no one/not anyone, nothing/not anything etc) are used in negations.** *I know **no one** at this party. I don't know **anyone** at this party.* **Any** and **its compounds** **are used with negative words (hardly, never, without, seldom, rarely etc).** *I **never** go **anywhere** alone at night. (not: I never go nowhere alone at night.)*
● **Every** **is used before singular countable nouns.** **Every** and **its compounds** **take a verb in singular.** *Every worker in the factory **has** been well trained. (= all the workers) We've bought **everything** we need. (= all the things)*

11 Determiners / Pronouns

249 Underline the correct item.

1 He didn't say anything / nothing to the police.
2 No one / Anyone was at home when I called.
3 There was hardly no one / anyone at the party.
4 I need any / some more milk for this cake.
5 I can't find my sister anywhere / nowhere.
6 Are you going nowhere / anywhere for your holiday?
7 John goes to sleep at 11.00 pm any / every evening.
8 Call round any / some time you like.
9 He needs any / some time to work out the answer.
10 Anybody / Nobody told me you were leaving.
11 Anybody / Everybody congratulated us.
12 She goes to school every / some day.
13 Is there everything / anything good on at the cinema?
14 Will you give them nothing / some homework tonight?
15 I think there's anything / something wrong with my car.
16 Sally isn't going anywhere / nowhere this weekend.
17 He doesn't want anything / nothing in particular for his birthday.
18 Shall I go and buy some / anything cheese?
19 There is nowhere / everywhere in the world I'd like to visit more than Egypt.
20 I didn't buy some / any milk.

250 Fill in: some, any, no, every or their compounds.

1 ...Everyone... knows that the sky is blue, but few people know why.
2 If you have .... questions, I'll be in my office.
3 .... wanted to miss the match so .... arrived early.
4 The teacher asked if .... knew the answer to her question.
5 Would you like .... cheese or maybe .... sweeter?
6 Have you seen Jim ....? I've been looking .... for him.
7 If you have .... spare time, there's .... I want to talk to you about.
8 .... is looking for John but .... has seen him since this morning.
9 I've never been .... without finding .... interesting to see.
10 If .... is going to the supermarket could they get me .... milk?
11 Don't speak to me. There is .... you can say to me that will make .... difference to how I feel.
12 We never go .... for our holidays. Why don't we go .... this year?
13 Jerry is very tidy; he won't tolerate .... being out of place.
14 "I'll get you .... coffee." "Have you got .... cold - .... milk perhaps?"

● **Ever** can be added to certain **question words** to mean **"any"**. These words are: whoever (anyone who), whatever (anything that), whichever (any of), whenever (any time that), wherever (any place that), however (in any way that). *You can come **whenever** you like. (= any time that you like)*

251 Fill in: whoever, whatever, whichever, whenever, wherever or however.

1 I'm not sure how to advise you. I suggest you do ...whatever... you think best.
2 .... mum decides to put the washing out, it always starts raining.
3 My pen is missing! .... has borrowed it kindly return it, immediately.
4 "Welcome! Come in and sit down .... you can find an empty seat."
5 Red and green both look good on you. .... colour you choose, I'm sure it will suit you.
6 The interview is informal so you can dress .... you want.
7 You know where to find me - come round .... you want and we'll talk over your problem.
8 .... wins the elections is sure to be the best candidate.
9 You must get some advice about the career you wish to follow so that .... one you choose, you won't regret it.
10 There are two different routes from here to Manchester. Why not take .... is the shortest to save time?

Else

- **Else** (= more; different) is followed by a singular verb and can be used with the **indefinite pronouns** and adverbs **everyone, something, nobody, anywhere** etc.
  You'd better ask Joanne. **Nobody else knows** *better than her.* It can also be used with **who, what, where** and **how** to refer to people, things, places etc. *What else can be done to prevent crime?*
- **Else** forms its possessive case with **'s**. *Don't use my pen. Take* **someone else's**.
- **Or else** means "otherwise". *Get an umbrella* **or else** *you'll get wet.*

252 *Complete the sentences using "else" structures.*

1 You must study for the test ...*or else*... you won't do well.
2 We always go to this restaurant. Can't we go ....?
3 She wasn't in the bank when they robbed it; you'd better ask ....
4 You have to speak to Mary; .... can make such an important decision.
5 I've only bought two tickets for the concert, as I wasn't sure if .... would want to go.
6 .... can cook as well as my mother.
7 When he was moving, he brought the big things in a van and .... in his car.
8 We always watch the football; can't we watch .... for a change?
9 Sandra and Cilla will be there, but I don't have a clue if .... is coming.
10 The waiter asked if we wanted to order ....

"Other" structures

- **the other(s)** = **the rest.** *These books are Tom's;* **the others** *are mine.*
- **others** = **several more apart from those already mentioned.** *People have different opinions when it comes to vegetarianism; some believe it's unhealthy and unnatural not to eat meat while* **others** *believe it is much better for our health.*
- **each other** = **one another.** *Good friends always help* **each other** *out.*
- **every other** = **alternate.** *I go jogging* **every other** *day.*
- **the other day** = **a few days ago.** *I bumped into George* **the other day**; *he looked well.*
- **the other one(s)** = **not this/these but something else.** *No, not that shirt. I want* **the other one**; *the black one please. These shoes are too small - can I try* **the other ones**, *please?*
- **another** = **one more apart from those already mentioned.** *Can you give me* **another** *cup of coffee?* **Another** can also be used with expressions of distance, money and time. *It'll cost* **another** *£5 to get it.*

253 *Fill in: another, (the) other(s), each other, every other.*

1 They went skiing ...*the other*... day. It was fun.
2 Only four people turned up at the christening. All .... guests had to go somewhere else.
3 This shirt doesn't fit me - can I try .... one on, please?
4 In .... four years Tom will have qualified as a doctor.
5 Those magazines belong to Jim, ... belong to me.
6 There were only enough seats for 20 passengers on the bus - .... had to stand.
7 Some commuters believe it's economical to cycle to work while .... prefer to use a car-sharing scheme.
8 No, we're not close to our destination yet - we have .... six miles to go.
9 Even though they see .... every day, they still want to spend more time together.
10 Kate is very keen on playing the piano - she has lessons .... day and in between she practises at home.

11 Determiners / Pronouns

In Other Words

- Tom, Steve and Paul don't like tennis.
  None of them like/likes tennis.
- Ann is a typist. Mary is a typist, too.
  Both Ann and Mary are typists.
- Sally, Sue and Pam enjoy swimming.
  All three of them enjoy swimming.

- There isn't anything in the garden.
  There is nothing in the garden.
- No one will make me stay.
  There isn't anyone that/who will make me stay.
- Lynn doesn't like yogurt. Fiona doesn't like yogurt either. Neither of them likes yogurt.
  Neither Lynn nor Fiona likes yogurt.

254 *Complete the sentences using the words in bold. Use two to five words.*

1 No one knows the answer to my question.
   anyone   There ...*isn't anyone who knows*... the answer to my question.
2 There isn't anything I can do to help.
   is   There .... do to help.
3 Bob lives in Rome. John lives in Rome, too.
   live   Both .... in Rome.
4 Pete, Robert and Bill cook delicious meals.
   them   All .... delicious meals.
5 Mr Green can't drive. Mr Smythe can't drive either.
   can   Neither Mr Green .... drive.
6 The boys all dislike brussel sprouts.
   likes   None .... brussel sprouts.
7 These computers are not difficult to operate.
   of   None .... difficult to operate.
8 There wasn't anything he could do to avoid crashing.
   nothing There .... to avoid crashing.
9 Five is an odd number. Seven is an odd number, too.
   are   Both .... odd numbers.
10 No one in the jury believed the witness.
   anyone   There .... jury that believed the witness.

Oral Development 15

*Use **both, all, neither** and **none** to compare the three women.* **eg. All three of them look happy.**

Lynn

25, single, two brothers, no sisters, likes cinema, didn't go to university, works in a company

Sarah

25, single, no brothers, no sisters, likes cinema, went to university, is self-employed

Pamela

33, single, two brothers, no sisters, likes cinema, went to university, works in a company

Pronouns

Personal pronouns		Possessive adjectives	Possessive pronouns	Reflexive-Emphatic pronouns
before verbs as subjects	**after verbs as objects**	**followed by nouns**	**not followed by nouns**	
I	me	my	mine	myself
you	you	your	yours	yourself
he	him	his	his	himself
she	her	her	hers	herself
it	it	its	---	itself
we	us	our	ours	ourselves
you	you	your	yours	yourselves
they	them	their	theirs	themselves

Note: We use **the** instead of a possessive adjective with parts of the body after prepositions. **Verbs used in this pattern include: bite, hit, kiss, pat, punch, slap, sting, touch etc.** *She slapped the boy on the face. (not: on his face)*

Own + possessive adjective is used to emphasise the fact that something belongs to one person and no one else. *She's got her **own** car.* or *She's got a car **of her own**.*

255 *Fill in the correct pronouns or possessives.*

Dear Jean,

1) ...*We*...'re really enjoying 2) .... on holiday in Clacton and have found something different to do every day. 3) ....'ll never guess what happened to 4) .... last night. Fred and 5) .... went to see a comedy show. Stan Blair was the star attraction. Have 6) .... heard of 7) ....? He is a young, up-and-coming comedian who is just starting to make a name for 8) .... At the end of 9) .... act he asked if anyone in the audience was celebrating 10) .... birthday that night. To 11) .... embarrassment Fred shouted out that it was 12) ....! I was invited onto the stage and Stan presented 13) .... with a bunch of flowers. After the show he met Fred and 14) .... in the bar for a drink and introduced 15) .... to the other members of the cast and they all signed 16) .... names on the back of one of 17) .... programmes. I haven't enjoyed 18) .... so much in ages. We both agreed that Stan had definitely made 19) .... holiday. Hope 20) .... was just as memorable.

Love,
Stella

256 *Fill in the gaps with "the" or a possessive adjective.*

1 He was crying because a wasp had stung him on ...*the*... nose.
2 She patted him lightly on .... shoulder to get .... attention.
3 He hugged .... son and said, "I'm proud of you."
4 The little boy kissed .... sister on .... cheek.
5 The boxer punched his opponent on .... nose.
6 She stroked .... hair and told him not to worry.
7 A falling brick nearly hit me on .... head.

11 Determiners / Pronouns

Reflexive - Emphatic Pronouns (myself - yourself etc)

- **Reflexive pronouns** are used after certain verbs (**behave, burn, cut, enjoy, hurt, kill, look at** etc) when the subject and the object of the verb are the same. *Did you cut* **yourself**? They can also be used after **be, feel, look, seem** to describe emotions or states. *She hasn't been* **herself** *recently.* Reflexive pronouns can be used after prepositions but not after prepositions of place. *She is very pleased with* **herself**. *but: She looked behind her. (not: behind herself)*
  Certain verbs (**wash, shave, dress, undress, meet, rest, relax, stand up, get up, sit down, wake up** etc) do not normally take a reflexive pronoun. *She woke up and dressed. (not: She woke up herself and dressed herself.)* **Wash** or **dress** can be used with a reflexive pronoun to talk about young children or animals. *The little girl is* **washing herself**.
- **Emphatic pronouns** have the same form as reflexive pronouns but a different meaning. They give emphasis to the noun, or the fact that a certain person performs an action. *She* **herself** *organised the feast.* They can also mean "without help". *He painted the house* **himself**. *(without help)*
- Note these idioms: **Enjoy yourselves!** (= Have a good time!) **Behave yourself!** (= Be good!) **He likes being by himself.** (= He likes being alone.) **He lives by himself.** (= He lives on his own.) **By myself, by yourself, by himself etc** (= on my own, on your own, on his own etc) **Help yourself to tea.** (= You're welcome to take some tea if you want some.) **Do it yourself.** (= Do it without being helped.) **Make yourself at home!** (= Feel comfortable.) **Make yourself heard.** (= Speak loudly enough to be heard by others.) **Make yourself understood.** (= Make your meaning clear.)

Note: each other means "one another". **Compare:** *Tom and Bill are brothers who have been brought up to look after* **each other**. *Tom and Bill are very independent for their ages and they are extremely capable of looking after* **themselves**.

257 *Fill in the pronouns then identify them: reflexive or emphatic.*

1 The Chinese girl decorated the pumpkin ...*herself*... . *(emphatic)*
2 The winner looked very proud of ....
3 She brought up her children by ....
4 The couple wrote to .... when they had to spend time apart.
5 The children enjoyed .... when they visited Disneyland.
6 Ann was afraid of spiders, so she didn't go into the room by ....
7 Instead of hiring a catering company for the party, she decided to do all the cooking ....
8 The boy was asked to behave .... at the wedding.
9 He shouted loudly above the noise to make .... understood.
10 Cats are very clean animals: they are always washing ....
11 Doctors advise us that we have to exercise regularly in order to keep .... healthy.
12 The weather is affecting me at the moment - I don't feel .... at all!
13 He's very vain and loves looking at .... in the mirror.

258 *Fill in with: of one's own, on one's own or one's own in the correct form.*

1 He left ...*his own*.. family to go and live abroad.
2 I would like to have a room ....
3 She couldn't lift the table .... so she asked her husband to help her.
4 Let me handle this matter ...., will you?
5 They had .... house designed by a top architect.
6 He's about to set up .... business and has asked me to help organise it.
7 He enjoys spending time ....
8 I'd really like a car .... so I don't have to rely on my friends all the time.
9 "Is this .... motorbike, young man?" the policeman asked.
10 Although she can afford domestic help, she insists on doing the housework ....

Possessive case

's / s' (people or animals)	of (inanimate things)
• **singular noun + 's** *the cat's claws, the boy's hats* • **regular plural noun + '** *the tourists' passports* • **irregular plural noun not ending in s + 's** *the men's room, the children's playroom* • **compound noun + 's** *his mother-in-law's car* • **'s after the last of two or more names to show common possession** *Ann and Sally's flat (They share the same flat) but: Ann's and Sally's flats (each one has got a flat)*	• **of + inanimate thing/abstract noun** *the door of the house, the beauty of the view* • **of + possessive case/pronouns when there is a determiner (this, any etc) before the nouns** *Look at this painting of Picasso's. (one of Picasso's paintings), a dress of hers (one of her dresses)* • **of + people (in longer phrases)** *That's the brother of one of my friends.* • **'s/of to talk about places or organisations** *London's attractions/the attractions of London*

Note: **phrases of place + 's** *(at the butcher's)* **time/distance expression + 's/'** *(last week's news, three days' visit)*

259 *Rewrite the following using the correct possessive form.*

1 the butterflies - the wings ...*the butterflies' wings*...
2 the students - the books ....
3 drive - three hours ....
4 the department store - the staff ....
5 living - the cost ....
6 some friends - my brother ....
7 bread - the price ....
8 the baby - the pram ....
9 John and Paul - the wives ....
10 the men - the changing rooms ....
11 the sea - the waves ....
12 a climb - two hundred metres ....
13 Lucy and Emily - the mother ....
14 the house - my father's closest friend ....
15 the president - the decision ....
16 my physics professor - the report ....
17 the park - the playground ....
18 the Smiths - the car ....
19 my mother-in-law - the garden ....

260 *Complete the following sentences using the words in bold. Use two to five words.*

1 In England, Elizabeth II is the Queen.
   of   Elizabeth II ...*is the Queen of*... England.
2 The gallery has just bought a painting by Monet.
   one   The gallery has just bought .... paintings.
3 I saw a play by Shakespeare at The Globe.
   plays   I saw .... at The Globe.
4 It takes half an hour to walk into town.
   is   It .... into town.
5 This necklace belonged to my mother-in-law.
   was   This .... necklace.
6 In France the president is elected every seven years.
   of   The .... every seven years.

11 Determiners / Pronouns

There - It

- **There + be**: used for something mentioned for the first time or to say that someone or something exists. **There are** some letters for you on your desk.
- **Personal pronoun + be/other verb**: used to give more details about something or someone already mentioned. **There's** someone at the door. **He** wants to see you.
- **It + be**: used for identification. There's someone outside. **It's** your landlord.
- **It + be ... to-inf/that-clause** is used to begin a sentence. **It's** nice to be with you. **It's** a pity **that** he **didn't** come.
- **It** is also used for distance, temperature, time expressions, weather and in the following expressions: It seems that, It appears that, It looks like, It is said that, It doesn't matter etc. **It's** freezing today, isn't it? **It appears that** he's been promoted; he's just bought a new car. **It seems that** there is a problem with the machine. (but we also say): **There seems to be** a problem with the machine. **It looks like** it's going to rain.

261 Fill in: there or it.

1 ...*It*...'s very cold today; .... has been snowing all night.
2 ....'s a policeman at the door; .... seems that the neighbour has complained about the noise.
3 ....'s a holiday tomorrow so no one has to go to work.
4 Let's go by taxi to the cinema; ....'s much too far to walk.
5 ....'s a letter on the doorstep; ....'s for you.
6 This report you've shown me is confusing - .... appears to be a mistake in it.
7 .... are many changes to be made to this report but .... shouldn't take us too long.
8 .... is my privilege to introduce our distinguished guest speaker.
9 ....'s nothing much on TV tonight - .... 's a pity we don't have a video recorder.
10 .... is a shame you weren't able to come to the party. .... were lots of people there.

262 Complete the sentences using the words in bold. Use two to five words.

1 Everyone thanked me except Paul.
person   The only ...*person who didn't thank*... me was Paul.
2 She said: "I dislike French films and so does Jim."
neither   She said that .... French films.
3 If you decorate the house on your own, it will be cheaper.
yourself   If you ...., it will be cheaper.
4 I take twenty minutes to drive to work every morning.
drive   It's .... to my work every morning.
5 Try to watch your behaviour at the wedding reception.
yourself   Try .... at the wedding reception.
6 I don't like being alone in the house at night.
by   I don't like .... in the house at night.
7 There are only a few people who can speak Welsh.
not   There .... can speak Welsh.
8 She left the shop with another person's bag by mistake.
someone   She left the shop .... by mistake.
9 We spent all afternoon cleaning the living room.
whole   We spent .... the living room.
10 We don't know much about supernatural phenomena.
knowledge   We have .... about supernatural phenomena.
11 She passed the written exam and the oral exam as well.
both   She passed .... exams.

12 She sat alone waiting for her friends to turn up.

own She sat .... her friends to turn up.

13 Nobody can find the solution to the problem.

anybody There .... can find the solution to the problem.

14 He has been everywhere except Australia.

country The .... been to is Australia.

15 In Australia the first inhabitants were the Aborigines.

of The .... were the Aborigines.

16 "You can call me whenever you want," he said.

time He said I .... that I wanted.

17 She told the children to go and play in another place.

else "Go ....," she told the children.

18 There aren't many chefs who can make Creme Bavaroise well.

few There are .... Creme Bavaroise well.

19 She invited both her relatives and her colleagues to the engagement party.

only She invited .... also her colleagues to the engagement party.

20 He has seen to everything except the orchestra.

thing The .... seen to is the orchestra.

21 We haven't had any luck finding a flat.

no We have .... finding a flat.

22 It takes three hours to climb to the top of the hill.

is It .... to the top of the hill.

263 Find the word which should not be in the sentence.

1	she
2	
3	
4	
5	
6	
7	
8	
9	
10	
11	
12	
13	
14	
15	
16	
17	
18	
19	
20	
21	
22	
23	
24	
25	

1 My sister she gave birth to a lovely baby boy last week.

2 There he is a man at the door. It must be the postman.

3 Our children want themselves to go camping this summer; what about yours?

4 We felt ourselves relieved when the plane landed at the airport.

5 "This it is your captain speaking. Welcome on board!"

6 He kept talking about how so expensive their holiday had turned out to be.

7 She spent the all morning buying gifts for her family.

8 Computers are not easy to use them unless you know the software.

9 There it seems that we are in for a long hot summer.

10 The manager wants all of applicants to be called for an interview.

11 She likes to wake up herself early in the morning.

12 We haven't got an our own camera but we intend to buy one.

13 If anyone person arrives late, they will not be allowed to enter the room.

14 You can call on us any one day you want.

15 He's got a little patience so he wouldn't be any good at teaching.

16 These books are out of print but the others ones are available.

17 He could very hardly understand what was going on.

18 Every one employee has to clock in at 9.00.

19 All that we can do it is to wait for their phone call.

20 Unless the both parties agree to start discussions, there won't be any progress.

21 Neither of the teacher nor the students enjoyed the trip to Aspen.

22 We know a very few people here so we feel lonely at times.

23 A lots of people gathered at the airport to welcome the Olympic winners.

24 Would you like to spend the whole all month with us?

25 Some people enjoy going to the opera but others themselves don't.

Consolidation 11

Phrasal Verbs

stand by: 1) remain loyal esp in a difficult situation, 2) watch passively, 3) be ready for action

stand for: 1) represent, 2) (usu in questions and negations) tolerate; put up with

stand in for: replace sb temporarily

stand out: be very noticeable, prominent

stand up for: support; defend

stand up to: resist; stay in good condition

● ● ● ● ● ● ● ● ● ● ● ● ● ●

be taken aback: be strongly surprised

take after: look like

take sth back: admit that one was wrong in what one said

take down: 1) lengthen a garment (let down), 2) separate into pieces in order to repair or remove, 3) write down

take in: 1) give accommodation, 2) deceive

take for: identify sb or sth wrongly

take off: 1) remove clothes, 2) copy sb's speech or manners esp for fun; imitate

take on: 1) undertake responsibility, 2) employ

take sb out: take sb to the theatre etc

take over: take control or responsibility

take to: like

take up: begin to do sth as a hobby

264 Fill in the correct particle(s).

1   More and more people are beginning to stand ...*up for*... their rights.
2   She's so tall, she stands .... in any crowd.
3   The initials EU stand .... European Union.
4   Although he's in prison, his wife is standing .... him.
5   The star of the show was ill, so someone had to stand .... her.
6   We're not going to stand .... this injustice any longer.
7   I was taken .... by his offensive manner.
8   He wanted an energetic hobby so he took .... water skiing.
9   I'm sorry, I take .... what I said. You're not lazy and selfish.
10 My mother takes .... foreign students to make extra money.
11 The vice president took .... the company when the president retired.
12 I took you .... your brother from a distance. You look so alike.
13 She takes .... her mother; they have the same eyes.
14 He was talking too fast and we didn't manage to take .... the whole lecture.
15 They're taking .... extra staff at the car factory.

265 Think of the word which best fits each space. Write only one word in each space.

Paris

Paris, the capital **(0)** ...*of*... France, is a city where **(1)** .... the modern and the historical can be appreciated at the **(2)** .... time. One of the best examples of **(3)** .... is the Louvre. The world-famous art gallery was **(4)** .... a royal palace and now houses five thousand works of art including the Mona Lisa. Visitors come from all **(5)** .... the world to see these and to admire the grand architecture of the building itself. However, in the eighties, a more contemporary attraction **(6)** .... built in the gallery's courtyard; giant glass pyramids which, because **(7)** .... their sharp contrast, look surprisingly spectacular.

The Musée d' Orsay is another art gallery **(8)** .... present function differs greatly from its original use. Now filled **(9)** .... paintings by Van Gogh and Monet, the building was once a railway station. On the other hand, the Beaubourg, also known **(10)** .... the Pompidou Centre, is a thoroughly modern building. The home of contemporary culture, it is unique in that all of **(11)** .... pipes and ducts are on the outside.

For those **(12)** .... prefer to watch the world go by rather **(13)** .... look at the world in pictures, Les Deux Magots and the Café de Flore are definitely **(14)** .... a visit. These two street cafés are **(15)** .... many famous writers and intellectuals from the past met for coffee and stimulating discussions.

266 *Complete the sentences using the words in bold. Use two to five words.*

1 "You broke the television!" she said to me.
   of   She ...*accused me of breaking*... the television.
2 Is it necessary to write this report today?
   have   Does this report .... today?
3 I can't meet you at the airport.
   impossible It's .... you at the airport.
4 You'd better hurry or else you won't be home on time.
   will   If .... home on time.
5 He always locks the windows so that he won't be burgled at night.
   fear   He always locks the windows .... at night.
6 There was only a little food left after the party.
   any   There .... after the party.
7 He didn't call me; he didn't send me a letter either.
   did   He neither called me .... a letter.
8 I didn't have a chance to say goodbye.
   opportunity I had .... goodbye.
9 He found success after facing many difficulties.
   against   He .... before he found success.
10 She lost her passport at the airport.
   got   Her .... at the airport.
11 He can't make people understand him when he speaks French.
   himself   He .... when he speaks French.
12 Sally is coming to the party and Pam is coming too.
   also   Not only Sally .... to the party.

267 *Fill in the correct form of the verbs in brackets.*

Jason's uncle, who was a sailor, **1)** ...*had been travelling*... (travel) around the world for years. On his return, he **2)** .... (come) to the house with presents for everyone. To Jason he gave an old lamp which he **3)** .... (buy) in Saudi Arabia. Jason tried **4)** .... (hide) his disappointment at such a dirty old gift, but thanked his uncle for **5)** .... (bring) it anyway. When his uncle **6)** .... (go), Jason's mother wanted **7)** .... (take) the lamp to an antique shop and **8)** .... (it/clean). "That's OK," said Jason. "I **9)** .... (do) it myself." So he took it away and started **10)** .... (polish) it. As he **11)** .... (rub) away the dirt some smoke **12)** .... (come) out of it and, out of the smoke, appeared a large, rather frightening man. "Who are you?" **13)** .... (cry) Jason. "I am the Genie of the Lamp," the man **14)** .... (reply). "You can have three wishes. But be careful! If you **15)** .... (wish) well, you **16)** .... (reward), but if you

17) .... (wish) badly, you **18)** .... (bring) disaster on yourself and your family." Jason thought for a while and said, "I wish everyone in the world **19)** .... (have) enough food." "Good boy," said the Genie. "And I wish the peoples of the world **20)** .... (stop) fighting each other," he said. "One more." Now Jason thought really hard. "My mum **21)** .... (work) a lot recently and she's really tired all the time. If she **22)** .... (have) a car, she **23)** .... (not/be) so tired." So he wished for a car. "You **24)** .... (choose) well," said the Genie and disappeared. Jason **25)** .... (not/tell) his mum about what **26)** .... (happen), but the next day a letter arrived for her saying: "You **27)** .... (win) first prize in our car competition. A brand new Mercedes **28)** .... (deliver) to your home within the next few days."

Consolidation 11

268 *Fill in the correct prepositions of place or movement.*

between, down, on top of, over, in/inside, above, in front of, past, up, among, next to/by/beside, from...to, through, under, below, behind, along, opposite, at, round/around, near, outside, on, against, onto, out of, across, to/towards/in the direction of, into

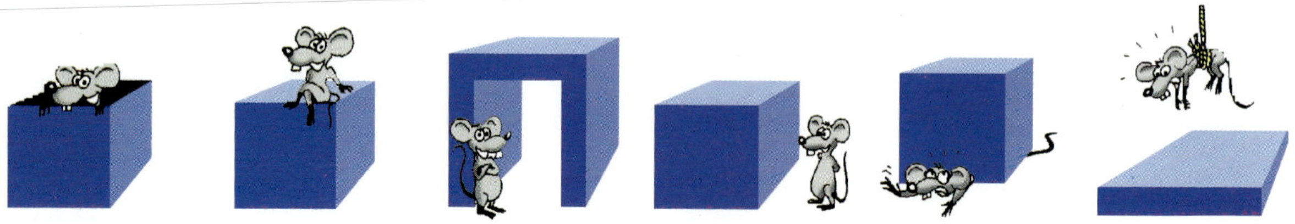

1 .....in/inside.... 2 .... 3 .... 4 .... 5 .... 6 ....

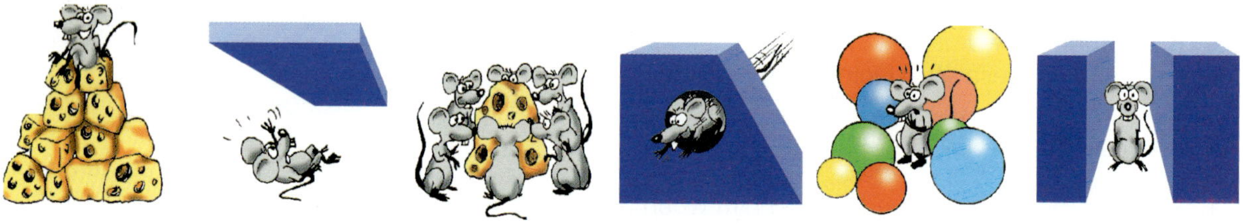

7 .... 8 .... 9 .... 10 .... 11 .... 12 ....

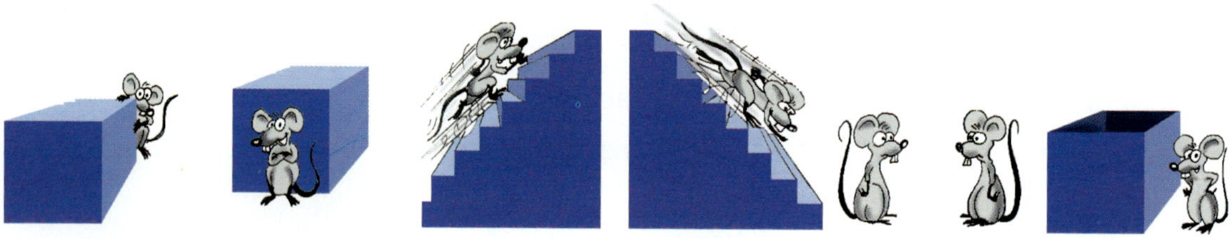

13 .... 14 .... 15 .... 16 .... 17 .... 18 ....

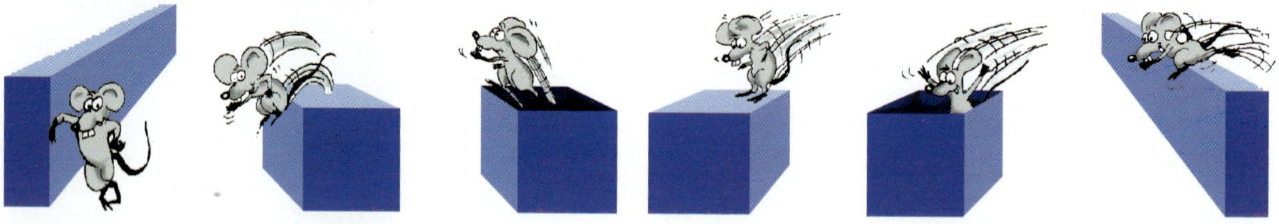

19 .... 20 .... 21 .... 22 .... 23 .... 24 ....

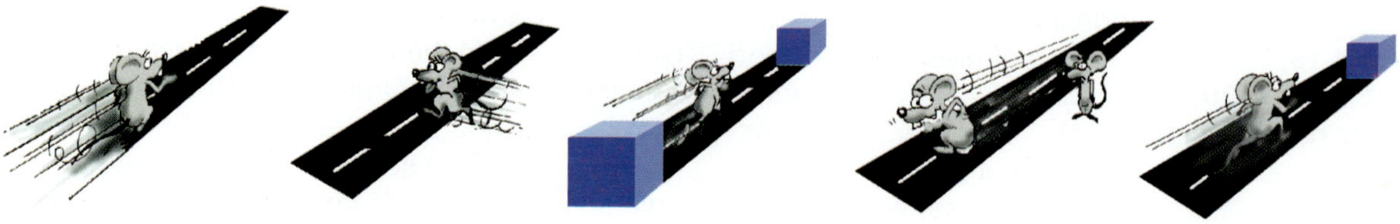

25 .... 26 .... 27 .... 28 .... 29 ....

269

Read the text carefully. Some of the lines are correct and some have a word which should not be there. If a line is correct, put a tick (✔) in the space provided. If a line has a word which should not be there, write it in the space provided.

The Dangers of the Sun

0	Holiday beaches are as like huge barbecues where	
00	people lie like burgers on a grill. Many	
1	people do not realise that the dangers of baking	
2	themselves in the sun. By following on some	
3	sensible advice, holidaymakers can to achieve a	
4	perfect tan, yet avoid such a dangers as sunburn	
5	and even skin cancer. The sun is at its strongest	
6	between 11 am and 3 pm, so that sit in the	
7	shade at this time. Babies should have be kept	
8	out of direct sun, and children they should	
9	wear sunblock and a hat. Remember to	
10	reapply suncream regularly, in particularly	
11	after the swimming. Sunglasses are not just a	
12	fashion accessory. They provide vital protection	
13	as from the sun's rays. Never wear sunglasses	
14	with much cheap lenses; they do more harm than	
15	good. Summer is a great season, but be sensible!	

0	*as*
00	✔
1	
2	
3	
4	
5	
6	
7	
8	
9	
10	
11	
12	
13	
14	
15	

270

For questions 1 - 10, read the text below. Use the word given in capitals at the end of each line to form a word that fits in the space in the same line. Write your word in the answer boxes provided.

Child Development

(0) .... children who have a good

(1) ...., whether in writing or speaking, benefit from

(2) .... . Many parents wrongly make the

(3) .... that this should occur in the classroom only,

giving teachers sole (4) .... for this. But parental

(5) .... is important too. A good

(6) .... is to get your child to enter writing

(7) .... which will give writing a sense of purpose and

fun. Making young minds realise the

(8) .... of keeping a diary is useful too. However, the

best idea is to encourage your child with (9) ....

storytelling and (10) .... game playing.

CREATE	
IMAGINE	
ENCOURAGE	
ASSUME	
RESPONSE	
GUIDE	
SUGGEST	
COMPETE	
IMPORTANT	
DRAMA	
ENJOY	

0	*Creative*
1	
2	
3	
4	
5	
6	
7	
8	
9	
10	

12 Questions / Short Answers

To form **Yes/No questions** (questions which ask for "Yes" or "No" in the answer) we put the auxiliary or modal verb (be, have, can etc) before the subject. *He is watching TV.* ➡ *Is he watching TV?* With all other verbs we form Yes/No questions with **Do/Does** (Present Simple) or **Did** (Past Simple) *He likes pizza.* ➡ *Does he like pizza? Did you go to the library?* Yes/No questions are asked with a rising intonation. *Do you enjoy cartoons?* ↗

Wh-questions begin with a question word (**who, what, where, why, when, whose, which, how** etc) "*How old is he?*" When there is a preposition, it usually goes at the end of the question. In formal English it can be put before the question word. *Who was he accused by? (more usual)* **By whom** was he accused? (formal English)

Questions are used to ask for information or permission. They are also used to make suggestions, requests, offers or invitations. *How far is the station? (information)*, **May I** go out? (permission), **Shall we** play tennis? (suggestion), **Could you** help me with the dishes? (request), **Would you like** some more coffee? (offer), **Would you like to** come to the beach with me? (invitation)

271 *Form questions, then identify the speech situation.*

1 (you look after/the baby tonight?)   *Could you look after the baby tonight? (request)*
2 (we go/the cinema this weekend?)
3 (How old/be Mary on her birthday?)
4 (I get/you another cup of coffee?)
5 (you like/come to my party on Saturday?)
6 (What time/the next bus leave?)
7 (I use/the phone?)
8 (we buy/Joan a book for Christmas?)
9 (you/give me a lift to the station?)
10 (you see/Mick at school yesterday?)

We normally use the following question words to ask about:

people	things/animals	place	time	quantity	manner	reason
Who Whose (possession) Which (of) What	What Which (of)	Where	How long How often What time When	How many How much	How	Why

- **Which** is used when there is a **limited choice**. "*Which is your favourite film star - Meryl Streep or Glenn Close?*" It can also be used with the **comparative** and **superlative**. "*Which is more comfortable, a bicycle or a motorcycle?*" "*Which is the quickest route to Birmingham?*"
- **What** is used when there is an **unlimited choice**. "*What kind of music do you like?*" It can also be used in the following patterns: **What...look like?** (asking for a description of physical appearance), **What...for?, What colour?, What size?, What kind/sort?, What time?, What is he like?** (asking for a description of character), **What is it used for?** etc "*What colour are his eyes?*" "*What is your new teacher like?*" "*He's friendly and patient.*" "*What does Ann look like?*" "*She's slim with a fair complexion.*"
- **What** and **which** are sometimes both possible. *Which/What fruit does he like eating?*

272 *Fill in: who, whose, which, what, where, how long, how often, what time, when, how many, how much, how or why.*

1 "...*Who*...starred in the film "The Godfather?" "Al Pacino."
2 "..................................... calories do you consume every day?" "About 1,800."

3 "..................................... of these skirts do you prefer, the blue or the pink?" "The blue one."
4 "..................................... do you go to the gym?" "About once a week."
5 "..................................... sugar do you take in your coffee?" "One spoonful."
6 "..................................... are we going to the restaurant?" "At 6 o'clock."
7 "..................................... did it take you to write your essay?" "About five hours."
8 "..................................... are you crying?" "I've hurt my arm."
9 "..................................... does your sister get back from Portugal?" "Next Wednesday."
10 "..................................... is your favourite colour?" "Purple."
11 "..................................... are you going on holiday this year?" "South Africa."
12 "..................................... pen is this? I found it on the floor." "It's mine."
13 "..................................... do you leave home in the morning?" "About 8 o'clock."
14 "..................................... did you manage to break your arm?" "I fell off my bicycle."
15 "..................................... is the new restaurant like?" "It's extremely elegant."
16 "..................................... are the children up to?" "I don't know."
17 "..................................... is the fastest way to get to Paris from here?" "By plane."
18 "..................................... didn't you call me earlier?" "I was busy."
19 "..................................... is your favourite subject at school?" "Latin."
20 "..................................... money have you got left?" "None."

273 *Ask questions where the word/phrase in bold is the answer.*

1 Pete works for **British Telecom**.
   ...*Who does Pete work for?*...
2 Sara owns **two** cars. ....
3 She's **tall and fair**. ....
4 It's **nearly seven o'clock**. ....
5 I have French lessons **twice a week**. ....
6 She's **very shy and quiet**. ....
7 I went to **Hawaii** on holiday. ....
8 There are **six students** in my class. ....
9 I wasn't at work today **because I was ill**. ......
10 **David's** car was stolen. ....

11 **Shakespeare** wrote "King Lear". ....
12 We've lived here **for ten years**. ....
13 My new car cost **£10,000**. ....
14 Kay's gone out **shopping**. ....
15 I'm not going out **because it's cold**. ....
16 Shirley got married to **Ben**. ....
17 That's **my** pen. ....
18 The **history exam** was the most difficult. ....
19 I get up at **eight o'clock** in the morning. ....
20 That man is **the new director**. ....
21 She lives **in the suburbs**. ....

Subject/Object Questions

If **who, which** or **what** are the subject of the question, the word order is the same as in statements (subject questions). If they are the object of the question, the verb is in question form (object questions).

subject		object		subject		object
Greg	*hit*	*David.*		*David*	*hit*	*Paul.*

Who hit David? (not: ~~Who did hit David?~~)   **Who did** David **hit**?

274 *Write questions for the sentences below. The words in bold should be the answer.*

1 **Tom** broke the window. ...*Who broke the window?*...
2 Jill invited **Paul** to the party. ....
3 Lions live in **Africa**. ....
4 **Anthony** arrived late. ....
5 Peter opened **the door**. ....
6 Kate gave the letter **to Julie**. ....
7 **Jenny** forgot to do her homework. ....
8 He likes **basketball**. ....
9 **Hugh** was rude to Jill. ....

10 **Jo** lost her purse. ....
11 **Professor Evans** gave the lecture. ....
12 **Jane** lost the keys to her car. ....
13 **Phil** borrowed your car. ....
14 Sue dropped **her glasses**. ....
15 **Tracy** loves ice cream. ....
16 Jeremy saw **his teacher**. ....
17 James bought **a Coke**. ....
18 Jenny married **Bill**. ....

12 Questions / Short Answers

Negative Questions

- **Negative questions** are formed with **not** but there is a difference in word order for the short and full form.
  auxiliary + n't + subject + verb (short form) *Hasn't* she called you yet? *(everyday speech)*
  auxiliary + subject + not + verb (full form) *Has she not* called you yet? *(used for emphasis)*

- **Negative questions** are used to express: **surprise** (***Didn't you*** *know she was my Mum?*), **annoyance** or **sarcasm** (***Can't you*** *be more patient?*), **a wish to persuade someone** (***Won't you*** *tell me who you went out with?*) and **expectation of a "Yes" - answer** (*Don't you know she got promoted?*)

275 *In the following dialogues, make negative questions using the words given and decide if the expected response would be Yes or No, as in the example:*

1 A: You're still in your pyjamas. ...*Aren't you supposed to be getting ready?*... (supposed to/get ready)
   B: ...*No,*... I've still got plenty of time.
2 A: Your mother is shouting for you. ....? (hear her)
   B: ...., but I want to play basketball a little longer.
3 A: You've been learning German for years. ....? (speak yet)
   B: ...., but I'm too shy to try in front of strangers.
4 A: What a lovely hairdo! ....? (tell me who does it for you)
   B: ...., because you always copy everything I do!
5 A: Why aren't you coming to the party? ....? (feel like going out)
   B: ...., but I've got to babysit tonight.
6 A: You look down. ....? (enjoy the film)
   B: .... It was the kind of film that really depresses me.
7 A: She had her tenants evicted. ....? (a mean thing to do)
   B: .... She's got a reputation for being heartless.
8 A: That was a rather tactless thing to say. ....? (realise she was Anne's sister)
   B: .... You could have mentioned it earlier.
9 A: There was a terrible car crash. ....? (see it on the news)
   B: ...., I didn't get home until late last night.
10 A: It's past your bedtime. ....? (be in bed by now)
   B: .... I'm allowed to stay up late at the weekend.

276 *Write questions to which the bold type words are the answers.*

Although it is commonly assumed that **tortoises are simply small domestic pets**, a number of large species of tortoise have been living **in their natural environment** for centuries. Tortoises **in tropical regions** can exceed three feet in length and records show that before it became extinct, the atlas tortoise measured **almost six feet**. The turtle is very similar to the tortoise but lives **in the sea** rather than on the land. In recent years turtles have been fished for **food and their valuable oil**. **Conservationists** are concerned about this trend, as **turtles may soon become extinct**.

1 ...*What is commonly assumed?*...
2 ....
3 ....
4 ....
5 ....
6 ....
7 ....
8 ....

Question Tags

● Question tags are short questions added to the end of a statement to ask for **confirmation** of, or **agreement** with, the statement. They are formed with an auxiliary verb and the appropriate personal pronoun. They take the same auxiliary verb as in the statement if there is one, otherwise they take **do/does** (Present S.) or **did** (Past S.). *She speaks French, **doesn't she**? He isn't rich, **is he**?*

● A positive statement is followed by a negative question tag, and a negative statement is followed by a positive question tag. *He plays well, **doesn't he**? He can't do it, **can he**?* Note that **everyone/someone/anyone/no one** form their question tags with an **auxiliary verb + they**. *Everyone offered to help, didn't **they**?*

● Study the following question tags.

1	"I am"	"aren't I?"	*I am older than you, aren't I?*
2	"I used to"	"didn't I?"	*He used to go to school with you, didn't he?*
3	Imperative	"will you/won't you?" "can you/could you?"	*Phone me later, will you?/won't you?/ can you?/could you?*
4	"Let's"	"shall we?"	*Let's go home now, shall we?*
5	"Let me/him" etc	"will you/won't you?"	*Let her decide for herself, will you/won't you?*
6	"Don't" (negative imperative)	"will you?"	*Don't come round so late again, will you?*
7	"I have" (= possess)	"haven't I?"	*She has got her own office, hasn't she?*
8	"I have" (idiomatic use)	"don't I?"	*We had a great time, didn't we?*
9	"There is/are"	"isn't/aren't there?"	*There is some mail for me, isn't there?*
10	"This/That is"	"isn't it?"	*That's your car over there, isn't it?*

● **Questions tags** can be said with a **rising intonation** when we are not sure and expect an answer, or a **falling intonation** when we are sure and don't really expect an answer. *They're moving house,* **aren't they**? ↗ *(not sure) He caused the accident, **didn't he**? (sure)* ↘

277 *Add the appropriate question tag.*

1 That book is new, ...*isn't it*...?
2 Don't forget to go to the supermarket, ...?
3 Let's go out for dinner, ...?
4 They had a fight last night, ...?
5 There is a hospital near you, ...?

6 Let him finish his coffee, ...?
7 I'm due at your house at six, ...?
8 He has got a Harley Davidson, ...?
9 He used to work with Ann at Fosters, ...?
10 Pass me that pencil, ...?

● Question tags can also be **affirmative-affirmative.** If said with a rising intonation, we ask for more information. *She is seeing John, **is she**?* If said with a falling intonation, we express negative feelings such as disappointment or disapproval. We don't expect an answer. *I'll be punished, **will I**?*

● **Echo tags** are a response to an affirmative or negative sentence. They are used in everyday speech to ask for more **information** or to show **anger, concern, confirmation, interest, surprise** etc.
Affirmative: *He quit his job. - **He did, didn't he**? (confirmation) He quit his job. - **He did**? (surprise)*
Negative: *He hasn't called. - **He hasn't, has he**? (confirmation) He hasn't called. - **He hasn't**? (surprise)*

278 *Add an appropriate response expressing disappointment/ disapproval, confirmation or surprise.*

1 "Tulips grow in Holland." "...*They do, don't they?*..." (confirmation)
2 "It's ten o'clock already." " ...." (surprise)
3 "I'll have to sit the exam again." " ...." (disappointment)
4 "She's been to Paris." " ...." (surprise)
5 "He's started smoking again." " ...." (disapproval)

6 "He seems to be having a hard time." " ...." (confirmation)
7 "She didn't accept the job offer." " ...." (surprise)
8 "She's going out with him again " " ...." (disapproval)
9 "They got engaged." " ...." (confirmation)
10 "He could have been killed." " ...." (surprise)

Short Answers

Short answers are used to avoid repetition of the question asked before. Positive short answers are formed with **Yes + personal pronoun + auxiliary verb** (do, can, have, will etc).
"*Can she do it?*" "*Yes, she can.*"
Negative short answers are formed with No + personal pronoun + negative auxiliary verb.
"*Did he mention anything?*" " *No, he didn't.*"

279 *Add question tags and short answers to the statements below.*

1 "There's room for me in your car, ...*isn't there*...?" "Yes, ..*there is*... ."
2 "He's got a friendly face, ...?" "Yes, ..."
3 "Leave me more space, ...?" "No, ..."
4 "You will help me with my suitcases, ...?" "Yes, ..."
5 "They are still in France, ...?" "No, ..."
6 "This is the way to Brian's house, ...?" "Yes, ..."
7 "They had a holiday in Florida last year, ...?" "Yes, ..."
8 "Don't ask for my opinion, ...?" "No, ..."
9 "He used to have a moustache, ...?" "Yes, ..."
10 "You went to Crete last month, ...?" "No, ..."

Oral Development 16

Look at the pictures, then make sentences with question tags and short answers.

S1: He seems to be enjoying himself, doesn't he?
S2: Yes, he does. It takes a lot of courage to do something like that, doesn't it?   etc

So - Neither/Nor - But

- **So + auxiliary verb + personal pronoun/noun** (positive addition to a positive sentence). *She speaks Spanish.* **So do we.** *(We speak Spanish too.) John went to Florida.* **So did Kate.** *(Kate went to Florida too.)*
- **Neither/Nor + auxiliary verb + personal pronoun/noun** (negative addition to a negative sentence). *Sheila can't play the drums.* **Neither/Nor can I.** *(not:* ~~So can I.~~*)*
- **But + personal pronoun/noun + affirmative auxiliary verb** (positive contrast to negative statement) *Jim has never been to a pop concert,* **but I have.** *She hasn't done her homework,* **but he has.**
- **But + personal pronoun/noun + negative auxiliary verb** (negative contrast to positive statement) *John looks happy,* **but Jane doesn't.** *John has done his homework,* **but she hasn't.**
- **When we wish to express surprise at what somebody has said, we use so + subject + auxiliary verb.** *Michael: Look, that woman's got pink hair! Alison:* **So she has!**

280 *Rephrase the sentences using so, neither/nor or but as in the example:*

1 Both George and Mary sing really well. ...*George sings really well. So does Mary.*...
2 John has passed his test. Emily hasn't passed her test. ....
3 Both Mark and Louise are English. ....
4 I have never been to Australia. David has been to Australia. ....
5 Both Sarah and Marion went to Leeds University. ....
6 Neither Cathy nor Sally saw the accident happen. ....
7 Not only Maria but also Lisa has been awarded a prize. ....
8 John and Paul don't need any help. ....

281 *Add an appropriate response to the following sentences.*

1 He's extremely angry. (surprise) ...*So he is!*...
2 I can't explain his behaviour. (addition - I) ....
3 She's gone on a three-month cruise. (addition - he). ....
4 Betty doesn't like being kept waiting. (addition - Jim) ....
5 He's been voted Best Dressed Man of the Year. (surprise) ....
6 She's going in for a beauty contest. (surprise) ....

Asking for permission / Making requests	Giving/Refusing Permission / Answering requests
Can I/Could I close the window? I'm freezing. **May I/Might I** use your computer?	**Yes, you can./Yes, of course (you can)./No, you can't. Yes, you may./Yes, of course (you may)./No, you may not./I'd rather you didn't./I'm afraid not.**

Making suggestions/invitations	Answering suggestions/invitations
Will you/Would you/Would you like to join me for dinner? **Shall we** go out for a walk?	**I'd like to./I'd love to./Yes, all right./I'm afraid I can't./ I'd love to but I can't./I'm sorry, I can't.**

Making offers	Answering offers
Shall I/we, Can I/we, Would you like me to help you?	**Yes, please./No, thank you./No, thanks.**

282 *Fill in short answers as in the example:*

1 A: Shall we spend the afternoon by the lake?
  B: ...*Yes, all right*... . The kids would love to feed the ducks.

12 Questions / Short Answers

2 A: Dad, can we go to the rodeo?
   B: .... They might even let you ride.
3 A: Would you like to meet for coffee this afternoon?
   B: .... I'm working late tonight.
4 A: Can I turn the volume down on the radio?
   B: .... I won't be able to hear it then!
5 A: Can you close the door before you go out, please?
   B: .... Shall I lock it too?
6 A: Shall I water your plants for you while you're on holiday?
   B: .... That would be very kind of you!
7 A: Would you like me to give you a lift to work tomorrow?
   B: .... I prefer to cycle.
8 A: Could I borrow some money from you, please?
   B: .... And don't worry about when to pay me back.
9 A: Will you let me know if you can't come to my party?
   B: .... I'll phone you tomorrow.
10 A: Can I have the last piece of cake?
   B: .... That piece is for your brother.

So - Not

So and **not** can be used in short answers after: think, hope, expect, suppose, I'm afraid, guess, it seems, say, tell sb, it appears, believe or imagine.

I'm afraid so - I'm afraid not	I imagine so - I don't imagine so/I imagine not
It appears so - It doesn't appear so/It appears not	He says so/He said so - He didn't say so
I believe so - I don't believe so/I believe not	It seems so - It doesn't seem so/It seems not
I expect so - I don't expect so/I expect not	I suppose so - I don't suppose so/I suppose not
I guess so - I guess not	He told me so - He didn't tell me so
I hope so - I hope not	I think so - I don't think so/I think not

"Will he pass his exams?" ***"I hope so."*** *"Could he be lying?"* ***"I don't believe so."***

283 *Fill in the blanks with phrases using the verbs in brackets and so or not.*

1 A: Is Jenny really going on safari this summer? (say)
   B: ...*She says so*... . She's always wanted to see a lion.
2 A: Are you going to Mary's wedding? (afraid)
   B: .... I'll be in Brussels that day.
3 A: Has the postman been yet? It's 11 o'clock. (expect)
   B: .... He usually comes at 9 o'clock.
4 A: Do you think Bill will come tonight? (imagine)
   B: .... He was feeling really ill earlier.
5 A: Will you be having a holiday this year? (suppose)
   B: .... We usually go to our villa on Crete.
6 A: You need a special visa to go to America, don't you? (think)
   B: .... My friend needed one last year.
7 A: Will we be paid today? (hope)
   B: .... I need to pay the rent.
8 A: Have the next-door neighbours moved out? (appear)
   B: .... The place is empty.
9 A: Is Dave going to do up the house himself? (tell)
   B: .... He's trying to save some money.
10 A: Do you think it's going to rain? (appear)
   B: .... The sky is rather cloudy.

11 A: Will you be throwing a party this year? (think)
    B: .... Last year's was a disaster.
12 A: Will the island be very crowded when we are there? (imagine)
    B: .... It's very busy all year round.
13 A: Is Janet coming to the school reunion? (hope)
    B: .... It wouldn't be the same without her.
14 A: Is the chairman of the company going to retire? (seem)
    B: .... He is suffering from poor health.
15 A: Is Susie playing badminton tonight as usual? (guess)
    B: .... She hasn't told me otherwise.
16 A: Has Karen lost weight? (appear)
    B: .... She bought herself a dress a size smaller than usual.

284 *Find the word which should not be in the sentence.*

1	*mind*
2	
3	
4	
5	
6	
7	
8	
9	
10	
11	
12	
13	
14	

1 Could you mind come a bit earlier tomorrow?
2 How far is it the cinema?
3 He used to work in a bank, didn't use he?
4 Didn't they not go to the concert last night?
5 Would you like have a piece of cake?
6 Let's stay for another few days, shall we stay?
7 How long is she be spending in America?
8 What Anne does she plan to do in the summer?
9 There was a fax for you this morning, wasn't it there?
10 Who did left the gate open?
11 You can't be serious, can you be?
12 Would you mind to photocopying this letter for me?
13 Don't forget to take some spare socks, will you not?
14 That was Jeremy's brother, wasn't it he?

Oral Development 17

Look at the pictures below, then, working in pairs, have short dialogues. One student asks a question and the other answers using so or not and a reason of his/her own as in the example:

S1: *Is she having a nice time?*
S2: *I think so. She seems to be enjoying herself.*

S1: *Is she at the funfair?*
S2: *I don't think so. She's probably in a playground. etc*

Consolidation 12

▶ Phrasal Verbs

turn away: 1) refuse to let in, 2) refuse to help
turn down: 1) reduce volume, power etc (**opp:** turn up), 2) reject
turn in: go to bed
turn into: convert into
turn off: switch off (opp: **turn on**)
turn on: switch on
turn out: 1) prove to be in the end, 2) force sb to leave, 3) produce
turn to: go to sb for help, advice etc
turn over: go to the next page
turn up: increase the volume, pressure etc (**opp:** turn down)

● ● ● ● ● ● ● ● ● ● ●

work on: be busy with
work out: 1) find by reasoning, 2) turn out successfully
work up: develop

285 Fill in the correct particle(s).

1 I'm so tired, I think I'll turn ...*in*... early tonight.
2 I always turn .... my mother for help and advice.
3 Turn the radio .... a little bit - it's too loud.
4 The club was turning people .... because it was full.
5 Turn .... the TV. It's time for the news.
6 They turned the old warehouse .... a new office block.
7 Don't forget to turn .... the TV before you leave the house.
8 I turned .... the job because the money wasn't good enough.
9 We trusted him but he turned .... to be a thief.
10 If you turn .... the page you'll find the answer.
11 After a day working in the fields, I had really worked .... an appetite.
12 We can't work .... this mathematical equation.
13 I wanted to become a dancer but it didn't work ....
14 Let's work .... the best route from London to Birmingham.
15 He is working .... his new novel at the moment.

286 Look at Appendix 1, then fill in the correct preposition.

1 It never occured ...*to*... me that you were right.
2 She is an attorney .... profession.
3 We mustn't dispose ..... our waste in the sea.
4 He denied any knowledge .... the scandal.
5 She acts as if she were superior ... everyone.
6 The film star came accompanied .... her agent.
7 I'm tired .... commuting to work every day.
8 A car collided ...... a taxi but no one was hurt.
9 Prince Charles is the heir .... the British throne.
10 He plays squash .... his free time.
11 He was asked to leave .... short notice.
12 You're .... colour. Aren't you feeling well?
13 My brother is brilliant .... mathematics.
14 Can I pay you .... cheque?
15 My name's Elizabeth; they call me Liz .... short.
16 Watermelons are .... season now.
17 He failed .... his attempt to break the world record.
18 Ted reminds me .... an old acquaintance.
19 They left the country .... dawn.
20 Could you give me some advice .... this matter?
21 I can't cope .... this situation any longer.
22 The teacher glared .... the student who was causing trouble.
23 He was sentenced .... life imprisonment.
24 They arrived .... good time for the lecture.
25 Pollution is a threat .... the environment.
26 We entered .... a contract with the other party.
27 The students acted out the dialogue ..... turn.
28 She took no notice .... the warning.
29 He invested all his money .... shares.
30 They let me have this antique chair .... nothing.

287 Complete the sentences using the words in bold. Use two to five words.

1 He regrets not applying for the job.
   wishes He ...*wishes he had applied for*... the job.
2 She wants to pursue a singing career and no one can stop her.
   pursuing No one .... a singing career.
3 The moment she left they started talking.
   sooner No .... they started talking.

▶194

4 If he hadn't helped us, we wouldn't have finished on time.
  his   But ...., we wouldn't have finished on time.
5 This tea is so strong that I can't drink it.
  me   This tea is .... drink.
6 They gave him a gold watch as a present.
  was   He .... a gold watch as a present.
7 I think that this law should be abolished.
  do   I think they .... this law.
8 They bought very little furniture for their new flat.
  much   They .... for their new flat.
9 They are installing a new computer in our office today.
  having   We are .... in our office today.
10 You can go to the party, but be home by midnight.
  long   So .... by midnight, you can go to the party.
11 The mistake wasn't her fault.
  blame   She .... the mistake.
12 Gill sent him three letters before getting an answer.
  until   Gill didn't get an answer .... three letters.

288 *Fill in the gaps with an appropriate form of the verb in brackets.*

Laura **1)** ...*looked up*... (look up) her boyfriend's phone number in the telephone directory because she **2)** .... (forget) it. She was quite surprised when his phone **3)** .... (answer) by a woman. "Er, hello ... . Is John there?" "Yes, but he **4)** .... (have) a shower at the moment."So Laura asked the woman **5)** .... (tell) him that his girlfriend **6)** .... (phone). Half an hour passed and she **7)** .... (begin) to get impatient. She said to herself, "If he **8)** .... (not/ring) in two minutes, I **9)** .... (phone) him back." Two minutes later she phoned him back. This time a man **10)** .... (answer). "John Jacobs **11)** .... (speak)." "You aren't my boyfriend!" exclaimed Laura."I **12)** .... (know)," he replied. "That's what I **13)** .... (try) to tell my wife for the past half hour!"

289 *Think of the word which best fits each space. Write only one word in each space.*

Stonehenge

Stonehenge is a prehistoric monument **(0)** ...*on*... an area of land called Salisbury Plain - about seven miles north of the town of Salisbury in England. Stonehenge consists **(1)** .... a series of stone settings arranged **(2)** .... a circle and is considered one of the **(3)** .... complex stone circles in the world. Built as a religious temple, Stonehenge was first recorded **(4)** .... John Aubrey in the 17th century, although excavation of the site did not begin **(5)** .... 1919. Research has shown that there were three main periods of construction, beginning around 1800 BC and

finishing **(6)** .... the 15th century BC, when Stonehenge **(7)** .... completely reconstructed. The fact that the monument is **(8)** .... large implies that many people must **(9)** .... worked together in a team to help build it. There has always been controversy **(10)** .... the exact function of Stonehenge. Although**(11)** .... is no doubt that it had religious importance, it was also known to have a special significance **(12)** .... regard to the sun. Records show that the site was used **(13)** .... a place of worship during the summer months and especially **(14)** .... June 21st, the longest day of the year. Today, Stonehenge is a major tourist attraction and is still believed to have a spiritual force, **(15)** .... to this day.

For questions 1 - 15, read the text below and decide which word A, B, C or D best fits each space. There's an example at the beginning (0).

Jersey

Over recent years Jersey, an island in the English Channel, has **(0)** .... a very popular holiday destination for British tourists. They are attracted by its **(1)** .... climate and magnificent scenery.
Jersey was popularised as a resort by an English television series **(2)** .... "Bergerac", which follows a police detective on his adventures around the island. The producers of the series were **(3)** .... to show the island at its **(4)** .... Scenes were shot in all the most beautiful **(5)** .... of the island so, although "Bergerac" was not **(6)** .... to boost the island's tourist industry, the number of visitors to the island steadily **(7)** .... as the series became more popular. Most of the tourists who come to Jersey are English. Jersey appeals **(8)** .... them because the ferry crossing or plane journey gives the **(9)** .... of travelling abroad, yet the island has all the conveniences of home. For **(10)** ...., English is spoken all over the island (only the older **(11)** .... still speak Jersey French) and the currency and many of the shops are familiar. Yet, because the island is so close to France, it is **(12)** .... to sense a French **(13)** .... in the food, the architecture and the **(14)** .... of life. It is this added cultural element that **(15)** .... Jersey a popular holiday destination.

0	**A** been	**B** become	**C** made	**D** changed		0	A☐ B■ C☐ D☐
1	**A** easy	**B** shy	**C** mild	**D** calm		1	A☐ B☐ C☐ D☐
2	**A** said	**B** pronounced	**C** told	**D** called		2	A☐ B☐ C☐ D☐
3	**A** careful	**B** accurate	**C** cautious	**D** exact		3	A☐ B☐ C☐ D☐
4	**A** best	**B** excellence	**C** prime	**D** advantage		4	A☐ B☐ C☐ D☐
5	**A** countries	**B** parts	**C** regions	**D** divisions		5	A☐ B☐ C☐ D☐
6	**A** aimed	**B** intended	**C** determined	**D** proposed		6	A☐ B☐ C☐ D☐
7	**A** rose	**B** raised	**C** arose	**D** appeared		7	A☐ B☐ C☐ D☐
8	**A** from	**B** by	**C** to	**D** for		8	A☐ B☐ C☐ D☐
9	**A** sense	**B** meaning	**C** perception	**D** understanding		9	A☐ B☐ C☐ D☐
10	**A** case	**B** instance	**C** illustration	**D** point		10	A☐ B☐ C☐ D☐
11	**A** age	**B** group	**C** peoples	**D** generation		11	A☐ B☐ C☐ D☐
12	**A** easy	**B** painless	**C** obvious	**D** casual		12	A☐ B☐ C☐ D☐
13	**A** effect	**B** influence	**C** power	**D** pressure		13	A☐ B☐ C☐ D☐
14	**A** method	**B** means	**C** way	**D** type		14	A☐ B☐ C☐ D☐
15	**A** makes	**B** creates	**C** does	**D** gives		15	A☐ B☐ C☐ D☐

291

Read the text carefully. Some of the lines are correct and some have a word which should not be there. If a line is correct, put a tick (✔) in the space provided. If a line has a word which should not be there, write it in the space provided.

Contact Sports

0	The old sports of boxing and wrestling are still popular	**0** ✔
00	today, despite of the dangers. Films like "Rocky",	**00** *of*
1	although they show the blood and violence which	**1**
2	go with these sports, glamorise the risks involved within.	**2**
3	The relevant authorities try to enforce rules and	**3**
4	regulations to be prevent serious injuries from occurring,	**4**
5	but the risk of brain damage and even the death has	**5**
6	not been completely removed from out the game. While	**6**
7	the argument it continues in the media about harmful	**7**
8	images on the TV, people seem to have been neglected the	**8**
9	roughness of sports where man physically hurts with	**9**
10	his fellow man. Surely that this kind of an example must	**10**
11	have a bad effect on the youngsters who watch TV every	**11**
12	day. Some supporters of these contact sports claim to it's	**12**
13	all a bit of fun and cannot see what could be wrong	**13**
14	with two adults competing as to decide who is the	**14**
15	fittest. I disagree, however; such dangers can't be a fun.	**15**

292

For questions 1 - 10, read the text below. Use the word given in capitals at the end of each line to form a word that fits in the space in the same line. Write your word in the answer boxes provided.

Learning an Instrument

When you are only a **(0)** .... at learning an
instrument, it is difficult to imagine ever
becoming a **(1)** .... musician. Even if you are very
(2) .... about the piano or violin, unless you begin
serious training in your **(3)** .... you will find
it difficult to achieve the level of **(4)** ....
necessary for a concert **(5)** .... . Not
many **(6)** .... start out their career in the
(7) .... of fame and fortune. Many are simply
(8) .... people and are able to express the
(9) .... side of their character through the playing of
music. To receive public attention you have to have
(10) .... to succeed and be confident of your abilities.

BEGIN	**0** *beginner*	
	1	
PROFESSION	**2**	
ENTHUSE		
CHILD	**3**	
PERFECT	**4**	
PERFORM	**5**	
ART	**6**	
PURSUE	**7**	
MUSIC	**8**	
CREATE	**9**	
DETERMINE	**10**	

Practice test 6

For questions 1 - 15, read the text below and decide which word A, B, C or D best fits each space. Mark your answers in the answer boxes provided.

Graffiti

The history of writing and drawing on walls, nowadays **(0)** ..... as graffiti, is much longer than **(1)** ..... of us realise. People were painting on walls thousands of years ago. **(2)** ..... the paintings could have been done for religious reasons, there is also the **(3)** ..... that the artists wanted to **(4)** ..... their individuality at the same time. **(5)** ..... days graffiti can be seen almost everywhere, from the Paris Metro to the outside walls of houses in Northern Ireland. It is often viewed as the **(6)** ..... of vandals, but some people actually claim that it is a **(7)** ..... of art. Certainly, there have been a number of **(8)** ..... of graffiti which have been shown at art exhibitions.

However, as most graffiti is not appreciated, there are continuous **(9)** .... to have it removed, which **(10)** ..... a great deal of money. **(11)** ..... instance, London Underground has to spend £5 million a year **(12)** ..... cleaning its stations. Unfortunately the stations do not **(13)** ..... clean for very long. But recent research has **(14)** ..... to the development of a new type of paint. This is effective in the fight **(15)** .... graffiti because paint will not dry on it, so it is much easier to clean the walls.

0	**A** believed	**B** said	**C** known	**D** concerned				
1	**A** most	**B** much	**C** every	**D** lot				
2	**A** But	**B** Although	**C** However	**D** Moreover				
3	**A** possibility	**B** risk	**C** ability	**D** circumstance				
4	**A** explain	**B** describe	**C** tell	**D** express				
5	**A** Now	**B** Our	**C** These	**D** Modern				
6	**A** work	**B** operation	**C** job	**D** career				
7	**A** mark	**B** make	**C** form	**D** name				
8	**A** drawings	**B** shows	**C** models	**D** examples				
9	**A** tries	**B** attempts	**C** trials	**D** tests				
10	**A** spends	**B** charges	**C** costs	**D** saves				
11	**A** As	**B** By	**C** For	**D** In				
12	**A** on	**B** at	**C** with	**D** to				
13	**A** stop	**B** remain	**C** maintain	**D** hold				
14	**A** reached	**B** found	**C** led	**D** arrived				
15	**A** for	**B** versus	**C** counter	**D** against				

Answer boxes:

	A	B	C	D
0			■	
1				
2				
3				
4				
5				
6				
7				
8				
9				
10				
11				
12				
13				
14				
15				

Part 2

For questions 16 - 30, read the text below and think of the word which best fits each space.
Use only one word in each space. Write your answers in the answer boxes provided.

Beating Stress

Do you grab quick snacks **(0)** .... work, eat late at night and drink too **(16)** .... tea and coffee? If so, you're probably **(17)** .... stress, and your eating habits are **(18)** .... the problem worse. The effects of stress can be beaten by following **(19)** .... simple advice. First, cut **(20)** .... on coffee, tea and cola drinks. They all contain caffeine, which **(21)** .... you feel better for a **(22)** .... minutes, but which also destroys the vitamins **(23)** .... our bodies. Try not to eat sweets, biscuits and cakes. A quick burst of sugar suddenly increases blood-sugar levels; however, **(24)** .... 2 or 3 minutes, you **(25)** .... left feeling tired and irritable. Don't drink alcohol to forget **(26)** .... worries. In the long term, alcohol **(27)** .... depression. Eat plenty **(28)** .... citrus fruit and green vegetables as they contain Vitamin C. Red meat and seafood contain iron, **(29)** .... helps fight nervous tiredness. Remember to eat a good breakfast to start the day well. Take **(30)** .... to eat properly and try to avoid eating late at night. Avoid junk food. Fresh is best!

0	*at*	0 ▭ ■
16		16 ▭ ▭
17		17 ▭ ▭
18		18 ▭ ▭
19		19 ▭ ▭
20		20 ▭ ▭
21		21 ▭ ▭
22		22 ▭ ▭
23		23 ▭ ▭
24		24 ▭ ▭
25		25 ▭ ▭
26		26 ▭ ▭
27		27 ▭ ▭
28		28 ▭ ▭
29		29 ▭ ▭
30		30 ▭ ▭

Part 3

For questions 31 - 40, complete the second sentence so that it has a similar meaning to the first sentence. Use the word given and other words to complete each sentence. You must use between two and five words. Do not change the word given. Write your answers in the answer boxes provided.

0 I'm sure they worked hard on the project.
have
They .... on the project.

| 0 | *must have worked hard* | 0 ▬ |

31 I'd be grateful if you could check this for me.
checking
Would .... for me?

| 31 | | 31 |

32 Someone stole his credit card last week.
had
He .... last week.

| 32 | | 32 |

33 This music reminds me of my childhood.
brings
This music .... of my childhood.

| 33 | | 33 |

34 If I am told in advance, I can arrange things.
let
Provided .... in advance, I can arrange things.

| 34 | | 34 |

35 He had never seen such a huge plane.
before
Never .... such a huge plane.

| 35 | | 35 |

36 He was made to wait two hours to see the boss.
kept
The boss .... hours before he saw him.

| 36 | | 36 |

37 Sheila doesn't like fish. Ann doesn't like fish either.
nor
Neither .... fish.

| 37 | | 37 |

38 Paul regretted telling lies.
wished
Paul .... lies.

| 38 | | 38 |

39 The bus came late, so he was late.
earlier
If the bus .... not have been late.

| 39 | | 39 |

40 I hope you have fun at the reception.
yourself
I hope .... at the reception.

| 40 | | 40 |

Part 4

For questions 41 - 55, read the text below and look carefully at each line. Some of the lines are correct and some have a word which should not be there. If a line is correct, put a tick (✔) by the number in the answer boxes provided. If a line has a word which should not be there, write the word in the answer boxes provided.

Buying Toys

0	Bringing up children is as expensive enough with all the	**0**	*as*
00	clothes, equipment and other essentials without having to	**00**	✔
41	keep it up with the latest toy craze. With a limited budget,	**41**	
42	a parent needs to choose what toys with care. A toy	**42**	
43	should to be tough, childproof, safe and interesting.	**43**	
44	These things are difficult to judge by watching at a	**44**	
45	television commercial or looking at a magazine advert.	**45**	
46	Ideally a parent needs to go on alone to a toy shop,	**46**	
47	without being under pressure to buy up the latest	**47**	
48	advertised plaything. Sometimes the most simplest things	**48**	
49	are the best. Youngsters can have much hours of pleasure	**49**	
50	with paper, a glue and coloured pens and pencils.	**50**	
51	Nor is it not necessary to buy expensive	**51**	
52	educational games neither as children can learn	**52**	
53	just as well from nature and visits to museums with	**53**	
54	a caring parent. As long as learning is fun, children,	**54**	
55	full of natural curiosity, will always want to learn.	**55**	

Part 5

For questions 56 - 65, read the text below. Use the word given in capitals at the end of each line to form a word that fits in the space in the same line. Write your word in the answer boxes provided.

Factory Work

Factory work is often dull and **(0)** .... although it
(56) .... isn't difficult. Most people work on a
(57) .... line, where individuals are responsible for
the **(58)** .... of one stage of a process. Much of
the work doesn't require training and is **(59)** ....,
although it helps if you have **(60)** .... . Some
factory **(61)** .... enjoy their job because it provides
regular hours and a **(62)** .... income. They all have
the **(63)** .... of making friends, as factories are often
large and have lots of **(64)** .... . Others claim that they
are underpaid, and **(65)** .... scan the jobs column
of local newspapers hoping to find something better.

REPEAT	
GENERAL	
PRODUCT	
COMPLETE	
SKILLED	
PATIENT	
WORK	
RELY	
POSSIBLE	
EMPLOY	
FREQUENT	

0	*repetitive*
56	
57	
58	
59	
60	
61	
62	
63	
64	
65	

Pre - test 3

A Choose the correct item.

1 I .... the walls painted next week.
A had B would have
C have had D will have

2 Don't ever say that to me again, ...?
A do you B don't you
C will you D won't you

3 Very .... people bought the group's latest album.
A many B much
C few D little

4 Simon hasn't graduated yet, ... his sister has.
A and B but
C so D nor

5 I won't know the results for .... days.
A much B a great deal of
C a couple of D a little

6 No sooner .... the garden than a storm broke out.
A do we water B had we watered
C have we watered D will we water

7 Jane feeds the fish once .... day.
A a B the
C --- D any

8 There were hardly ...... people at the bus stop.
A no B some
C every D any

9 .... Frank and Fiona are going to Ireland.
A Both B All
C Each D Either

10 I've never seen .... fashionable clothes before.
A so B what
C such D such a

11 She has .... hope of getting the job.
A little B few
C several D both

12 .... idea was it to visit the exhibition?
A What B Whose
C Who D Where

13 "I love playing tennis." "......... do I."
A Nor B Neither
C So D Too

14 It was so cold I had to spend the .... day indoors.
A whole B every
C all D each

15 Although Jack speaks fluent Italian, he has never .... Italy.
A gone to B been to
C gone at D been in

16 .... were several celebrities at the party.
A There B They
C It D These

17 If .... sees Sophie, can they give her a message?
A anything B any
C anyone D anywhere

18 "I've never been fined." "......... have I."
A Too B Neither
C But D So

19 ...... of these two rings do you prefer?
A What B Who
C Whose D Which

20 .... said Ireland is dry?
A Whoever B Whatever
C Whenever D Wherever

21 New drugs .... tested at the moment.
A were being B have been
C will be D are being

22 Everyone has to comply with the law, ... ?
A don't you B don't we
C don't they D doesn't one

23 He's appearing in .... court next week.
A --- B one
C a D the

24 Seldom .... them these days.
A do we see B have we seen
C did we see D will we see

B *Complete the sentences using the words in bold. Use two to five words.*

1 In spite of appearing calm, he was really quite nervous.
appeared Although .... really quite nervous.

2 It's a pity I didn't invite her to the party.
wish I .... to the party.

3 Sarah prefers swimming to jogging.
than Sarah prefers .... jog.

4 "Why don't we go to the theatre?" he said.
suggested He .... to the theatre.

5 Jim won't apologise under any circumstances.
will Under .... apologise.

6 It's possible that he has already informed them.
have He .... them.

7 He invited twenty people but only half of them turned up.
whom He invited twenty people .... turned up.

8 Martha got a new job. She wanted to get more money.
view Martha got a new job .... more money.

9 I crashed my car so I was late for my meeting.
crashed If .... my car, I wouldn't have been late for my meeting.

10 Jane wants to go to the party but her parents won't let her.
would If Jane's parents .... to the party.

11 Could you look after the children until I get home?
mind Would .... the children until I get home.

12 Ted can't read Greek. Emily can't read Greek either.
nor Neither .... read Greek.

13 She speaks Japanese and Chinese.
only She speaks .... Chinese.

14 When did you last spend Christmas with your family?
since How long is .... Christmas with your family?

15 Bread is sliced with a knife.
used A knife .... bread.

16 Mark rang them three times before getting an answer.
until Mark didn't get an answer .... three times.

17 Did you have a good time in America?
yourself Did .... in America?

18 I packed several sweaters because I was afraid I would be cold.
case I packed several sweaters .... cold.

19 Julie had just put the phone down when it rang again.
sooner No .... the phone down than it rang again.

20 Spanish and Portuguese are alike.
similar Spanish .... Portuguese.

21 Paul checked the tyre pressure for me.
had I .... by Paul.

22 This film is so violent that I can't watch it.
me This film is .... watch.

23 There are only a few people who have the time to take long holidays.
not There .... have the time to take long holidays.

24 Experts say drinking a lot of water is good for your health.
said Drinking a lot of water .... for your health.

25 Skiing is more difficult than windsurfing.
not Windsurfing .... as skiing.

26 The woman screamed so loudly that she was heard by everyone.
scream So .... that she was heard by everyone.

27 Susie wants to become a professional hairdresser and no one can stop her.
becoming No one .... a professional hairdresser.

28 "I didn't exceed the speed limit," Sam said.
   denied   Sam .... the speed limit.
29 Columbus first discovered America.
   who   It was .... discovered America.
30 I haven't very much knowledge of French history.
   little   I .... of French history.
31 Mark is working; Melissa is working too.
   are   Both .... working.
32 I'm sure Frank didn't see the burglar.
   seen   Frank .... the burglar.
33 I'd prefer him to drive us there.
   rather   I .... us there.
34 The last time we went out was three months ago.
   for   We .... three months.
35 My friends have never been abroad.
   have   None .... been abroad.
36 We didn't think she would be turned down for the part.
   think   Little .... she would be turned down for the part.

C   *Fill in the blanks with the correct particle(s).*

1 I must stand .... for Tom, who is absent.
2 The meeting has been put .... until tomorrow.
3 I've run .... coffee. Can you get me some?
4 My penfriend saw me .... at the airport.

5 He set .... his own firm last year.
6 Please turn .... the TV. I'm studying.
7 I can't work .... this equation.
8 I took ..... the company when my father died.

D   *Fill in the blanks with the correct preposition.*

1 He was accompanied .... his wife.
2 He gave me advice .... how to act.
3 I'm leaving for Italy .... Sunday night.
4 He's tired .... living in the city.

5 She reminds me .... an old friend.
6 Transportation costs are included ..... the price.
7 Mr Biggs is busy .... the moment.
8 Criminals are a threat .... society.

E   *Correct the following sentences by taking out the inappropriate word.*

1 I asked for a friend to give me a lift.
2 I left school before seven years ago.
3 When I will go to Paris, I'll visit my aunt.
4 I bought for my mum a silk scarf.
5 Make sure you are lock all the windows.
6 We went out when the rain was stopped.

7 Never you leave matches near children.
8 John couldn't to steer the boat.
9 Both Alison and also Olivia are English.
10 He never keeps up any of his promises.
11 I had called him early this morning.
12 The park can to be seen from my window.

F   *Fill in the correct word derived from the words in bold.*

1 John apologised and said he was .... to go to Janet's party.
2 There was a very .... smell in the house, so we opened all the windows.
3 There is not much .... of me winning the lottery.
4 Bringing up children is a big ....
5 The teacher spoke about the .... of studying hard in order to pass the exams.
6 The police set off in .... of the bank robbers.
7 You need a lot of .... if you want to be a successful musician.
8 Jane was filled with .... to know what her birthday present was going to be.
9 It is not very .... living in a big city, with its noise and pollution.
10 He had the .... of attending lessons either in the morning or in the evening.
11 The children were very .... about going to the beach for the day.
12 On completing the course ...., Tony was awarded a diploma.

ABLE
PLEASANT
LIKELY
RESPONSIBLE
IMPORTANT
PURSUE
DETERMINE
CURIOUS
HEALTH
OPT
ENTHUSE
SUCCESS

Appendix 1

A

abide by (v)
absent from (adj)
abstain from (v)
accompanied by (adj)
according to (prep)
account for (v)
accuse sb of (v)
accustomed to (adj)
acquainted with (adj)
addicted to (adj)
adequate for (adj)
adjacent to (adj)
advantage of (n) (but: there's an **advantage in** - (have) an **advantage over** sb)
advice on (n)

afraid of (adj)
agree to/on sth (v)
agree with sb (v)
ahead of (prep)
aim at (v)
allergic to (adj)
amazed at/by (adj)
amount to (v)
amused at/with (adj)
angry at what sb does (adj)
angry with sb about sth (adj)
angry with sb for doing sth (adj)
annoyed with sb about sth (adj)
(in) answer to (n)
anxious about sth (adj)
(be) anxious for sth to happen (adj)
apologise to sb for sth (v)
(make an) appeal to sb for sth (n)

appeal to/against (v)
apply to sb for sth (v)
approve of (v)
argue with sb about sth (v)
arrest sb for sth (v)
arrive at (a small place) (v)
arrive in (a town) (v)
ashamed of (adj)
ask for (v) (but: **ask sb a question**)
assure (sb) of (v)
astonished at/by (adj)
attached to (adj)
attack on (n)
attend to (v)
(un)aware of (adj)

B

bad at (adj) (but: He was very **bad to** me.)
base on (v)
basis for (n)
beg for (v)
begin with (v)
believe in (v)
belong to (v)

benefit from (v)
bet on (v)
beware of (v)
(put the) blame on sb (n)
blame sb for sth (v)
blame sth on sb (v)

boast about/of (v)
bored with/of (adj)
borrow sth from sb (v)
brilliant at (adj)
bump into (v)
busy with (adj)

C

call at/on (phr v)
call for (= demand) (phr v)
campaign against/for (v)
capable of (adj)
care about (v)
care for sb (v) (= like)
(take) care of (n)
care for sth (v) (= like to do sth)
careful of (adj)
careless about (adj)
cause of (n)
certain of (adj)
change into (v)
characteristic of (n/adj)
charge for (v)
charge sb with (v)
cheque for (n)
choice between/of (n)
clever at (adj) (but: It was very **clever of** you to buy it.)
close to (adj)
coax sb into (v)
coincide with (v)

collaborate with (v)
collide with (v)
comment on (v)
communicate with (v)
compare with (v) (how people and things are alike and how they are different)
compare to (v) (show the likeness between sb/sth and sb/sth else)
comparison between (n)
complain of (v) (= suffer from)
complain to sb about sth (v) (= be annoyed at)
compliment sb on (v)
comply with (v)
conceal sth from sb (v)
concentrate on (v)
(have) confidence in sb (n)
confine to (v)
confusion over (n)
congratulate sb on sth (v)
connection between (n) (but: **in connection with**)
conscious of (adj)
connect to/with (v)

consist of (v)
contact between (n) (but: **in contact with**)
content with (adj)
contrary to (prep)
contrast with (v)
contribute to (v)
convert to/into (v)
cope with (v)
correspond to/with (v)
count against (v)
count on sb (phr v)
cover in/with (v)
covered in/with (adj)
crash into (v)
(have) a craving for sth (n)
crazy about (adj)
crowded with (adj)
cruel to (adj)
cruelty towards/to (n)
cure for (n)
curious about (adj)
cut into (phr v) (= interrupt sb/a conversation)

Verbs, Adjectives, Nouns with Prepositions

D

damage to (n)
date back to (v)
date from (v)
deal with (v)
dear to (adj)
decide on/against (v)
decrease in (n)
dedicate to (v)
deficient in (adj)
definition of (n)
delay in (n)
delight in (v)
delighted with (adj)
demand for (n)
demand from (v)
depart from (v)
departure from (n)

depend on/upon (v)
dependent on (adj)
deputise for (v)
descended from (adj)
describe sb/sth to sb else (v)
description of (n)
die of/from (v)
die in an accident (v)
differ from (v)
(have) difference between/of (n)
different from (adj)
difficulty in/with (n)
disadvantage of (n) (but: **there's a disadvantage in doing sth**)
disagree with (v)
disappointed with/about (adj)
disapprove of (v)

discharge sb from (v)
discouraged from (adj)
discussion about/on (n)
disgusted by/at (adj)
dismiss from (v)
dispose of (v)
disqualified from (adj)
dissatisfied with (adj)
distinguish between (v)
divide between/among (v)
divide into/by (v)
do sth about (v)
doubtful about (adj)
dream about (v)
dream of (v) (= imagine)
dressed in (adj)

E

eager for (adj)
economise on (v)
efficient at (adj)
(put) effort into sth (n)
emphasis on (n)
engaged to sb/in sth (adj)
engagement to sb (n)
enter into (= start) (v)
enthusiastic about (adj)
envious of (adj)

equal to (adj)
escape from/to (v)
example of (n)
excellent at (adj)
exception to (n)
exchange sth for sth else (v)
excited about (adj)
exclaim at (v)
excuse for (n)
excuse sb for (v)

exempt from (adj)
expel from (v)
experienced in (adj)
experiment on/with (v)
expert at/in (sth/doing sth) (n)
(= person good at)
expert at/in/on (sth/doing sth) (adj)
(= done with skill or involving great knowledge)
expert with sth (n) (= good at using sth)
expert on (n) (= person knowledgeable about a subject)

F

face up to (phr v)
fail in an attempt (v)
fail to do sth (v)
failure in (an exam) (n)
failure to (do sth) (n)
faithful to (adj)
fall in (n)
familiar to sb (= known to sb) (adj)

familiar with (= have knowledge of) (adj)
famous for (adj)
fed up with (adj)
fill sth with sth else (v)
finish with (v)
fire at (v)
flee from (v)
fond of (adj)

forget about (v)
forgive sb for (v)
fortunate in (adj)
friendly with/to (adj)
frightened of (adj)
full of (adj)
furious with sb about/at sth (adj)

G

generosity to/towards (n)
genius at (n)
glance at (v)
glare at (v)

good at (adj) (but: He was very **good to** me.)
grateful to sb for sth (adj)
grudge against (n)

guess at (v)
guilty of (adj) (but: he felt **guilty about** his crime)

H

happen to (v)
happy about/with (adj)
harmful to (adj)
hear about (v) (= be told)
hear from (v) (= receive a letter)

hear of (v) (= learn that sth or sb exists)
heir to (n)
hinder from (v)
hint to sb about sth (v) (but: **hint at** sth)

hope for (v)
hope to do sth (v)
(no) hope of (n)
hopeless at (adj)

Verbs, Adjectives, Nouns with Prepositions

I

idea of (n)
identical to (adj)
ignorant of/about (adj)
ill with (adj)
impact on (n)
impressed by/with (adj)
(make an) impression on sb (n)
improvement in/on (n)
incapable of (adj)
include in (v)

increase in (n)
independent of (adj)
indifferent to (adj)
indulge in (v)
inferior to (adj)
information about/on (n)
(be) informed about (adj)
inoculate against (v)
insist on (v)
insure against (v)
intelligent at (adj)

intent on (adj)
(have no) intention of (n)
interest in (n)
interested in (adj)
interfere with/in (v)
invasion of (n)
invest in (v)
invitation to (n)
invite sb to (v)
involve in (v)
irritated by (adj)

J

jealous of (adj)

join in (v)

joke about (v)

K

knock at/on (v)
know about/of (v)
keen on sth (adj)

keen to do sth (adj)
kind to (adj)

key to (n)
knowledge of (n)

L

lack in (v)
lack of (n)
laugh at (v)
lean on/against (v)

leave for (v) (= head for)
lend sth to sb (v)
listen to (v)
live on (v)

long for (v)
look after (phr v) (= take care of)
look at (v)
look for (= search for) (phr v)

M

married to (adj)
marvel at (v)

mean to (adj)
mention to (v)

mistake sb for (v)
mix with (v)

N

name after (v)
necessary for (adj)
need for (n)
neglect of (n)

nervous about (adj)
new to (adj)
nice to (adj)

nominate sb (for/as sth) (v)
(take) (no) notice of (n)
notorious for doing sth (adj)

O

obedient to (adj)
object to (v)
objection to (n)
obliged to sb for sth (adj)

obvious to (adj)
occur to (v)
offence against (n)

operate on (v)
opinion of/on (n)
opposite of/to (n)

P

part with (v)
patient with (adj)
pay by (cheque) (v)
pay for (v) (but: **pay a bill**)
pay in (cash) (v)
peculiar to (adj)
persist in (v)
(but: **insist on**)
(take a) photograph of (n)
picture of (n)
pity for (n)
take pity on sb (exp)
pleasant to (adj)

pleased with (adj)
(take) pleasure in (n)
(have the) pleasure of (n)
point at/to (v)
(im)polite to (adj)
popular with (adj)
praise sb for (v)
pray for sth/sb (v)
prefer sth to sth else (v)
(have a) preference for (n)
prepare for (v)
present sb with (v)
prevent sb from (v)

(take) pride in (n)
pride oneself on sth/on doing (v)
prohibit sb from doing sth (v)
prone to (adj)
protect against/from (v)
protection from (n)
protest about/at (v)
proud of (adj)
provide sb with (v)
punish sb for (v)
puzzled about/by (adj)

Q

quarrel about sth/with sb (v/n)

qualified for (adj)
quick at (adj)

quotation from (n)

Verbs, Adjectives, Nouns with Prepositions

R

rave about (v)
react to (v)
reaction to (n)
ready for (adj)
reason for (n)
reason with (v)
rebel against (v)
receive from (v)
(keep) a record of (n)
recover from (v)
reduction in (n)
refer to (v)
(in/with) reference to (n)
refrain from (v)
regard as (v)

regardless of (prep)
related to (adj)
relationship between (n) (but: a **relationship with** sb)
relevant to (adj)
rely on (v)
remind sb of/about (v)
remove from (v)
replace sth with sth else (v)
reply to (n/v)
report on (n/v)
reputation for/of (n)
research on/into (n)
respect for (n)
respected for (adj)

respond to (v)
responsiblity for (n)
responsible for (adj)
result from (v) (= be the consequence of)
result in (v) (= cause)
result of (n)
resulting from (adj)
rhyme with (v)
rich in (adj)
(get) rid of (phr)
rise in (n)
(make) room for (n)
rude to (adj)
run into (phr v)

S

safe from (adj)
same as (adj)
satisfied with/by (adj)
save sb from (v)
scared of (adj)
search for (v/n)
(be) in search of (n)
sensible of sth (adj) (= aware of sth)
sensitive to (adj)
sentence sb to (v)
separate from (v)
serious about (adj)
share in/of sth (n)
shelter from (v)
shocked at/by (adj)
shoot at (v)
short of (adj)
shout at (v)

shy of (adj)
sick of (adj)
silly to do sth (adj) (but: it was **silly of** him)
similar to (adj)
skilful/skilled at (adj)
slow in/about doing sth/to sth (adj)
smell of (n/v)
smile at (v)
solution to (n)
sorry about (adj) (= feel sorry for sb) (but: I'm **sorry for** doing sth)
speak to/with sb about (v)
specialise in (v)
specialist in (n)
spend money on sth (v)
spend time in/doing sth (v)
split into/in (v)
spy on (v)

stand for (phr v)
stare at (v)
strain on (n)
subject to (adj/v)
submit to (v) (but: **submit sth for** publication)
subscribe to (v)
succeed in (v)
suffer from (v)
sufficient for sth/sb (adj)
superior to (adj)
sure of/about (adj)
surprised at/by (adj)
surrender to (v)
surrounded by (adj)
suspect sb of (v)
suspicious of (adj)
sympathetic to/towards (adj)
sympathise with (v)

T

take sth to sb/sth (v)
talent for sth (n)
talk to sb about sth (v)
(have) taste in (n)
taste of (v)
terrible at (adj)
terrified of (adj)

thank sb for (v)
thankful for (adj)
think about/of (v)
threat to sb/sth/of sth (n)
threaten sb with sth (v)
throw at (v) (in order to hit)
throw to (v) (in order to catch)

tired from (adj)
tired of (adj) (= fed up with)
translate from ... into (v)
tread on (v)
trip over (v)
trouble with (n)
typical of (adj)

U

unaware of (adj)
understanding of (n)

uneasy about (adj)
upset about/over sth (adj)

(make) use of (n)
used to (adj)

V

valid for (length of time) (adj)

valid in (places) (adj)
value sth at (v)

vote against/for (v)
vouch for (v)

W

wait for (v)
warn sb against/about/of (v)
waste (time/money) on (v)

weak in/at (adj)
wink at (v)
wonder about (v)
worry about (v)

worthy of (adj)
write to sb (v)
wrong about (adj)

Prepositional Phrases

At

at the age of
at the airport
at an auction
at the beginning of (when sth started) (but: **in the beginning** = originally)
at one's best
at breakfast/lunch etc
at the bottom of
at the bus stop
at church
at the corner/on the corner
at all costs
at the crossroads
at dawn
at one's desk
at the door
at ease
at the end (= when sth is finished) (but: **in the end** = finally; at all events)
at fault
at first

at first hand
at first sight
at a glance
at a guess
at hand
at heart
at home
at/in a hotel
at ... km per hour
at large
at last
at the latest
at least
at length
at liberty
at a loss
at the match
at midnight
at the moment
at most
at night (but: **in the** night)
at noon
at once

at peace/war
at present
at a profit
at the prospect
at random
at any rate
at one's request
at the same time
at school
at sea
at the seaside
at short notice
at/in the station
at sunset
at the table
at the time
at times
at the top of (but: **on top of**)
at university
at the weekend
at work
at 23 Oxford St.

By

by accident
by all accounts
by appointment
by the arm/hand
by auction
by birth
by bus/train/plane/ helicopter/taxi/ coach/ ship/boat/sea/air/car etc (but: **on a/the** bus/plane/ train/coach/ship/boat **in a** taxi/car helicopter/ plane)
by chance
by cheque

by correspondence
by day/night
by degrees
by the dozen
by far
by force
by hand
by heart
by invitation
by land/sea/air
by law
by luck
by marriage
by means of
by mistake

by nature
by now
by oneself
by order of
by phone
by post/airmail
by profession
by request
by (the/one's) side
by sight
by surprise
by the time
by the way
by oneself
by one's watch

For

for ages
for breakfast/lunch/dinner
for certain
for a change
for ever
for fear (of)
for fun (= for amusement)
for good
for granted

for hire
for keeps
for instance
for luck
for life
for love
for nothing
for once
for the rest of

for safe keeping
for one's sake
for the sake of
for sale
for short
for the time being
for a visit/holiday
for a walk
for a while

Prepositional Phrases

In

in action
in addition to (+ -ing form)
in advance (of)
in agreement (with)
in aid of
in all (= all in all)
in answer to
in an armchair
in a bad temper
in bed
in the beginning
(= originally)
in blossom
in a book
in brief
in any case
in cash
in the centre of
in charge (of)
in cities
in code
in colour
in comfort
in common
in comparison with
in conclusion (to)
in (good/bad) condition
in confidence
in control (of)
in the country
in danger
in the dark
in debt
in demand
in detail
(be) in difficulty
in the direction of
in doubt
in a ... dress
in due course
in the end (= finally)
in exchange for
in existence
in fact
in fashion
in favour of/with
in flames
in the flesh
in focus
in one's free time
in full swing
in fun

in future
in gear
in general
in good time
in half
in hand
in haste
in good/bad health
in hiding
in honour of
in the hope of
in hospital
in a hotel
in a hurry
in ink/pencil/pen
in sb's interest
in length/width etc
in all sb's life
in the limelight
in a line
in the long run
in love (with)
in luxury
in the meantime
in a mess
in the middle of
in a mirror
in moderation
in a moment
in a good/bad mood
in the mood
in the morning
in mourning
in name only (= not in reality)
in need of
in the news
in a newspaper
in the name of (= on behalf of)
in the nick of time
in the north/south
in a nutshell
in oils
in the open
in one's opinion
in orbit
in order of/to
in other words
in pain
in pairs
in the park
in particular
in the past

in person
in pieces
in place of
in politics
in pounds
in practice/theory
in principle
in prison
in private/public
in all probability
in progress
in a queue
in reality
in return
in the right/wrong
in a row/rows
in ruins
in safety
in season
in secret
in self-defence
in short
in sight (of)
in the sky
in some respects
in stock
in the streets
in succession
in the suburbs
in the sun/shade
in good/bad taste
in tears
in theory
in a tick
in time
in no time
in touch
in town
in tune (with)
in turn
in two/half
in uniform
in use
in vain
in view of
in a loud/low voice
in a way (= in a manner)
in the way
in writing
in a word

Prepositional Phrases

On

on account of	on duty	on order
on a ... afternoon/ evening	on earth	on the outskirts
on the agenda	on edge	on one's own
on the air	on an expedition	on page ...
on approval	on a farm (but: **in a field**)	on parade
on arrival	on fire	on the pavement
on average	on the (4th) floor (of)	on the phone
on bail	on the floor	on a platform
on balance	on foot	on principle
on the beach	on the one hand	on purpose
on behalf of	on the other hand	on the radio/TV
on one's birthday	on holiday	on the right
on board	on horseback	on the River Seine
on the border	on impulse	on sale
on business	on the increase	on schedule
on call	on an island (but: **in the mountains**)	on the screen
on a campsite (at a campsite)	on a journey	on second thoughts
on the coast	on one's knees	on sight
on condition	on leave	on the sofa
on the contrary	on the left	on this street/on the street(s)
on credit	on loan	on strike
on a cruise/excursion/ trip/tour	on the market (= available to the public)	on good/bad terms
on (a ...) day	on one's mind	on time
on demand	on that morning	on top of
on a diet	on the move	on the trail of
on the dole	on New Year's Day	on a trip
	on the news	on the way (to) (= as I was going)
		on the whole

Out of

out of breath	out of focus	out of reach
out of character	out of hand	out of season
out of condition	out of luck	out of sight
out of control	out of order	out of step
out of danger	out of the ordinary	out of stock
out of date	out of place	out of tune
out of debt	out of practice	out of turn
out of doors	out of print	out of use
out of fashion	out of the question	out of work

Off

off the air	off the map	off the record
off colour	off the peg	off the road
off duty	off the point	off school/work
off limits		

Under

under age	under discussion	under pressure
under arrest	under the impression	under repair
under one's breath	under orders	under the weather
under control		

Against

against the law

Ahead	ahead of schedule, ahead of one's time
Before	before long
Behind	behind schedule, behind the times
From	from time to time, from now on, from experience, from memory, from scratch
Into	into pieces
To	to one's astonishment, to one's surprise, to this day, to some extent
With	with regard to, with a view to (+ -ing form)
Within	within minutes
Without	without delay, without fail, without success, without warning

Spelling Rules

1 -(e)s ending

a. words ending in -s, -ss, -ch, -x, -sh, -z, -o add -es

bus - buses, mass - masses, pitch - pitches, mix - mixes, topaz - topazes, tomato - tomatoes, zoo - zoos

b. nouns ending in vowel + o, double o, short forms/ musical instruments/proper nouns ending in -o add -s

rodeo - rodeos, igloo - igloos, radio - radios, piano - pianos, Filipino - Filipinos

2 -f/-fe ending

nouns ending in -f/-fe drop -f/-fe and add -ves

wife - wives, leaf - leaves

3 -y ending

a. words ending in consonant + y drop -y and add -ies, -ied, -ier, -iest, -ily

hurry - hurries - hurried, funny - funnier - funniest, worry - worrying

b. words ending in consonant + y add -ing

employ - employs - employed - employing

c. words ending in vowel + y add -s, -ed, -ing, -er, -est

coy - coyer - coyest

4 -ie ending

words ending in -ie change -ie to -y before -ing

die - dying

5 dropping -e

a. words ending in -e drop -e and add -ing, -ed, -er, -est

save - saving - saved (but: be - being)
tame - tamer - tamest

b. adjectives ending in -e add -ly to form their adverbs

rare - rarely, nice - nicely (but: true - truly)

c. adjectives ending in -le change -le to -ly to form their adverbs

incredible - incredibly (but: whole - wholly)

d. verbs ending in -ee add -ing

see - seeing

Pronunciation

Pronunciation of -(e)s ending (noun plurals and the 3rd person singular of verbs in the Present Simple)

/s/ after /f/, /t/, /p/, /k/	**/ɪz/ after /z/, /dʒ/, /tʃ/, /s/, /ʃ/**	**/z/ after /b/, /g/, /m/, /d/, /l/, /n/, /v/ or any vowel sound**
laughs, spots, drips, racks	*houses, dodges, ditches, passes, lashes*	*dabs, rigs, beams, thrills, pains, leaves, toys*

Pronunciation of -ed ending

/ɪd/ after /t/, /d/	**/t/ after /k/, /tʃ/, /f/, /s/, /ʃ/, /p/**	**/d/ after /b/, /dʒ/, /m/, /v/, /g/, /l/, /n/, /z/, vowel + /r/**
lifted, branded	*baked, matched, laughed, lanced, dashed, trapped*	*snubbed, nudged, dimmed, craved, drugged, spilled, opened, cruised, cared*

Concrete noun	Abstract noun	Verb	Adjective
	(in/dis)ability	disable, enable	able, disabled
	acceptance, acceptability	accept	acceptable
	accident		accidental
	achievement	achieve	achievable
actor, actress	action, act, activity, acting, activation	activate, act	active
admirer	admiration	admire	admiring, admirable
admission	admittance, admission	admit	admissible
adventurer	adventure		adventurous
adviser	advice, advisability	advise	advisable, advisory
alarm	alarm	alarm	alarming, alarmed
analyst	analysis	analyse	analytic(al)
	anxiety		anxious
applicant, applicator	application	apply	applicable, applied
artist	art, artistry		artistic
	assumption	assume	
attendant	attendance, (in)attention	attend	attendant, (in)attentive
beginner	beginning	begin	beginning
behaviourist	behaviour, behaviourism	behave	behavioural
benefit, benefactor, beneficiary	benefit	benefit	beneficial
	breath, breathing	breathe	breathless, breathy, breathtaking, (un)breathable
calculator	calculation	calculate	calculating, calculable
celebrity	celebration	celebrate	celebrated
centre	centre	centralise, centre	central
character, characteristic	character, characterisation	characterise	characteristic, characterless
child	childhood, childbirth		childless, childish, childlike
	choice	choose	choos(e)y
	classification	classify	classified, classifiable
collection, collector	collection	collect	collected, collective
comforter	comfort	comfort	comfortable, comfortless, comforting
	commitment, committal	commit	committed
	communication	communicate	communicable, communicative
competitor	competition	compete	competitive
	complaint	complain	
	completeness, completion	complete	complete
confidant(e)	confidence, confidentiality	confide	confident, confidential, confiding
	consciousness		conscious
	conservation	conserve	conservative
	(in)consideration	consider	considerable, considerate
construction, constructor	construction	construct	constructive
correction	(in)correctness, correction	correct	correct, corrective
correspondent, correspondence	correspondence	correspond	corresponding
creation, creator, creature	creation, creativeness, creativity	create	creative

Concrete noun	Abstract noun	Verb	Adjective
cure	cure	cure	curable, curative
	curiosity		curious
	danger	endanger	dangerous, endangered
daily	day, daylight		daily
	decision, (in)decisiveness	decide	decided, decisive
demonstrator	demonstration	demonstrate	demonstrative
	depression	depress	depressed, depressing, depressive
	depth, deepness	deepen	deep
	description	describe	describable, descriptive
	despair, desperation	despair	despairing, desperate
destroyer	destruction, destructiveness	destroy	destructible, destructive
	determination	determine	determined
discovery, discoverer	discovery	discover	discoverable
dramatist	drama	dramatise	dramatic
	ease	ease	easy
economist	economy, economics	economise	economic, economical
educator	education	educate	educated, educational
elector	election	elect	elective, electoral
electrician	electricity, electrocution	electrify, electrocute	electric, electrical
employer, employee	(un)employment	employ	employed, employable
	encouragement	encourage	encouraging
end	end, ending	end	endless
	energy	energise	energetic
	enjoyment	enjoy	enjoyable
enthusiast	enthusiasm	enthuse	enthusiastic
	envy	envy	envious, envied, enviable
escapee, escapist	escape, escapism	escape	
	exactness, exactitude	exact	exact, exacting
examiner, examinee	exam(ination)	examine	
	excitement	excite	exciting, excited, excitable
exhaust	exhaustion	exhaust	exhausted, exhausting, exhaustive
	existence	exist	existent, existing
	expectation, expentancy	expect	expected, expectant
expenses	expense, expenditure	expend	expensive, expendable
	explanation	explain	explanatory
	fame		famed, famous, infamous
	fascination	fascinate	fascinating
	fashion	fashion	fashionable
	fault	fault	faulty, faultless
finance, financier	finance	finance	financial
	fluency		fluent
fortune	fortune, misfortune		fortunate

Concrete noun	Abstract noun	Verb	Adjective
	(in)frequency	frequent	frequent
	generalisation, generality	generalise	general, generalised
globe	globalisation	globalise	global
government, governor	government, governance	govern	governing, governmental
guide	guidance	guide	guided, guiding
	happiness		happy
	health, healthiness		healthy
	honesty		honest
host, hostess	hospitality	host	hospitable
human, humanist, humanity	humanisim, humanity, inhumanity		human, humanly, humane, humanitarian
	idiom		idiomatic
	illness, ill		ill
image	imagination, image, imagery	imagine	imaginary, imaginable, imaginative
	importance		important
	impression	impress	impressive, impressionable
	inspiration	inspire	inspirational, inspired, inspiring
insurance, insurer	insurance	insure	insured
intelligence	intelligence		intelligent
	interest	interest	interested, interesting
interpreter	interpretation	interpret	
	introduction	introduce	introductory
intruder	intrusion	intrude	intrusive
investigator	investigation	investigate	investigative, investigatory
invitation	invitation	invite	inviting, invited
	isolation	isolate	isolated, isolating
jewel, jeweller, jewellery			jewelled
learner	learning	learn	learned
	likelihood		likely
likeness	likeness	liken	like, alike
	loudness		loud
luxuriance	luxury	luxuriate	luxurious, luxuriant
	madness	madden	mad
	majority		major
medicine	medicine, medication		medical, medicated, medicinal
(im)mortal	(im)mortality	immortalise	mortal
mover	movement, move, motion	move	moving, movable, motionless
musician	music, musical		musical
	mystification, mystery, mysteriousness	mystify	mysterious
nature	nature	naturalise	natural
necessaries	necessity	necessitate	necessary
nerve	nerve, nervousness	nerve	nervous, nerveless, nervy

Concrete noun	Abstract noun	Verb	Adjective
	norm, normal, normality, normalisation	normalise	(ab)normal
operator	operation	operate	operable, operational, operative
opportunist	opportunity, opportunism		opportune
	option	opt	optional
organisation, organiser	organisation	organise	organised
	(im)patience		(im)patient
	peace, peacefulness		peaceful, peaceable
	percent, percentage		
perfectionist	(im)perfection, perfectionism	perfect	perfect, perfectible
performer	performance	perform	
personality, person, personnel	personality, personification	personalise, personify	personal
pessimist	pessimism		pessimistic
	pleasure, pleasantness	please	pleasant, pleasurable, pleased, pleasing
politician	policy, politics	politicise	political
pollutant	pollution	pollute	polluted, polluting
population	popularity	populate	popular
	possibility		possible
	power	empower, power	powerful, powered, powerless
practitioner	practicality, practice	practise	practical, practicable
	prevention	prevent	preventable, preventive
	privacy, privatisation	privatise	private
	probability		probable
product, produce, producer, productivity	production, productivity	produce	productive
professional	profession		professional
promoter	promotion	promote	promotional
	proposal, proposition	propose	proposed
protector	protection	protect	protective, protected
psychologist	psychology, psyche, psychosis	psych(e)	psychological, psychic, psychotic
public	publicity	publicise	public
pursuer	pursuit	pursue	
qualification	qualification	(dis)qualify	qualified, unqualified, disqualified
realist	reality, realism, realisation	realise	real, realistic
	recognition	recognise	recognisable
reference	reference	refer	referable
reject	rejection	reject	reject, rejecting
relation, relative	relation, relationship, relativity,	relate	related, relative
	relaxation	relax	relaxing, relaxed
	reliability, reliance	rely	(un)reliable, reliant

Concrete noun	Abstract noun	Verb	Adjective
repeater	repetition, repeat	repeat	repeatable, repetitive
replacement	replacement	replace	(ir)replaceable
	requirement	require	
response	response, responsiveness	respond	responsive
	(ir)responsibility		(ir)responsible
	restriction, restrictiveness	restrict	restricted, restrictive
safe, saver, saviour, savings	safety	save	safe
	(dis)satisfaction	satisfy	(dis)satisfied,
			satisfactory,
			satisfying
scenery	scene		scenic
scientist	science		scientific
	security	secure	secure
sense, sensor	sense, sensation, sensitivity,	sense	sensible,
	sensibility		sensitive,
			sensory, sensational,
			senseless
	skill		skilled, skillful
spectacles, spectator	spectacle	spectate	spectacular
	starvation	starve	starving, starved
stranger	strangeness		strange
	stress	stress	stressful
	success	succeed	successful
suit	suit	suit	suitable, suited
	suggestion	suggest	suggestive,
			suggestible
summary	summary	summarise	summary
	surprise	surprise	surprising, surprised
surroundings		surround	surrounding
sympathiser	sympathy	sympathise	sympathetic
tempter	temptation	tempt	tempting, tempted
	tendency	tend	
	threat	threaten	threatening
trainer, trainee	training	train	trained, training
	trend	trend	trendy
	truth		true, truthful
type	type		typical
	understanding	understand	understandable,
			understanding
valuer	value, valuation	value	valuable, valueless,
			invaluable
variety	variety, variation, variability	vary	various, varied,
			variable
warmer	warmth, warm	warm	warm
westerner, west	west	westernise	western, west,
			westerly, westward
watch, watcher	watch	watch	watchful
worker, work	work	work	workable, working

Irregular Verbs

Infinitive	Past	Past Participle	Infinitive	Past	Past Participle
be	was	been	lie	lay	lain
bear	bore	born(e)	light	lit	lit
beat	beat	beaten	lose	lost	lost
become	became	become	make	made	made
begin	began	begun	mean	meant	meant
bite	bit	bitten	meet	met	met
blow	blew	blown	pay	paid	paid
break	broke	broken	put	put	put
bring	brought	brought	read	read	read
build	built	built	ride	rode	ridden
burn	burnt	burnt	ring	rang	rung
burst	burst	burst	rise	rose	risen
buy	bought	bought	run	ran	run
can	could	(been able to)	say	said	said
catch	caught	caught	see	saw	seen
choose	chose	chosen	seek	sought	sought
come	came	come	sell	sold	sold
cost	cost	cost	send	sent	sent
cut	cut	cut	set	set	set
deal	dealt	dealt	sew	sewed	sewn
dig	dug	dug	shake	shook	shaken
do	did	done	shine	shone	shone
draw	drew	drawn	shoot	shot	shot
dream	dreamt	dreamt	show	showed	shown
drink	drank	drunk	shut	shut	shut
drive	drove	driven	sing	sang	sung
eat	ate	eaten	sit	sat	sat
fall	fell	fallen	sleep	slept	slept
feed	fed	fed	smell	smelt	smelt
feel	felt	felt	speak	spoke	spoken
fight	fought	fought	spell	spelt	spelt
find	found	found	spend	spent	spent
fly	flew	flown	spill	spilt	spilt
forbid	forbade	forbidden	split	split	split
forget	forgot	forgotten	spoil	spoilt	spoilt
forgive	forgave	forgiven	spread	spread	spread
freeze	froze	frozen	spring	sprang	sprung
get	got	got	stand	stood	stood
give	gave	given	steal	stole	stolen
go	went	gone	stick	stuck	stuck
grow	grew	grown	sting	stung	stung
hang	hung	hung	strike	struck	struck
have	had	had	swear	swore	sworn
hear	heard	heard	sweep	swept	swept
hide	hid	hidden	swim	swam	swum
hit	hit	hit	take	took	taken
hold	held	held	teach	taught	taught
hurt	hurt	hurt	tear	tore	torn
keep	kept	kept	tell	told	told
know	knew	known	think	thought	thought
lay	laid	laid	throw	threw	thrown
lead	led	led	understand	understood	understood
learn	learnt	learnt	wake	woke	woken
leave	left	left	wear	wore	worn
lend	lent	lent	win	won	won
let	let	let	write	wrote	written

Acknowledgements

The author and publishers wish to thank the following who have kindly given permission for the use of copyright material:

Pears Cyclopaedia for *The English Language* on p. 13, *Developing Countries* on p. 100 and *World Population* on p. 120; Focus magazine for the passages *Christmas* on p. 17, *Dangerous Work* on p. 26, *The Surprising Season* on p. 26, *Eccentric or Mad* on p. 27, *Electronic Noses* on p. 30, *Mountain Biking* on p. 69, *Flying on the Flag* on p. 71, *Choose Your Sport Carefully* on p. 88, *Does the Moon Affect Your Behaviour* on p. 102, *Diamonds are Forever* on p. 135, *Buying a New Bike* on p. 138, *Women Drivers* on p. 140, *How Strange Are They* on p. 164, *Why Are Broken Mirrors Believed to be Unlucky* on p. 165, *Brain* on p. 166 and *Grafitti* on p. 198; The European for *The Lost Art of Old Masters* on p. 25; Best magazine for *Vegetables* on p. 28, *Channel Tunnel* on p. 44, *The Isle of Wight* on p. 103 and *Snoring* on p. 155; Caxton encyclopedia for *Mecca* on p. 45, *Big Ben* on p. 105, and *Diaries* on p. 137; Reader's Digest for the extract from *Anorexia* by Elise Piquet on p. 66 reprinted from the February 1993 Reader's Digest, the extract from *What Women Do Better* by Susan Seligson on p. 134 reprinted from the May 1994 Reader's Digest and *Wake up to Milk* on p. 155 reprinted from the June 1993 Reader's Digest; The Greek News for *Alternative Therapy* on p. 68; Premier Magazines Ltd for *In Flight Video Magic* on p. 136; Woman's Own for *Stress* on p. 163, *Burglars* on p. 168, *Paris* on p. 182 and *Beating Stress* on p. 199.

Ideal Photo for photographs on pages: 10, 18, 30, 34, 38, 45, 46, 52, 57, 63, 67, 69, 71, 86 (doctor, businessman), 89, 94, 95, 97, 105, 113, 114, 115, 118, 125, 151, 160, 165, 166, 169, 172, 173, 176, 177, 183, 185, 201